SPORTS STARS

STARS

SERIES 3

SPORTS STARS

SERIES 3

Michael A. Paré

AN IMPRINT OF GALE

Detroit • NewYork • Toronto • London

SPORTS STARS, SERIES 3

Michael A. Paré

Staff

Julie L. Carnagie, *U·X·L Associate Developmental Editor*
Carol DeKane Nagel, *U·X·L Managing Editor*
Thomas L. Romig, *U·X·L Publisher*

Margaret A. Chamberlain, *Permissions Specialist*
The Graphix Group, *Typesetting*

Shanna P. Heilveil, *Production Assistant*
Evi Seoud, *Assistant Production Manager*
Mary Beth Trimper, *Production Director*

Cynthia Baldwin, *Product Design Manager*
Michelle DiMercurio, *Art Director*

Library of Congress Cataloging-in-Publication Data

Sports stars. Series 3 / edited by Michael A. Paré
     p. cm.
    Includes bibliographical references and index.
    Summary: Presents thirty biographical sketches of popular athletes active in a variety of sports.
    ISBN 0-7876-1749-0
    1. Athletes—Biography—Juvenile literature.   [1. Athletes.]
I. Paré, Michael A.
GV697.A1S657   1997
796'.092'2—dc21
[B]

97-622
CIP
AC

Cover photographs (clockwise from top left): Kerri Strug, Lisa Leslie, and Alex Rodriguez, reproduced by permission of AP/Wide World Photos. Donovan Bailey reproduced by permisson of Reuters/Nick Didlick/Archive Photos.

♾™ This book is printed on acid-free paper that meets the minimum requirements of American National Standard for Information Sciences—Permanence Paper for Printed Library Materials, ANSI Z39.48-1984.

Printed in the United States of America

Contents

Biographical Listings

Athletes by Sport

Italics indicate series. Entries in Series 3 are **bolded.**

BASKETBALL

TRACK AND FIELD

YACHTING

Reader's Guide

Sports Stars, Series 3, presents biographies of thirty amateur and professional athletes, including Jim Harbaugh, Gary Payton, and Tara Lipinski. Besides offering biographies of baseball, basketball, and football sports figures, *Sports Stars,* Series 3, provides increased coverage of athletes in a greater variety of sports, such as swimming, gymnastics, and figure skating, and features biographies of women, including Lisa Leslie and Christy Martin, who have broken the sex barrier to participate in the male-dominated sports of basketball and boxing.

Athletes profiled in *Sports Stars,* Series 3, meet one or more of the following criteria. The featured athletes are:

- Currently active in amateur or professional sports

- Considered top performers in their fields

- Role models who have overcome physical obstacles or societal constraints to reach the top of their professions.

Format

The thirty profiles of *Sports Stars,* Series 3, are arranged alphabetically. Each biography opens with the birth date and place of the individual as well as a "Scoreboard" box listing the athlete's top awards. Every essay contains a "Growing Up" section focusing on the early life and motivations of the individual and a "Superstar" section highlighting the featured athlete's career. The profiles also contain portraits and often additional action shots of the individual. A "Where to Write" section listing an address and a list of sources for further reading conclude each profile. Additionally, sidebars containing interesting details about the individuals are sprinkled throughout the text.

Additional Features

Sports Stars, Series 3, includes a listing by sport of all the athletes featured in Series 1, Series 2, and Series 3, as well as a cumulative name and subject index covering athletes found in all three series.

Acknowledgments

The author would like to thank the U•X•L staff and give special thanks to Julie Carnagie, who handled *Sports Stars,* Series 3 so efficiently. Most of all, the author would like to thank his wife Ellen for her support, his daughter Chloe for her hugs, and his newest daughter, Grace, for her smiles that made completing this project a little easier.

Comments and Suggestions

We welcome your comments on this work as well as your suggestions for individuals to be featured in future editions of *Sports Stars.* Please write: Editor, *Sports Stars,* U•X•L, 835 Penobscot Bldg., Detroit, Michigan 48226-4094; call toll-free: 800-877-4253; or fax toll-free: 800-414-5043.

Photo Credits

The photographs featured in *Sports Stars,* Series 3, were received from the following sources:

Lance Armstrong

1971—

Cyclist Lance Armstrong has always been a fighter. When he was in high school, he became a national champion in one of the toughest sports in the world—the triathlon—an event that combines swimming, running, and cycling. When Armstrong took up cycling full time, he won the world championship in 1993. In 1995 and 1996, he won the Tour Du Pont, the most prestigious bicycling race in the United States. Just when his career and life seemed to be going so well, Armstrong faced the most difficult challenge of his life—being diagnosed with cancer. Never a quitter, he promises to be back on the road in no time.

"He is superman."— cyclist Tony Rominger.

Growing Up

SINGLE PARENT. Lance Armstrong was born September 18, 1971. He is the only child of his mother, Linda, a 17-year-old single parent who worked as a secretary. Armstrong's mother married twice while she was still a teenager, but both marriages ended in divorce. "My mother never went to college and had no opportunities," Armstrong explained in *Bicycling*. "When she had me, she was up against the wall. People said her life was over."

Armstrong never met his father and relied on his mother for support. "You only have your children around for a short time," his mother told *Sports Illustrated*. "You better spend your time with them while you can, because then they're gone. For a long time there were just the two of us. All I did, my life, was going to work and raising my son, and I was happy to do it."

LONG DISTANCE OPERATOR. Armstrong developed a relationship with John Walling, a friend of his mother. "He was high-energy all the time," Walling recalled in *People Weekly*. "I had to channel that energy into something positive." Walling and Armstrong's mother married in 1992.

Armstrong took up sports in fifth grade. He played football, baseball, and basketball, but he did not have the speed and coordination to be successful. Armstrong soon realized that his strength was his endurance—his ability to work out for a long time without becoming tired. He began training to become a distance runner and ran six miles a day after school. Armstrong ran in races against adult men and won championships in several age groups.

TRIATHLETE. In high school, Armstrong decided to combine his running with two other sports he enjoyed—swimming and bicycling—and competed in triathlons. When he was 16, *Triathlete* named him the 1988 Rookie of the Year, saying he could become "one of the greatest athletes the sport has ever seen."

Armstrong won back-to-back national sprint-course triathlon championships while in high school (1989 and

1990). "But one problem with the triathlon was that I didn't like the swimming all that much," Armstrong admitted in *Sports Illustrated*. "I looked at what I did best, what I liked best. Riding the bicycle. I went with that."

LEAVES HOME. When he turned 18, Armstrong moved out of his mother's home. He got an apartment in Austin, Texas, because he wanted to be closer to the rock music scene in that city. Having her son leave home was difficult for Armstrong's mother. "It's terrible sometimes, but you have to have confidence in what you teach your child," Linda Walling explained in *Sports Illustrated*. "I've always marched to the beat of a different drum. I didn't raise him to go to college but to be his own person. Self-sufficient. You have to let them go."

Soon cycling took Armstrong around the world. In 1990 coach Eddie Borysewicz, the 1984 U.S. Olympic cycling coach, recruited him to join the Subaru-Montgomery team. Armstrong soon became one of the team's stars, earning eleventh place in the 1990 World Championship Road Race and second place in the National Team Time Trial Championship that same year.

Armstrong spent weeks racing in Europe against the world's best. In 1991, he won the 11-day Settimana Bergamasca race in Italy. Armstrong defeated an Italian racer, so the Italian fans threw tacks on the street in order to slow him down. He won by more than a minute despite these dirty tactics. "Bergamasca was my biggest accomplishment," Armstrong told *Bicycling*. "After some races you come out with a whole new confidence. Your attitude is different, and people treat you differently. After I won that race, I said, 'Hey, maybe I'm onto something here.'"

TURNS PROFESSIONAL. By the time he turned 20, Armstrong was the best cyclist in the United States. In 1990, he was the U.S. amateur (unpaid) champion and also won the First Union Grand Prix and Thrift Drug Classic, races that are both usually captured by professional riders. Armstrong finished second in the 1992 U.S. Olympic Trials and represented his country at the 1992 Summer Olympics in Barcelona, Spain. In a dis-

Armstrong celebrates his win of the Tour de France's eighth stage.

appointing performance, he finished fourteenth in the Olympic road race. "Lance had one bad race all year," Chris Carmichael, national coaching director of the U.S. Cycling Federation, told *Bicycling*. "Unfortunately, it was the Olympic road race."

LAST PLACE. The day after the Olympic race Armstrong turned professional. In his first race as a professional, the San Sebastian Classic in Spain, he finished last out of 111 riders who finished the race. Despite being so far behind, Armstrong insisted on finishing the race. "That night my teammates realized I wasn't normal," he admitted in *Bicycling*. "I didn't do it to impress anyone, just to finish. It goes back to my mother. She didn't raise a quitter."

His performance in his first professional race greatly disappointed Armstrong. "I was devastated," he confessed in the *Los Angeles Times*. "I felt like quitting on the spot. I was ready to get on the plane and go straight home. My coach talked me out of it. He said it was just a bad day."

Two weeks later, Armstrong finished second in a World Cup race in Zurich, Switzerland. The result earned him respect, but he was not satisfied. "I define success as winning races," Armstrong admitted in *Sports Illustrated*. "Otherwise, this sport is too hard." Before the year was over he had won two races and finished second in another. "Finishing last in San Sebastian may have been the best thing that ever happened to me," Armstrong explained in *Bicycling*. "In two weeks, I'd forgotten all about the Olympics."

TEAM LEADER. Armstrong became a professional star in 1993. He won six races for his Motorola team and received a $1 million bonus for finishing first in all three races of the Thrift Drug Triple Crown. A victory in the last race of the series, the CoreStates U.S. Professional Championship, made Armstrong the national champion. "It's easy to forget that he's only 21," Carmichael told *Bicycling*. "The pro ranks are so unforgiving, he's got to be careful. But the world is waiting for Lance."

The Tour Du Pont is America's most prestigious road race. The tour winds its way for over 1000 miles through several states along the east coast of the United States. In 1993, Armstrong arrived at the race as the leader of the Motorola team because the squad's best rider, Andy Hampsten, was competing in another race. He had participated in the race the two previous years, but finished seventy-third and twelfth. This time, Armstrong was determined to do better.

As in other multi-day road races, the Tour Du Pont is broken up into stages, with each stage lasting about 7 hours,

TEAM SPORT

Even though individuals win bicycle races, cycling is a team sport. For Armstrong to win a race, he must have the support of the other members of his team. Each team has a leader, the racer with the best chance to win. The leader's teammates do everything they can to help him win the race. They block riders from other teams, set the pace for their leader, give him their bike if his breaks, and ride in front of him to break the wind, a maneuver called drafting. Without a strong team, even a talented rider will not win.

Armstrong credits his teammates with all his victories, and splits his prize money with them. "When the star rider wins, then everyone feels like he has won," he explained to *Boys' Life*. Even with the help of his teammates, Armstrong knows it is still up to him to win races. "I'm expected to do a lot of things," he admitted in *USA Today*. "My team wants Lance Armstrong to be successful, and they can help. But when it comes down to it, I'm the guy that has to do it."

beginning and ending in a different city. (The Tour Du Pont is a 12-stage race.) In 1993, Armstrong won 2 stages of the race and stayed close to the leader, Raul Alcala of Mexico. He trailed Alcala by mere seconds entering the last stage of the race, a 36.5-mile time trial. Alcala won this last stage by almost 2 minutes over Armstrong and captured the championship. "It was a painful experience, demoralizing," Armstrong admitted in *Bicycling*. "But I'm only 21. I'll have my day in this race."

WORLD CHAMPION. In July 1993, Armstrong traveled to France for the most important bicycle race in the world—the Tour de France. Though he dropped out halfway through—he was in sixty-second place and had no chance to win—he became the third-youngest rider to ever win a stage in the famous race. Armstrong won the eighth stage, winding from Chalons-sur-Marne to Verdun. He was only the fifth American to ever win a stage of the Tour de France.

On August 29 of that same year, Armstrong squared off against the best riders in the world at the World Road Race Championship, a one-day race that covered 161 miles around Oslo, Norway. Although a rookie in the big race, he was now the established leader of his team. The weather was wet and rainy the day of the race, conditions that made cycling dangerous. "I'm still terrified of the wet just from that day," Armstrong recalled in *Bicycling*. "It's stuck in the minds of a lot of racers. Everyone talks about it."

Halfway through the race, Armstrong hit a wet spot and crashed, sliding across the slick pavement. "I didn't get hurt, and my bike was OK," he told *Jack & Jill*. The other riders passed Armstrong, but his teammates helped get him back into the race. They put their leader in their "draft," blocking the wind for him and allowing Armstrong to save his strength. Soon he had caught up to the pack. "That's when I knew I could win," Armstrong told the same magazine.

Armstrong made his move on the final sprint of the race, pushing his bike hard despite the wet conditions. He broke away from the lead pack and held on to win the race. "I told myself, 'Go like you've never gone before,'" Armstrong explained to *Bicycling*. "I thought that I had it, but you never know. I thought maybe I'd forgotten what lap I was on, so I checked my computer. Sure enough, it was the last lap." Armstrong became the second-youngest world champion of all time.

The new world champion brought his mother to the victory stand with him to share the victory. "It means a lot to have my mother there—she enjoys it so much," Armstrong explained in *Bicycling*. King Harland of Norway invited Armstrong to visit, but did not invite his mother. Armstrong angrily turned down the invitation. "You don't check your mother at the door," he stated in *Sports Illustrated*. The king changed his mind, however, and invited Armstrong's mother to the reception.

BURDEN OF THE BEST. Armstrong finished second in the Tour Du Pont again in 1994. That was his best result during the year, and the burden of being the defending world champion—who wears a rainbow colored striped jersey at each race for the next year—was hard on the young athlete. "It's not an easy jersey to wear," Armstrong told *USA Today*. "I feel like a marked man. I feel a responsibility to do well."

Armstrong realized that most Americans did not know about cycling. "Who knows who I am?" he asked in *Sports Illustrated*. "I don't know. Who knows what the Tour de France even is?" As the defending world champion, Armstrong put the pressure on himself to make cycling more popular in the United States. "I don't want to disappoint myself, my teammates, or my fans," he confessed in *Sports Illustrated*. "I have to carry the sport in this country, and the best way to do that is to win and win big."

Superstar

COMEBACK. Armstrong was determined to win the Tour Du Pont in 1995. He arrived early, riding along the 1130-mile course that wound through Delaware, Virginia, North Carolina, and South Carolina to learn where he could gain time. "I don't want to finish second again," Armstrong told *Sports Illustrated*. "I took time off before this race, but I was very disciplined."

Armstrong's weakness in the last two Tour Du Pont races was the time trials. In a time trial, the rider is alone, racing against the clock. Armstrong worked hard to improve in this important aspect of the tour, changing his position on the bike to become more aerodynamic and smoothing out his technique. "I think I'm stronger," he stated in *Sports Illustrated*. "I've never felt better. I just hope I can keep this form for as long as it takes."

TOUR CHAMP. The hard work paid off for Armstrong. He took control of the race in the fourth stage, a trip through Virginia that included four mountain climbs. Armstrong then won the fifth stage, the first of two time trials, with an impressive triumph that wiped out the memories of his poor performances in the past. He now had an almost insurmountable lead, but he did not let up. "Anything could happen," Armstrong explained in *Sports Illustrated*. "There could be an injury. There could be a crash. Anything."

Armstrong need not have worried. He won three of the twelve individual stages and finished two minutes ahead of his nearest competitor, Viatcheslav Ekimov of Russia, the man who defeated him the previous year. "It's as big as anything I've ever won," Armstrong confessed in *Sports Illustrated*. "I won the world championship two years ago, but that was a one-day race. This was over a number of days. And this was here [in the United States]."

FALLEN TEAMMATE. After his big victory, Armstrong got a close-up view of how dangerous cycling can be. At the 1995 Tour de France, his teammate, Fabio Casartelli, hit a wall and died from head injuries. The death of his teammate affected Armstrong, who three days later won his second career stage in the tour. "I was definitely possessed," he told *USA Today.* "Fabio was on my mind every meter of the breakaway. I felt so much stronger, so powerful. I knew they would never catch me." Only weeks later, Armstrong won the San Sebastian Classic, becoming the first American to win a European one-day classic.

TOUR TWICE. Armstrong won the Tour Du Pont for the second year in a row in 1996. Fans lined the route from Virginia to Georgia to cheer him on. "It's incredible the way the fans respond to Lance," his Motorola teammate Sean Yates told *Sports Illustrated.* "You might say they're making fools of themselves. You never see anything like it in this sport, even in Europe with their best riders." Armstrong won five of the twelve stages, blowing away the competition. "He is superman," cyclist Tony Rominger of Switzerland told *Sports Illustrated.*

Armstrong participated in the 1996 Tour de France, but pulled out of the race early with a case of bronchitis. He was not disappointed with his performance, however. "I will contend for the Tour de France," Armstrong explained in *Sports Illustrated.* "I could kill myself to finish third, but what's the use with the Olympics just 10 days later? I'm going to the tour strictly for preparation."

OLYMPIC FAVORITE. Armstrong was one of the favorites to win the road race and time trial at the 1996 Summer Olympics in Atlanta, Georgia. For the first time professional cyclists could compete at the Games. Having a U.S. crowd cheering for him was an advantage for Armstrong. "I have too much respect for the other riders' abilities to say I'm expecting to

THE NEXT LeMOND?

The last American to win the Tour Du Pont before Armstrong was the greatest American cyclist ever, Greg LeMond. LeMond is the only American to win the Tour de France, a feat he accomplished three times, and he also won the world championship on three occasions. The legendary cyclist helped make the sport more popular in the United States, and Armstrong recognizes the debt he owes his fellow countryman. "I owe him a lot," Armstrong admitted in *Bicycling.* "If it wasn't for him, I wouldn't be here now."

Even though Armstrong gives LeMond credit for what the great cyclist accomplished, he wants to be remembered in his own right. "But I'm not the next Greg Lemond," he stated in *Jack & Jill.* "I'm the first Lance Armstrong."

win the gold," he told *Sports Illustrated*. "But I'll be up there. And the Tour Du Pont has shown me what kind of support I'm going to get. It's going to be huge."

The 138-mile Olympic road race was a one-day event. "It's basically like the world championships," Armstrong explained to the Associated Press. "This is professional cycling and the best from each country are here." The field featured Miguel Indurain, the five-time Tour de France winner from Spain, and Sweden's Djarn Riis, the 1996 tour champion. Most of the professional riders had competed in the Tour de France earlier in the month.

Armstrong launched a final attack with 24 miles to go, but the effort drained him. "I took the attack," he explained in the *Los Angeles Times*. "I always feel like I need to give it a try." Pascal Richard of Switzerland won the race, barely edging Rolf Sorensen of Denmark. "It's disappointing," Armstrong admitted in the *Los Angeles Times* after finishing twelfth in the race. "This is not a sport you can predict or guarantee. We did our best. It didn't go our way today." The other professional riders did not fair well in the race either. Indurain finished twenty-sixth and Riis eighty-seventh.

After failing to win the road race, Armstrong still had one more chance to win a gold medal in the Olympic time trial. Unfortunately, Indurain was also in the race. The Spanish champion blew away the competition to win the gold medal. Armstrong was unlucky because rain drenched the course during his ride while Indurain raced under drier conditions. He finished sixth, more than two minutes behind Indurain.

BIGGEST CHALLENGE. Armstrong ranked seventh among the world's road racers, and he signed a $2 million contract to compete for France's Team Cofidis. In October 1996, however, he was suffering from what he thought was a groin injury. At first Armstrong tried to ignore the pain. "You have to perform with pain as an athlete," he explained in *People Weekly*. "Twenty-five and entering the peak of my career. I felt bulletproof."

Finally Armstrong went to see a doctor, and he received some shocking news. The doctor told him he had testicular cancer that had spread to his lungs and lymph nodes (numerous structures located throughout the body for the distribution of white blood cells and the removal of bacteria). "I was in shock," Armstrong recalled in *People Weekly*. "I put my head down on the doctor's desk and thought about it for a couple of minutes. But there was no point denying it, so I looked up and said, 'Let's get started. Let's kill this stuff.' With my fitness level, my drive and my desire, I'm not going to lose. I can't lose."

Armstrong had the cancerous testicle surgically removed and began chemotherapy to fight the disease. He later had to have brain surgery to remove more tumors. "Testicular cancer is highly curable now," Armstrong's doctor, J. Dudley Youman, explained in *People Weekly*. Doctor's estimate Armstrong has a 65 to 85 percent chance to recover fully from the disease. St. Louis Cardinals infielder Mark Gallego and former Philadelphia Phillie John Kruk have recovered from testicular cancer.

Armstrong now wants to be a role model for men between the ages of 20 and 34, prime candidates for the disease that strikes 7400 Americans every year. "I never thought I'd get cancer," he confessed in *People Weekly*. "But young, strong men should realize that this can happen."

OFF THE ROAD. Armstrong lives in Austin, Texas, in a three-bedroom home that has a swimming pool and a jacuzzi. He has a girlfriend, Lisa Shiels, who attends the University of Texas.

Even though he travels throughout the world, Armstrong will always be from Texas. He likes to wear cowboy hats and denim jackets. "I'm from the country of Texas," Armstrong told *Bicycling*. "My ultimate goal is to never leave Austin. If you come back here in 20 years, I'll still be here. There's a feeling, an attitude." He loves rock and blues music and lives in Austin to be near his favorite bands.

Armstrong has become a fan favorite, both in the United States and in Europe, but he tries not to become conceited. "I get embarrassed by all this stuff. I really do," Armstrong stated in *Sports Illustrated*. "All this attention makes me a little uncomfortable. I'm just a regular guy."

Despite his popularity, Armstrong has not accepted deals that could make him a lot of money. "People tell me I should do all these things outside the sport," he told *Bicycling*. "No, man, I want to ride my bike. If I win races for 10 years I'm never going to have to work again, anyway. If I just ride my bike I'm going to be set."

Armstrong has not yet won the Tour de France, but he hopes to in the future. A rider does not usually peak in the Tour until he is 24 or 25 because experience in dealing with the rigors of the race is so important. "You have to be seasoned for the Tour," Motorola team general manager Jim Ochowicz explained in *Sports Illustrated*. "Lance hasn't had much experience with the big mountains. To win the Tour . . . there are no timeouts. There can be no injuries. A cold can be a nightmare. The Tour takes victims, during the race and after. You can be out for a month, for a year after the Tour. You don't just go and win it. It's a process of testing limits, learning. That is what Lance has to do. He has to get the miles."

Finishing first in the Tour de France is every cyclist's dream, but Armstrong does not like to talk about winning the premier event in his sport. "I don't have the miles inside me yet," he admitted in *Sports Illustrated*. "I'm hesitant to even talk about the Tour de France. I don't know if I'm capable of winning it. Even the riders don't talk about it. It's almost taboo to talk about it. It's just so big."

Despite his setback, Armstrong vowed to be back on his bike in the future. "I might have a bald head and might not be as fast, but I'll be out there," Armstrong stated in *Sports Illustrated*. "I'm going to race again."

Sources

Bicycling, May 1993; July 1993; December 1993; July 1994; July 1995; July 1996; August 1996.
Boys' Life, April 1, 1995.
Jack & Jill, July-August 1994.

Los Angeles Times, June 29, 1996; July 6, 1996; August 1, 1996; October 9, 1996.

People Weekly, October 28, 1996.

Sports Illustrated, May 24, 1993; July 4, 1994; May 15, 1995; May 20, 1996; October 21, 1996.

Time, March 11, 1996.

USA Today, May 4, 1994; June 29, 1995; April 29, 1996; May 1, 1996; May 13, 1996; July 30, 1996; November 19, 1996.

Additional information provided by the Associated Press, the Motorola Cycling Team, and Reuters News Service.

WHERE TO WRITE:

U.S. CYCLING FEDERATION, U.S. OLYMPIC TRAINING CENTER,
1750 E. BOULDER STREET,
COLORADO SPRINGS, CO 80909.

Donovan Bailey

1967—

"If I run a perfect race, I'm the best sprinter in history."—Donovan Bailey.

The Olympic 100-meter dash is the most exciting 10 seconds in sports. The winner earns the title of world's fastest man or woman. At the 1996 Summer Olympics in Atlanta, Georgia, Donovan Bailey of Canada etched his name in the record books. He not only won the 100-meter dash against the best field in history, but also broke the world record with a time of 9.84 seconds. Bailey followed his individual victory by leading the Canadian 400-meter relay team to an upset win over the United States. A national hero in his adopted country, Bailey's triumphs show it is never too late to go for your dream.

Growing Up

JAMAICAN CANADIAN. Donovan Bailey was born December 16, 1967, in Manchester, Jamaica. He is the fourth of Icilda and George Bailey's five sons. In 1981, his parents divorced and Bailey moved with his father to Oakville, Ontario, Canada, a suburb of Toronto. George Bailey worked for a chemical company that made wallpaper.

LIKE FATHER, LIKE SON. Bailey has always been competitive, a trait he learned from his father. "My father was never satisfied with any job that I ever did," Bailey recalled in *Maclean's*. "I was taught to always push for something better. If I ever got 99 per cent in a test, there was still one more per cent I could get."

Bailey carried his competitiveness into sports. "I've always had this thing about being the best," Bailey explained to *Maclean's*. "In high school, playing basketball, if someone on the other team scored 30 points in the first half, then look out for me in the second half. It's something I got growing up on the playground. 'Whatever you can do, I can match.'"

Bailey also worked hard as a child to keep up with his brothers and sisters. "I think Donovan wanted to emulate [be like] his brother," George Bailey told *Maclean's*. "He was always very aggressive. He'd set a goal for himself and then he'd just go after it in a very determined way. Of course, we wanted him to become a doctor or a lawyer. Every parent does. But after a certain age, they have to make their own decisions."

POWER FORWARD. Bailey ran track at Queen Elizabeth High School, but did not train very hard at the sport. His high school coach became so angry with his lack of effort that he kicked the young athlete off the team on several occasions. Each time, however, Bailey won back his spot on the team by beating every other runner in a winner-take-all race. Bailey admits now that he only joined the track team in high school to socialize and meet girls.

Bailey's favorite sport in high school was basketball, which he continued to play when he attended nearby Sheridan

---

SCOREBOARD

WON THE GOLD MEDAL AND BROKE THE WORLD RECORD IN THE 100-METER DASH AT 1996 SUMMER OLYMPICS IN ATLANTA, GEORGIA.

ANCHORED CANADIAN VICTORY IN 1996 OLYMPIC 400-METER RELAY FINAL.

WON 100-METER TITLE AT THE 1995 WORLD TRACK AND FIELD CHAMPIONSHIPS IN GOTEBURG, SWEDEN.

BAILEY HAS EARNED THE TITLE OF WORLD'S FASTEST MAN.

Pfaff had worked as an assistant for legendary track coach Tom Tellez, whose most famous pupil was Carl Lewis of the United States. He issued a challenge to Bailey. "I was told [by Pfaff] either to take my sport more seriously, or else give it up," Bailey admitted in *Saturday Night*. "When it was spelled out to me so starkly [clearly], I knew I had no real choice. For the first time, I began to give it [training] my full attention."

Bailey accepted Pfaff's challenge and followed his new coach to the University of Texas in Austin to train. The two men worked to improve Bailey's technique, especially his start. Pfaff explained to him how the slightest mistake could mean the difference between victory and defeat in a race that lasts less than ten seconds. Bailey took the advice to heart. "When I met Dan I was just an empty book," he explained in *Saturday Night*. "I knew that I was there for a reason but it was like I was lost. Basically, I decided I was going to quit everything I was doing and give this a shot."

WORLD CHAMPION. Bailey's times improved steadily, and he burst on the international track scene in 1995. At the Canadian Track and Field Championships, Bailey ran 9.91, his best time ever. It was the fastest time in the world for 1995 and the fourth fastest time ever. The victory earned Bailey a place on the Canadian team at the 1995 World Track and Field Championships in Goteburg, Sweden.

The field for the 100-meter final at the world championships was loaded with great competitors. The favorite was Linford Christie, the 1992 Olympic gold medalist in the event. The field also included speedster Ato Boldon of Trinidad and American champion Mike Marsh.

When the starting gun went off , Bailey came out of the blocks slowly, falling behind the other sprinters. Soon, however, he accelerated, and by the 70-meter mark he took the lead from Boldon. As he passed Boldon, Bailey screamed. Finding an additional reserve of strength, he had just enough speed to carry him to the tape in first place. "I was mad," Bailey told *Sports Illustrated,* explaining his scream. "I knew I was in front, but I'd run a technically bad race."

Bailey finished with a time of 9.97 seconds, a fraction of a second in front of teammate Bruny Surin. Boldon finished third. Christie pulled a muscle in his leg, barely finishing the race in sixth place. Bailey completed an impressive double gold medal performance when he anchored the Canadian 400-meter relay team to an upset of the favored American team. Bailey and Canada were at the top of the sprinting world.

Superstar

OLYMPIC BOUND. After his world championship win, Bailey began to prepare for the 1996 Summer Olympics in Atlanta, Georgia. During the 1995 indoor track season he broke the world 50-meter record in Reno, Nevada, which had stood for 28 years.

Bailey qualified for the Olympics by winning the 100-meters at the 1996 Canadian Olympic Trials, defeating Surin with a time of 9.98. He came into the Olympics a favorite, even though his times since the world championships had been much slower than his career best. Bailey explained that he was working on his technique, preparing for the Olympics. "Atlanta—it's coming," Bailey told *Maclean's*. "If I'm healthy, I'll run well. I see myself winning everything that I get into. I know that people now expect me to be No. 1, but I always expected that."

TRAGEDY AND TRIUMPH. The morning of the Olympic men's 100-meter final, a pipe bomb exploded in Centennial Park in the center of the Olympic village. The park had served as a meeting place for visitors to the Games and the explosion caused fear among the athletes and fans. "I think it's pathetic that you have these lunatics running around [bombing] at the one place where 197 countries can gather in peace," Bailey stated in *Sports Illustrated*.

Despite the explosion, 81,742 people packed Olympic Stadium for the men's 100-meter final. The race featured one of the strongest fields in Olympic history, including Christie, Boldon, and Bailey and his Canadian teammate Surin. In

BEN JOHNSON

Bailey's Olympic victory in the 100-meters helped erase one of the most painful memories in Canadian sports history. In 1988 Ben Johnson—a Canadian immigrant from Jamaica—won the Olympic 100-meter race in Seoul, South Korea, and broke the world record. In a shocking revelation, however, Johnson failed a drug test following the race. He had been taking steroids, an illegal drug that helped him run faster.

Because Bailey rose so quickly to the top of his sport, some people have accused him of using steroids. He denies the accusations and has never failed a drug test. "Everyone is scared about drugs," Bailey told *Maclean's*. "And it's easy to understand. They don't want another Ben. Sometimes, I think [the testing] is just a headache, but if this is what I have to do to be a role model, I will. The Ben Johnson thing is past tense. He was before our time."

addition to these speedsters, the gold-medal sprint featured Frankie Fredericks of Namibia, the only runner in the year leading up to the Olympics to defeat American Michael Johnson in the 200-meter dash. Fredericks, the 1992 100-meter Olympic silver medal winner, had repeatedly defeated Bailey in races prior to the Olympics.

FALSE STARTS. The sprinters lined up to start the race, and it soon became obvious that each runner knew he needed to make every second count. Christie false started (began to run before the starting gun) and then Boldon did the same thing. On the third attempt to start the race, Christie jumped the gun for the second time. According to the rules of track and field, the two false starts disqualified Christie from the race.

When told he had been disqualified, Christie got mad and refused to leave the track. The delay caused by Christie's tantrum caused other runners—especially Boldon and American champion Dennis Mitchell—to become nervous. Bailey, however, was concentrating so hard on what he had to do to win the race that he later claimed that he did not even know officials had disqualified Christie. "I wondered what the delay was," Bailey told *Sports Illustrated*.

Most importantly, the delay did not bother Bailey once the real race began. "Sometimes the track gods are with you," Pfaff explained in *Sports Illustrated*. "Good starters become unnerved when there are a lot of false starts. He's [Bailey's] not a [fast] starter, so it didn't upset him as much."

FASTEST MAN. The sprinters got off to a legal start on the fourth attempt. Bailey came out of the blocks slowly, but at the 70-meter mark he took the lead. "When I started to accelerate and guys were still within reach of me, I knew I had it then," Bailey recalled in *Maclean's*. Bailey blew by Fredericks and Boldon to win the race and the gold medal.

Bailey not only won the event, but broke the world record with a time of 9.84. His mouth dropped open in amazement when he saw his time and he let out a scream of joy. Bailey took a victory lap with a Canadian flag draped over his shoulders. "I ran my own race in the final," he told *Maclean's*. "And I ended up here with the gold medal and a world record." Fredericks finished second and Boldon third. The combined times for all three medalists was the lowest ever for a 100-meter race.

OH, CANADA! The Olympics were not over for Bailey. The Canadian 400-meter relay team—the defending world champions—still had to compete. Despite their number-one world ranking, many commentators favored the home team from the United States. Except by disqualification, the Americans had never lost an Olympic 400-meter relay.

A controversy distracted the American team in the week leading up to the 400-meter relay final. Some track fans wanted Carl Lewis added to the U.S. 400-meter relay team. Lewis, who had won his ninth Olympic gold medal in the long jump earlier in the Games, wanted a chance to win a record tenth Olympic championship. The Lewis controversy made the Canadian team more determined. "All we heard all week was that Carl was going to win his tenth gold medal," Bailey told *Sports Illustrated*.

Robert Esmie led off the 400-meter relay for Canada. He gave the team a slight lead after 100-meters, passing the baton to Glenroy Gilbert. Gilbert pulled away from American Tim Harden, turning over a big lead to Surin in the third leg. Surin maintained the lead, and by the time Bailey received the baton for the anchor leg, the result was no longer in doubt.

As he crossed the finish line, Bailey raised his arm in triumph. "I knew—I knew—that all they had to do was get the stick around to me and it was over," Bailey stated in the *Toronto Star*. "If there was going to be any one in front of me when I got it, they had better say some big prayers." The Canadian team finished with a time of 37.69—just off the world record of 37.40 held by the American team. The four runners gathered around and put the Canadian flag over them. Together, they took a victory lap. The United States finished second.

OFF THE TRACK. Bailey lives in Austin, Texas, with his girlfriend, Michelle Mullin, and his daughter, Adriana. Being away from his family is hard, and Bailey missed many of his daughter's important milestones because of racing. "The strain of being a track athlete is mainly in the fact that we are always on the road," Bailey admitted in *Maclean's*. "I miss seeing my daughter. When I'm done with track, I want to go home and play with Adriana, be there to watch her play soccer or go to parent-teacher meetings. I know I have sacrificed a lot, but I believe that what I am doing now will ultimately benefit her."

Bailey is interested in track history and the athletes that came before him. His idol is the immortal American sprinter Jesse Owens, who won four gold medals in the 1936 Summer Olympics in Berlin, Germany. "Jesse would just show up and race—he didn't care who else was there," Bailey told *Saturday Night*. "I'm the same way."

Bailey caused some controversy before the Olympics by talking about the problem of racism in Canada. "We know it exists," Bailey told *Sports Illustrated*. "People who don't appear to be Canadian don't get the same treatment. They associate you with your parents' birthplace or your birthplace." Bailey calls himself a "Jamaican Canadian," and every member of the victorious Canadian 400-meter relay team was born outside of Canada.

Bailey is a spokesperson for Adidas sporting goods, Coca-Cola, Air Canada, Kellogg's and Helene Curtis cologne. In his spare time, Bailey likes to play golf. He is still very competitive and confident in his ability, as he told *Sports Illustrated:* "If I run a perfect race, I'm the best sprinter in history."

Sources

Calgary Herald, August 8, 1995.
Chicago Tribune, August 7, 1995.
Dallas Morning News, August 7, 1995.
Maclean's, August 21, 1995; January 15, 1996; July 22, 1996; August 5, 1996; September 30, 1996; October 7, 1996.
Newsweek, August 5, 1996.
Saturday Night, June 1996.
Sports Illustrated, August 14, 1995; July 22, 1996; August 5, 1996; August 12, 1996.

WHERE TO WRITE:
C/O CANADIAN OLYMPIC ASSOCIATION, OLYMPIC HOUSE, 2380 AV. PIERRE DUPUY,
MONTREAL, QUEBEC, CANADA H3C 3R4.

Amanda Beard

1981—

"I want to keep swimming until I'm old."
—*Amanda Beard.*

One of the most popular athletes at the 1996 Summer Olympic Games in Atlanta, Georgia, was American swimmer Amanda Beard. She won silver medals in both the 100- and 200-meter breaststroke races and a gold medal as part of the victorious U.S. 400-meter medley relay team. The youngest member of the U.S. swim team, Beard and her lucky teddy bear swam their way into the hearts of fans throughout the world.

Growing Up

SWIMS FOR FUN. Amanda Beard was born October 29, 1981, in Irvine, California. Her father, Dan, is a hotel and restaurant management professor at Orange Coast College, and her mother, Gayle, is a high school art teacher. Beard's parents are divorced, but live near each other and remain friends.

Beard began swimming as a child on the Colony Red Hots Swim Team. There she joined her two sisters, Leah and

Taryn, who also swam. "I wanted to do everything they did," Beard recalled in *USA Today*. Before she was old enough to actually swim competitively, her sisters made Beard the team's mascot. Besides swimming, Beard played soccer and softball, took tap and jazz dance classes, and raised several pets.

Beard's parents encouraged their children to swim for exercise, but did not push them too hard. "There wasn't exactly a swimming gene pool here," Dan Beard explained in *Sports Illustrated*. "We weren't setting out to make champions. We just liked the benefits of the sport, the competition, the fact that it makes kids schedule their time, the friendships that it brings. Nothing really was predestined, although I will say that when Amanda was five years old, she did say she was going to swim in the Olympics. We just smiled."

MOVING UP. Beard joined the Irvine Novaquatics swim club in January 1994. The club's coach, Dave Salo, recognized the young swimmer's potential. He talked to Beard's parents about having their daughter train full-time in swimming. "There were a number of people who were talking to us, saying we had to make the commitment," Dan Beard stated in *Sports Illustrated*. Beard cried when she learned she would have to give up soccer, but she agreed that she wanted to train seriously in swimming.

Beard's specialty at the time was the butterfly, and she hated the breaststroke. That was until she began working out with Brian Pajer, a swimmer who was a finalist in the breaststroke at the 1992 U.S. Olympic Trials. Pajer taught Beard the correct kick for the breaststroke, and soon her times began to improve. In January 1994 she swam the 100-meter breaststroke in a time of 1:33. By August 1994 she had cut her time to 1:15.

TAKES ON THE WORLD. Beard progressed so quickly in 1995

Beard qualifying for the Women's 200 meter breaststroke final during the 1996 Summer Olympics.

that she skipped junior competitions and entered senior events. She earned Rookie of the Meet honors at the Phillips 66 Spring Nationals, then took first place in both the 100- and 200-meter breaststroke races at the Olympic Festival. At the Phillips 66 Summer Nationals, Beard won the 100-meter breaststroke and finished second at the 200-meter breaststroke to earn a spot on the U.S. Pan Pacific Championships team.

Beard admitted to being nervous in her first appearance as a member of the U.S. national team. "I was sitting up in the stands a half-hour before my race and my legs were shaking and I was feeling sick to my stomach," Beard admitted in the *Orange County Register.* "[I told myself] Just relax. If you don't do well, that's OK. It's not the end of the world."

In her first taste of international competition, Beard won bronze medals in both the 100- and 200-meter breaststroke finals at the Pan Pacific Championships. She added a silver medal in the 400-meter medley relay. "She's won over everybody she's gotten to know," teammate Lea Loveless stated in the *Orange County Register.* "The unique thing about Amanda is she's not looking for attention. She's been true to who she is and I think that's what people really appreciate."

CONCERNED PARENTS. Beard's success meant that the 14-year-old had to travel all over the world. Her parents worried about their daughter because they could not afford to travel with her. "It's all great, but it's scary now," Gayle Beard admitted in *Sports Illustrated.* "You have to put your trust in a lot of people, some of whom you really don't know very well. Ninth grade, in itself, is a tough time for a kid, going to high school for the first time. She's struggled sometimes with the workload. Ninth grade is a time when you really don't want to be singled out, to be different. I worry a lot. I worry about jealousy, somebody saying something mean and hurting Amanda's feelings. All of this is exciting, but some days I just want to cover her up in her bed and protect her."

HARD WORK. Beard trained hard, working out five afternoons and three mornings per week. Salo had one goal in mind for Beard. "I tell all the kids in our program that they're training for the Olympic trials," he explained to *Sports Illustrated.* "That is the goal. Maybe none of them will make it, maybe one or two or three, but that is the goal." To reach her goal, Beard swam 300 laps of the pool each day in addition to attending ninth grade at Irvine High School.

OLYMPIC BOUND. Beard entered the U.S. Olympic Trials in March 1996 at Indianapolis, Indiana. Her main competition was Anita Nall, a silver and bronze medalist in the breaststroke at the 1992 Summer Olympics in Barcelona, Spain. Nall had set the U.S. records in both the 100- and 200-meter breaststroke races that same year.

Once the racing began, however, it was clear that Beard had no competition. Her time of 2:26.26 in the 200-meter breaststroke was the fastest in the world in 1996 and her time of 1:08.36 in the 100-meter breaststroke was the second-fastest ever, behind only the world record of 1:07.46 set by Penny Heyns of South Africa. "I just wanted to swim fast," Beard admitted in the *Detroit Free Press*. "I didn't really know what to expect. I can't believe I made the Olympics. It won't hit me until I get there."

LOCAL HERO. Beard was the first swimmer from the Novaquatics club to qualify for the Olympics since 1984. When she returned from the Olympic Trials, Irvine High School held a pep rally for her. "I've had dreams where I win the gold medal," Beard explained in *USA Today*. "When I wake up in the morning, I feel great."

Superstar

DREAM COME TRUE. Beard was only 14 when the 1996 Summer Olympics in Atlanta, Georgia, began. She became the youngest swimmer to make the U.S. team since Nicole Kramer in 1976. "I've been dreaming about the Olympics since I was 4," Beard told the *Sacramento Bee*.

The pressure of being on the Olympic team did not seem to affect Beard. "She's a 14-year old girl," her teammate, Erik Namesnik, told the Associated Press. "She just wants to go out there and have fun. She doesn't know any better."

Beard faced a tough task in the breaststroke races. Swimming experts favored Penny Heyns of South Africa in the 100- and 200-meter breaststrokes. Heyns held the world record in the 100-meter breaststroke and was also strong at the longer distance. Beard defeated Heyns in a race leading up the Olympics and felt she could repeat her performance in Atlanta.

"AMANDA'S TEAM." Beard swam her first Olympic race in the preliminary heat of the 100-meter breaststroke. The race also marked the first appearance of her fan section. Beard's parents and other supporters sat in the stands wearing matching t-shirts with teddy bears on them along with the words "Amanda's Team." Her teddy bear, a good luck charm, was also in the stands, wearing a jacket from the Novaquatics Swim Club. Before the race, Beard painted her nails to say, "Go U.S.A."

STRONG FINISH. In the 100-meter finals Beard squared off for the first time against Heyns. In a preliminary heat earlier in the day, Heyns broke her own world record in the event by .44 seconds. Beard does not wear goggles when she swims, and it almost cost her when something got into her eye. She placed seventh out of eight swimmers after 50 meters. At that point, however, Beard began to make her move, passing one swimmer after another.

"I like to have somebody ahead of me so I have someone to race," Beard told the Associated Press after the race. "That person is my goal to try to catch. On the first 25 [meters], I got something in my eye and I couldn't see really well. All I saw was something in the water swimming next to me." The only person Beard could not catch was Heyns, who touched the wall just ahead of her American rival. "I didn't have any idea how close I was to winning," Beard admitted in the *Detroit Free Press*.

Beard finished .36 of a second beyond Heyns, but set a new American record, 1:08.09 seconds. "When I looked up at the board and saw my time I was like, 'Oh, yeah, I broke the American record,'" Beard explained to the Associated Press. "I wanted to break the record so bad because I was so close to it at [the U.S. Olympic] trials."

ROOMMATES

Beard got a big thrill rooming with legendary American swimmer Janet Evans. "It's been a fantastic experience for me to room with someone like Janet," Beard explained in the *Detroit Free Press*. "She's like a sweetheart. I love her. If I ever have to go to another place, I want her in my room. She even did my laundry for me." Beard impressed Evans. "Amanda reminds me of me," Evans told the same magazine. "That naive, innocent attitude like I had in Seoul. You just get out and swim it. She really doesn't feel what this is all about yet, and that's very good."

Heyns's gold medal was the first for South Africa since the 1952 Summer Olympics in Helsinki, Finland. The International Olympic Committee had banned South Africa from competing because of their policy of apartheid (the legal and economic discrimination of nonwhites). "I knew the country had a lot of big expectations," Heyns told the *Los Angeles Times*. "I tried not to let that weigh on me. I was just hoping to reach the wall."

GOOD AS GOLD. Beard won her only gold medal as a part of the victorious U.S. 400-meter individual medley relay team. This relay involves four swimmers, each swimming 100 meters in their specialty—the freestyle, backstroke, butterfly, or breaststroke. Beard swam the breaststroke leg, teaming up with Beth Botsford, Angel Martino, and **Amy Van Dyken.** The United States won with a time of 4:02.88.

MEDAL NUMBER THREE. The Olympic 200-meter breaststroke final was almost a carbon copy of the 100-meter final. Beard fell behind early, but came on strong at the end. Unfortunately, the result was the same: Heyns first, Beard second. "On the last 50 meters it really hurt so bad, but I just thought, it will be all over soon, and I just put my head down and went," Beard explained to the *Detroit Free Press*. "I just wanted a medal. I didn't care what color it was. I'm happy with silver."

Beard enjoyed her Olympic experience. On one occasion, she and fellow swimmer Kristine Quance chased each other around with markers in their Olympic dorm. "By the time we were done, you couldn't see our skin," Beard recalled in *People Weekly*. "I had to scrub to get it off. I've been thinking back on how much fun it [her Olympic experience] was. I think that, maybe, when I'm older, I'll have stories to tell my grandchildren."

OUT OF THE POOL. Beard lives in Irvine, California. She

owns two cats (Angel and Dodger), one dog (Jerry Garcia), two rabbits, and four birds. Beard donates $1 of her $6 weekly allowance to an animal shelter and likes to take in stray animals.

After her swimming career is over, Beard would like to be an interior decorator. She decorated her own bedroom in rainbow colors. Beard is very organized and always folds her clothes and puts them away. "We're probably the only family in America that has a teenager whose room is neater than the rest of the house," Dan Beard told *USA Today*.

Beard tries to organize her races in the same way she does her clothes. "I try to picture the whole race in my mind before it happens," Beard explained in *USA Today*. "I concentrate on all my muscles and breathing and heart rate. Then I visualize myself winning. I don't think about the people I'm racing against as much as I concentrate on myself. That's why I don't like swimming with goggles. I don't like to see the person right next to me."

Beard joined the high school swim team after the Olympics and plans to compete as long as she can. "In 2004, I'll be 22," Beard explained to the Associated Press. "It'll be my first year out of college. If I'm still swimming good times, I want to keep swimming until I'm old."

Sources

Baltimore Sun, July 25, 1996.
Detroit Free Press, May 22, 1996; July 18, 1996; July 21, 1996; July 22, 1996; July 23, 1996; July 24, 1996; July 25, 1996; July 29, 1996; August 8, 1996.
Orange County Register, June 1, 1995; August 13, 1995.
People Weekly, August 19, 1996.
Sacramento Bee, March 8, 1996.
USA Today, July 19-21, 1996.
Additional information provided by Associated Press, Reuters News Service, and USA Swimming.

WHERE TO WRITE:
C/O USA SWIMMING,
ONE OLYMPIC PLAZA,
COLORADO SPRINGS, CO 80909-5770.

Pavel Bure

1971—

Why do hockey fans call forward Pavel Bure of the Vancouver Canucks the "Russian Rocket?" Maybe it's because of his speed, which allows him to rush end-to-end through the opposing team to score. Maybe it's his wicked shot, one that has allowed Bure to become one of only eight players in National Hockey League (NHL) history to score sixty or more goals twice in their career. Because of his ability to produce highlights every time he touches the puck, hockey fans also call Bure one of the best players in the NHL and the world.

Growing Up

BORN TO SKATE. Pavel Bure was born March 31, 1971, in Moscow, Union of Soviet Socialist Republics (now Russia). He and his brother, Valerí, lived with their parents, Vladimir and Tanya, in a suburb of Moscow. Vladimir Bure was a great freestyle swimmer who won four Olympic medals and represented his country in three Summer Olympics (1968, 1972, and 1976). He twice finished behind Mark Spitz in the 1972 Summer Olympics in Munich, Germany, as the legendary American swimmer won a record seven gold medals.

After retiring from competition, Vladimir Bure became a coach for the Red Army and then the national swim team. He raised his sons to be swimmers, but both discovered a sport they enjoyed more—hockey. Bure began skating at the age of six when his father gave him a chair to push around the ice so he would not fall down.

Some people say that Bure, in fact, was born to skate—he has the same birthday as legendary NHL star Gordie Howe. His hero as a child was Valery Kharlamov, a winger on the Red Army team known for his beautiful moves on the ice. "He could go around everybody, make some nice plays," Bure recalled in *Maclean's*.

MAKES TEAM. In 1977, Vladimir Bure took Pavel, then only six years old, to the tryouts for the Soviet Red Army junior hockey team. He did not do well—mainly because he was wearing figure skates—and his performance disappointed his father, especially since Bure did not try very hard. "Every father think his son the best," Vladimir Bure admitted in *Sports Illustrated*. "At his first practice, Pavel was the worst. You do something—bus driver, journalist—you try to be best."

Vladimir Bure told his son that he would have to try harder or quit. "He is [a] coach," Bure explained in *Sports Illustrated*. "He understands training very well." Bure responded to his father's encouragement, going to bed early on the nights before practices and working hard in drills. "I didn't make him run and lift weights three hours a day," Vladimir Bure told the same magazine. "But I make sure he has focus." Soon Bure was the best player on the team.

TEAMMATES. Bure joined the powerful Red Army Team when he was 16. There he played on a line with future NHL stars Alexander Mogilny and Sergei Fedorov. Red Army coach Viktor Tikhonov was grooming this line to replace the legendary K-L-M line of Vladimir Krutov, Igor Larionov, and Sergei Makarov. "We were like kids playing together who had played together all our lives," Fedorov recalled in the *Sporting News*. "We had that great feeling you get when you understand a teammate so well. I don't know if we realized how good we all were individually, but we knew how well we worked together. It was fun."

NHL BOUND. In the late 1980s, the Soviet Union began to collapse. Soon the country had broken up into several smaller countries, and the tight controls the government had over their athletes began to loosen. The changes going on in his home country gave Bure and his teammates the opportunity to fulfill a dream—to play in the best hockey league in the world, the NHL. The first to leave was Mogilny, who defected in Sweden and signed with the Buffalo Sabres in 1989. In 1990, Fedorov left the Russian national team in Seattle, Washington, and signed with the Detroit Red Wings.

After leading the Soviet Union to two world junior hockey championships (1989 and 1990), Bure knew he could play in the NHL. The Vancouver Canucks drafted him in the sixth round of the 1989 NHL Draft, the one-hundred-thirteenth player taken overall. "When Mogilny left the country, it was a huge deal," Bure explained in the *Sporting News*. "When Fedorov left, it was still a big deal, but less. Things were changing. By the time I came to the U.S., knowing I could play with Vancouver, it wasn't a big deal at all."

LEAVES HOME. In August 1991, the Russian national team traveled to play in the Canada Cup tournament. Bure's Red Army coaches pressured him to sign a contract promising his services to the Red Army team for three years. When he refused to sign, the coaches did not let him go to Canada.

In September of that year, Bure, his brother, and his father, left Russia and flew to Los Angeles, California. (The

Montreal Canadiens had drafted Valerí Bure.) Two months later Tanya Bure joined them. The secret trip surprised both the Red Army team and the Canucks, who had not expected Bure to be available to play in the NHL for at least two more years. "The Red Army gave me no choice," he declared in the *Sporting News*. "I wanted better—for me and my family."

The Canucks could not begin negotiating with Bure until they received permission to do so from the Red Army team. The whole process took two months, during which time Vladimir Bure put both his sons through strenuous workouts. They ran on the beach, lifted weights, and skated whenever they could get ice time at the Culver City Ice Arena. In the evening they played tennis or soccer.

Bure's (left) mean checks makes him one of the best hockey players in the NHL.

BUYS FREEDOM. As the negotiations with the Red Army officials dragged on, Bure became worried that he would miss the entire 1991—92 NHL season. He finally offered $50,000 of his signing bonus with the Canucks to buy his freedom from the Soviet Ice Hockey Federation. Bure then signed a four-year, $2.7 million contract with Vancouver on October 31, 1991.

Vancouver fans were excited by their new star. Two thousand fans showed up for his first practice. Bure's big contract could have bothered his teammates, but he proved he was worth every penny. "We worried he might be a kid with a bit of a big head," Canucks alternate captain Ryan Walter confessed in *Sports Illustrated*. "But there was nothing to worry about. The fact that he reported in such great physical condition said a lot about his attitude."

ROOKIE OF THE YEAR. Despite joining the team late, Bure instantly energized his teammates. "He can take the puck from behind our net, carry it down the ice and score," Canucks captain Trevor Linden told *Sports Illustrated*. "That's rare." Put on a line centered by fellow Russian Igor Larionov, Bure scored 34 goals in only 65 games in his first season. He won the Calder Trophy as rookie of the year in the 1991—92 season. It was the first time a Vancouver player had ever won an NHL postseason award.

"I guess there were no real stars before Pavel, who holds the audience captive every time the puck is on his stick," Glen Ringdal, the Canucks marketing director, explained in *Sports Illustrated*. "What you have with Pavel is more of an idolization, like you get with certain musical artists. Like you got with Elvis."

"RUSSIAN ROCKET." Bure earned the nickname the "Russian Rocket" with his play during his rookie year. The Canucks put up billboards featuring the young star with a rocket strapped to his back around town. The billboards said "We have lift-off." "In Russia, I was not Rocket," Bure admitted in *Sports Illustrated*. "I was just regular guy."

The "Russian Rocket" exploded in his second season. He scored 60 goals and added 50 assists. Bure was the first Canuck to ever score over 50 goals or earn more than 100 points (110) in one season. He also became the first Vancouver player to be named to the NHL's first-team all-star squad.

Superstar

LEAGUE LEADER. Bure led the league with 60 goals in 1993—94, including 46 in the final 46 games of the season. At the NHL All-Star Game, Western Conference coach Barry Melrose of the Los Angeles Kings put Bure on a line with Fedorov, the first time the former teammates had played together since leaving Russia. "I couldn't resist putting Fedorov and Bure together," Melrose admitted in the *Sporting News*. The line— that also included Brendan Shanahan (playing for the St. Louis Blues at the time)—accounted for three goals and numerous breakaways, including three by Bure.

PLAYOFF RUN. The Canucks finished one game over .500 during the 1992—93 season, barely qualifying for the playoffs. Vancouver fell behind the Calgary Flames in the first round, three games to one, and Mike Sullivan of the Flames held Bure scoreless. The Canucks staged a remarkable comeback, however, winning three straight overtime games. Bure scored the winning goal in double overtime of Game Seven sending his team to the second round of the playoffs. When he saw the puck in the net he threw his stick and then his gloves into the air.

In the second round of the playoffs, the Dallas Stars tried to rough-up Bure. Stars' enforcer Shane Churla took several cheap shots at the Canuck star. Bure finally retaliated, knocking Churla out. The tough play by Bure inspired his team-

---

SUPER SCORERS

Bure joined an elite group during the 1993—94 season. He became one of only eight players in NHL history to score sixty or more goals per year in two or more seasons. The following chart lists these players and the teams they played for.

Player	Team
Mike Bossy	New York Islanders
Pavel Bure	Vancouver Canucks
Phil Esposito	Boston Bruins
Wayne Gretzky	Edmonton Oilers
Brett Hull	St. Louis Blues
Jari Kurri	Edmonton Oilers
Mario Lemieux	Pittsburgh Penguins
Steve Yzerman	Detroit Red Wings

mates, and Vancouver took off. Bure scored six goals in the series, and the Canucks defeated Dallas in five games.

STANLEY CUP FINALS. When the Canucks defeated the Toronto Maple Leafs in the Western Conference Finals, they were in the Stanley Cup Finals for the first time since 1982. That year they lost to the powerful New York Islanders, but this time the Canucks had a good chance to win against the Eastern Conference champion New York Rangers. "I've been here long enough to know what this means," Bure explained in *USA Today*. "I think it will be wild. It's a great feeling. I've never felt like this before."

The Rangers were a powerful team led by center Mark Messier. New York shut down Bure and the Canucks offense for much of the series and won the Stanley Cup in seven grueling games. Bure missed his chance to become the first Russian player to have his name engraved on the famous hockey trophy. "Once I had a dream of winning the [Olympic] gold medal, but times change, dreams change," Bure stated in the *Sporting News*. "The Stanley Cup is better than a gold medal."

Bure's production in the 1994 Stanley Cup Playoffs erased all doubts about his ability to produce in the clutch. He scored 16 postseason goals—best in the NHL. "Pavel's been outstanding—he's scored some big goals for us, no question," Vancouver coach Pat Quinn stated in *Maclean's*. "I don't think he could ever get enough credit."

GOES HOME. A contract dispute between NHL players and owners delayed the start of the 1994—95 season. During this time Bure returned to Russia to play in exhibition games. The reaction of his countrymen surprised him, as fans asked for his autographs and showed him scrapbooks full of information about his NHL career. "I couldn't believe it, because I didn't know how much people there would know about me anymore," Bure admitted in the *Sporting News*. When NHL play resumed, he scored 20 goals and had 23 assists in 44 games.

ROCKET GROUNDED. The Canucks pulled off a big trade with the Buffalo Sabres in the summer of 1995 to bring Bure's former Red Army teammate, Alexander Mogilny, to Vancouver. He and Mogilny teamed to form one of the most dangerous lines in the NHL. Bure started the new season fast, scoring 6 goals and 7 assists in 15 games.

Unfortunately, Bure's season came to a crashing end when Chicago Blackhawks defenseman Steve Smith checked him from behind. Bure slide into the boards and tore the anterior cruciate ligament (ACL) in his right knee. The injury required surgery and Bure missed the rest of the season. "There is nothing I can do about it," he confessed to the Reuters News Service. "I'll just have to have the surgery. I'm not scared. I'll go home, but it will be a different type of summer."

Bure's knee healed enough for him to play for Russia in the World Cup of Hockey in the summer of 1996. Once again he suffered an injury, however, when he collided with U.S. defenseman Brian Leetch of the New York Rangers in an exhibition game. The collision caused a bruised kidney that kept Bure out of the entire tournament.

WHY SO GOOD? Because he is small, other teams think they can push Bure around. Rough tactics, however, cannot slow him down. "People don't realize how strong Pavel is," Canucks center Cliff Ronning told *Sports Illustrated*. Bure credits the training program his father designed for him. "I think you've got to work every day, even if you're good, to try to be better," he explained in *Maclean's*.

Bure is best known for his end-to-end rushes. "When he touches the puck, there's a feeling in the arena that something's going to happen," former teammate Greg Adams told the *Sporting News*. "As soon as he starts up the ice, you can hear it in the building, the sighs and moans." Bure has an amazing ability to control and shoot the puck as well as any player in the NHL. "If you give him too much room, he's going to burn you," Ronning declared in *USA Today*. "When we're playing well as a team, it gives Pavel a chance to show his special talent."

RUSSIAN INVASION

During the 1990s, more and more Russian players have come to North America to play in the NHL. At first, Canadian and American players and commentators criticized these players, saying they could not survive in the tough league. "We've had a lot of highly talented Europeans come to our game," Canucks general manager and coach Pat Quinn told *Sports Illustrated.*

Igor Larionov, now with the Detroit Red Wings, was one of the first two Russian players, along with Sergei Priakin, to play in the NHL. Larionov feels that today's Russian stars have learned to play the North American style of hockey. "It makes me proud to see these youngsters and how well they're doing," he stated in the *Sporting News.* "Those of us in the first [wave] of players to come over were at the end of our careers, and we had spent too many years under a very different system to really make the adjustment. But this generation has been able to do it."

Bure feels that criticism of him and other Russian players is unfair. "It was right seven or eight years ago when we were just playing in Russia," he told *USA Today.* "But now guys have played five or six or seven [seasons] over here. We can play tough hockey, too."

OFF THE ICE. Bure lives with his father in Vancouver. He has worked hard to learn English, but the adjustment to living in Canada has been difficult for him. "It was just everything," Bure stated in *Maclean's.* "You know, you've got no friends, can't speak [the] language, nothing."

Bure is very popular in Vancouver, though, and gets sacks of fan mail. "I can go nowhere that I am not recognized," he explained in *Maclean's.* "If I put on a baseball cap and sunglasses, people don't recognize me. But people here love hockey, and for me to sign autographs is no problem."

Bure likes all kinds of music, and in 1995, he joined Bryan Adams on stage during a concert to sing Adams' hit "Cuts Like a Knife." He has a large collection of Russian movies and he also enjoys reading. Bure works with youth hockey teams and has visited the Ronald McDonald House in Vancouver. (The Ronald McDonald House provides low-income housing for seriously ill children and their families while receiving treatment from a nearby hospital.)

Hockey experts agree that Bure is one of the premier players in the NHL. "He's electric," ESPN analyst Barry Melrose told the *Sporting News.* "He is the most exciting player in the NHL right now."

Sources

Maclean's, April 26, 1993; June 6, 1994.
Sporting News, February 21, 1994; June 6, 1994; April 17, 1995.
Sports Illustrated, December 7, 1992; May 30, 1994.
USA Today, June 3, 1994; June 7, 1994; June 8, 1994; May 31, 1994; August 27, 1996; August 29, 1996.

Additional information provided by the Reuters News Service and the
Vancouver Canucks.

 WHERE TO WRITE:

C/O VANCOUVER CANUCKS, GENERAL MOTORS PLACE,
800 GRIFFITHS WAY,
VANCOUVER, BC, CANADA V6B 6G1.

Ken Caminiti

1963—

"I love to play. For me, it's easy to go out there. Playing baseball is what I love to do."—Ken Caminiti.

Third baseman Ken Caminiti has earned the nickname "Scary Man" from his San Diego Padres teammates because he concentrates so hard on the baseball diamond that he gets a frightening look in his eye. He scared opposing pitchers so much in 1996—hitting .326 with 40 home runs and 130 runs batted in (RBI)—that he earned the National League Most Valuable Player (MVP) award and led the Padres to the Western Division title. A virtually unknown player for several major-league seasons with the Houston Astros, Caminiti became a star after winning the most important battle of his life—against alcohol addiction.

Growing Up

TOP SECRET. Kenneth Gene Caminiti was born April 21, 1963, in Hanford, California. He grew up in San Jose, California, with his parents, Lee and Yvonne. Lee Caminiti worked at Lockheed Corporation, a company involved with secret government aerospace projects. Because the projects were secret, he could not even tell his children what he did for a living. Caminiti still does not know what his father worked on.

SPARTAN STAR. Caminiti earned letters in baseball, basketball, and football at Leigh High School. After graduating in 1981, he stayed close to home and played baseball for one year at San Jose City College. His play there earned Caminiti a baseball scholarship to San Jose State University.

Caminiti earned second-team All-American honors from the *Sporting News* during his junior year at San Jose State (1984) after batting .348 for the Spartans and leading the team in average, home runs (5), triples (4), doubles (18), hits (77), and RBI (45). He batted .327 in two seasons at San Jose State and set a school career record for doubles (29). Caminiti spent the summer of 1984 playing with the U.S. Olympic baseball team, but failed to make the squad that played in the Summer Olympics in Los Angeles, California.

ASTROS' CHOICE. The Houston Astros drafted Caminiti in the third round of the 1984 major league free agent draft. Lee Caminiti negotiated his son's first major league contract, demanding a $50,000 signing bonus. Caminiti admired his father greatly. "He [his father] was so mentally tough," he told *Sports Illustrated.*

Injuries to both of his knees forced Caminiti to spend parts of four seasons in the minor leagues before finally earning a starting spot with the Astros in 1989. That season he batted .255 with 10 home runs and 72 RBI in 161 games. Over the next four seasons Caminiti established himself as an average major leaguer, but never reached star status. His best batting average with the team was .294 in 1992, and his most home runs were 13, which he hit in 1991, 1992, and 1993.

SCOREBOARD

1996 NATIONAL LEAGUE MOST VALUABLE PLAYER.

TWO-TIME GOLD GLOVE WINNER (1995 AND 1996) AS THE BEST FIELDING THIRD BASEMAN IN THE NATIONAL LEAGUE.

TWO-TIME NATIONAL LEAGUE ALL-STAR (1994 AND 1996).

CAMINITI OVERCAME A SERIOUS ALCOHOL PROBLEM TO BECOME THE BEST PLAYER IN THE NATIONAL LEAGUE FOR 1996.

LIFE IN THE FAST LANE. Caminiti had a hard time adjusting to the fast-paced lifestyle of a major league ballplayer. He began to go out drinking every night on road trips. "I used to drink every night, basically," Caminiti told *Baseball Weekly*. "I didn't get drunk every night, but I drank. I drank hard stuff, beer, anything I got my hands on." He also took medication to help him deal with pain caused by sports injuries he had suffered.

Caminiti tried to stop drinking on his own. "I lasted 22 days," he admitted in *Baseball Weekly*. "Then I took a drink again. That's when I realized I couldn't do it by myself. I was honest with myself. I had to get help." Following the 1993 season, Caminiti did what he admitted was "the hardest thing I ever had to do in my life." After his family and teammates urged him to get help, he checked himself into a clinic. "He did it for the right reason, the right person: himself," his father told the *Los Angeles Times*.

NEW MAN. Defeating his drinking problem helped Caminiti revive his career. "If you drink a lot, you don't feel right the next day," he explained in *Baseball Weekly*. "You get to the park, your stomach is queasy. So you don't eat right. By the time the game starts, you think you're OK, but I guarantee you you're not. You still have chemicals in your body." A .257 hitter when he entered rehabilitation, Caminiti has hit over .300 since with increased power.

Caminiti earned his first all-star appearance in 1994. "It's no coincidence that I made the all-Star team for the first time the year I quit [drinking]," he confessed in the *Los Angeles Times*. "I was playing good baseball, hard baseball, but not to my potential. The night life was too good."

Caminiti batted .283 with 18 home runs and 75 RBI in 1994. He was one of Houston's young stars, along with second baseman Craig Biggio and 1994 National League Most Valuable Player, first baseman Jeff Bagwell. The Astros were one-half game out of first place in the newly formed National League Central Division when the season came to an abrupt end because of a baseball strike. The strike was caused by a

Caminiti watches another of his homeruns leave the ballpark.

disagreement between players and owners on issues concerning free agency and players' salaries. Although he did not know it at the time, the strike also ended Caminiti's career in Houston.

BIG TRADE. The Astros traded Caminiti to the San Diego Padres as part of an 11-player deal on December 28, 1994. The former Houston player was happy with the trade. "It was the best thing that could have happened," Caminiti declared in the *Los Angeles Times*. "I came here [to San Diego] with the feeling that I was wanted, that I was special. In Houston, it was like I was going to be traded every year. I felt like I had to get a hit every at-bat to justify staying there, or justify being traded."

The Padres had been the worst team in major league baseball for several years. In an effort to save money, San Diego had traded or lost to free-agency several star players, including first baseman Fred McGriff (Atlanta) and outfielder Gary Sheffield (Florida). One player San Diego kept, however, was outfielder Tony Gwynn, the perennial National League batting champion.

The trade involving Caminiti was the first step in bringing the Padres back. Their new third baseman had the best season of his career so far in 1995. Caminiti set career bests in batting average (.302), hits (159), home runs (26), RBI (94), runs scored (109), and stolen bases (12). Fellow players and managers also recognized his fielding ability by voting him the Gold Glove Award, given annually to one player per position in each league. Caminiti had always been a great fielder, with the strongest infield arm in the major leagues.

Caminiti led the Padres in home runs and RBI, and the switch-hitter (hitting as both a right- and left-handed batter) became the first player in major league history to homer from both sides of the plate in the same game three times in one season. Following the 1995 season, Caminiti could have left the team as a free-agent, but instead signed a two-year, $6.1 million contract to stay with the Padres.

Superstar

PADRES POWER. The Padres' rebuilding program started showing results in 1996. The team signed outfielder Ricky Henderson, the great lead-off hitter and all-time base stealing champ, to join Caminiti and Gwynn in a powerful lineup. These additions, plus the development of a young pitching staff, propelled San Diego into playoff contention. The Padres battled the Los Angeles Dodgers the entire season for the National League Western Division lead.

In August 1996, Caminiti set a record with 14 home runs, the most ever in one month by a switch-hitter. He also broke the National League record for most career games with home runs from both sides of the plate when he turned the trick for the seventh time on August 28 against the New York Mets. Caminiti accomplished the feat for an eighth time later in the season and broke his own major league record by hitting home runs from both sides of the plate four times in the same season. He made a big impression at the 1996 All-Star Game, hitting a solo home run, the first ever by a Padre in the big game.

PLAYS WITH PAIN. Caminiti overcame numerous injuries during the 1996 season. He played with a torn rotator cuff in his left shoulder, an injury causing him so much pain that he could not lift his elbow out from the side of his body. He also suffered from a severely strained groin muscle and pain in his back and hip. "If he can walk, he can play," Lee Caminiti explained in the *Los Angeles Times*. "That's always been his attitude."

The injuries were even worse for Caminiti, since he could not take pain killers because of his alcohol problem. "He lifts everyone on the team to a higher level," San Diego general manager Kevin Towers told the *Los Angeles Times*. "Teammates see him playing with a torn rotator and other injuries and they give a little more effort. They forget their own aches and pains."

SNICKER STREAK. Caminiti's most amazing performance came in August of 1996. The Padres played several games in Mexico because the Republican National Convention was being held in Jack Murphy Stadium. While in Mexico, Caminiti became ill from something he ate. He could not eat or sleep and had to have fluids pumped into his body because he became dehydrated.

Padres manager Bruce Bochy thought there was no way his star could play. "You really had to be there," he recalled in *Sports Illustrated*. "He looked so bad—I mean, all curled up in pain on the floor—that I figured he'd miss two or three days. Ken Caminiti is the toughest, most intense player I've ever been around."

Despite his illness, Caminiti insisted on playing. With nothing but a Snickers candy bar in his stomach, he hit two home runs in one game and a grand-slam and a two-run single in another. "In five at bats he had four hits, three home runs, ten RBIs, three IVs and two Snickers," Gwynn explained in *Sports Illustrated.* "The guy is amazing."

Caminiti's courageous play inspired his teammates to go on a 10-1 winning streak. He hit .472 during that stretch with 7 home runs and 22 RBI. Snickers decided to pay Caminiti an endorsement fee and San Diego fans flooded the Padres' locker room with the candy bars.

DIVISION CHAMPS. Caminiti's tough play lifted the Padres to the playoffs for the first time in 12 years. San Diego battled the Los Angeles Dodgers to the final game of the season. The two teams were tied, and when the Padres won that last game they captured the Western Division title with a 91-71 record.

"He has single-handedly kept us in this thing," San Diego pitcher Bob Tewksbury explained in *Sports Illustrated.* "He has the best combination of mental toughness and baseball ability of anyone I've ever played with." The St. Louis Cardinals swept the Padres in the first round of the playoffs, but Caminiti hit two home runs in the final game. "We came up big but they came up bigger," he admitted in the *Los Angeles Times.*

MVP. In addition to his leadership on the field, Caminiti put up big numbers for San Diego. He set career bests in batting average (.326, fifth in the league), home runs (40, fifth in the league), RBI (130, third in the league), and runs scored (109). Caminiti set Padres records in batting average, home runs, RBI, and slugging percentage (.621, third in the league). He also hit 37 doubles and finished fourth in the league with 79 extra-base hits. Caminiti also became only the third third-baseman in major league history to hit over .300 and knock out 40 home runs. (The others were Eddie Matthews in 1952 and Al Rosen in 1953.)

Down the stretch, under the pressure of the pennant race, Caminiti hit 23 home runs and drove in 61 runs during the last two months of the season. He led the league in batting (.360), home runs (28), and RBI (81) after the all-star break. Caminiti hit .387 with runners in scoring position and .397 with runners in scoring position and two out.

Caminiti's combination of courageous performance and outstanding production led to his election as only the fourth unanimous winner of the National League Most Valuable Player award. He was also the first Padre to win this prestigious trophy. "I'm excited, but I don't play for the awards," Caminiti told the *Los Angeles Times*. "I play to do the best I can. I consider myself a player who can help his team win, but I never felt I could put up the type of numbers that an MVP does. I got on my knees every night and said a prayer that I could play, but my attitude is that if I can get to the park, I'm going to play." Catcher Mike Piazza of the Dodgers finished a distant second in the voting.

THE FUTURE. Caminiti had surgery after the 1996 season to repair the torn rotator cuff in his left shoulder. Doctors said he may miss the start of the 1997 season, but he disagreed. "They say I'm moving better than scheduled," Caminiti stated in the *Los Angeles Times*. "They're [doctors are] trying to slow me down, but I don't need them slowing me down. I want to start the season."

OFF THE FIELD. Caminiti lives in Richmond, Texas, with his wife, Nancy, and their two daughters, Kendall and Lindsey. He loves riding his customized motorcycle and has a 1955 Chevy automobile that he takes to car shows. "When he gets back to the [locker] room after a game, he doesn't even like to watch himself on *SportsCenter* highlights," Livingstone stated in *Sports Illustrated*. "He just likes to talk about his motorcycle and his car." Caminiti is the co-owner of the Southern Rod and Custom shop in Houston, which fixes up classic cars and hot rods. He also likes to bow hunt.

IT'S UNANIMOUS

The following chart lists the only four National League players to be unanimous choices as Most Valuable Player:

Player	Year	Team
Orlando Cepeda	1967	St. Louis Cardinals
Mike Schmidt	1980	Philadelphia Phillies
Jeff Bagwell	1994	Houston Astros
Ken Caminiti	1996	San Diego Padres

"SCARY MAN"

Caminiti has earned the nickname "Scary Man" because of the intimidating way he looks on the field. "He's got that look," teammate Scott Livingstone told *Sports Illustrated.* "You've really got to know him before you joke around with him, and even if you do, he might take it the wrong way." Caminiti wears a goatee beard that makes him look even tougher.

Caminiti plays hard, running out routine ground balls and fly outs. "Whatever Ken does, he does all out," his wife, Nancy, told *Sports Illustrated.* His attitude about the game explains why Caminiti can play over pain. "This is the way I see it," he told the same magazine. "I love to play. We get paid a lot of money to go out and play, so I'm going to play. For me, it's easy to go out there. Playing baseball is what I love to do."

Since leaving the treatment clinic, Caminiti has been able to stay away from alcohol. "I kinda like the label of being a non-drinker," he told *Baseball Weekly.* "I like how I feel now. You want to go out with the boys, but they know my situation. So if they go to dinner, they'll ask me out. If they're going out drinking, they won't ask. I'll go to a movie or play cards instead."

Caminiti has learned how to take the ups-and-downs of major league life in stride. "I've learned to take it one day at a time, try not to get too high and try not to get too low," he declared in the *Blossom Valley/ Santa Teresa Community News.* "Many players don't want to play in pain because they don't want to have bad numbers. But baseball is a team game."

Sources

Baseball Weekly, December 6, 1995.
Los Angeles Times, September 27, 1996; September 28, 1996; October 6, 1996; November 14, 1996.
Sporting News, September 16, 1996.
Sports Illustrated, September 9, 1996.
USA Today, September 4, 1996.
Additional information provided by San Jose State University and the San Diego Padres.

WHERE TO WRITE:
C/O SAN DIEGO PADRES,
PO BOX 2000,
SAN DIEGO, CA 92112-2000.

Oscar De La Hoya

1973—

Boxers expect to get hit, but they do not like it. Oscar De La Hoya gets hit less than most fighters, and that is why he is a champion. De La Hoya was the only American to win a boxing gold medal at the 1992 Summer Olympics in Barcelona, Spain, earning the nickname "Golden Boy." Since his Olympic triumph, he is undefeated and has won three professional championships. In June 1996, De La Hoya established himself as one of the best pound-for-pound boxers in the world when he defeated the legendary Julio Cesar Chavez.

Growing Up

TOUGH NEIGHBORHOOD. Oscar De La Hoya was born February 4, 1973, in Los Angeles, California. His parents, Cecilia and Joel, moved to the United States from Mexico. The neighborhood in which De La Hoya grew up was safe, but trouble lurked right around the corner. "A half mile down that way it

"I fight for the whole world."—Oscar De La Hoya.

gets real bad," De La Hoya explained in *Sports Illustrated*. "There are killings all the time. There are lots of drug houses just up the road, too."

Gangs controlled De La Hoya's neighborhood. "I've been asked to join gangs, but I've never wanted to," De La Hoya admitted in *Sports Illustrated*. "I've always had something else." Once six men with guns stole a wallet and camera from De La Hoya. His father worked hard as a shipping and receiving clerk for a heating and cooling company, but the family had a hard time making ends meet. De La Hoya carries a food stamp in his wallet to remind him of how poor his family was.

ALL IN THE FAMILY. Boxing was important in De La Hoya's family. His grandfather, Vicente, fought as an amateur in the 1940s, and his father fought professionally in the 1960s. "My father boxed, my uncles, cousins—they all boxed," De La Hoya told *Hispanic*. "When my brother, Joel, Jr., was boxing, I would follow him to the gym—that's when my father started to see that I loved it too, so he started to take me."

De La Hoya began to box at the age of six. "I was a little kid who used to fight a lot in the street—and get beat up," De La Hoya recalled in *Sports Illustrated*. "But I liked it. So my dad took me to the gym." De La Hoya won his first bout by knocking out his opponent in the first round. "I was laughing so hard," Joel De La Hoya Sr. told *Sports Illustrated*. "I thought, 'maybe I got something here.'"

HOME AWAY FROM HOME. De La Hoya got his early training at the Resurrection Boy's Club Gym in East Los Angeles, where he started to work out at the age of ten. The gym, a former church, soon became his home away from home. De La Hoya's idol as a child was the legendary Sugar Ray Leonard, a gold medal winner at the 1976 Summer Olympics and a great professional boxer.

MOVING UP. De La Hoya quickly began to achieve success. In 1988, he won the national Junior Olympic 119-pound championship and the next year he won the 125-pound title. Two years later, De La Hoya won the national Golden Gloves 125-pound title, and the same year was the youngest U.S. boxer at the Goodwill Games, where he won a gold medal. He followed that success with a victory in the 1991 U.S. Amateur Boxing 132-pound tournament. USA Boxing named De La Hoya the 1991 Boxer of the Year.

Based on his success, experts made De La Hoya a favorite to win a gold medal at the 1992 Summer Olympics in Barcelona, Spain. He had lost only once in international competition and defeated two-time world champion Julio Gonzalez of Cuba on the day of his prom at Garfield High School in 1991. De La Hoya claimed a place on the U.S. boxing team by winning the 132-pound class gold medal at the 1991 U.S. Olympic Festival, defeating Patrice Brooks. "How good is Oscar?" asked Manuel Torres, director of boxing at the Resurrection gym, in *Sports Illustrated.* "One in a million."

TOUGH TIMES. Just when De La Hoya's career seemed to be unstoppable, he faced two difficult adjustments. First, he split with his longtime trainer, Al Stankie, who had helped train another East Los Angeles boxer, Paul Gonzales, to an Olympic gold medal. Stankie had a serious problem with alcohol addiction. "It was very hard, but I had to let him go," De La Hoya admitted in *Sports Illustrated.*

De La Hoya then began training with Robert Alcazar, a friend of his father. "Oscar is so different from the boxers that I have worked with because he knew what he wanted to do with his life at an early age," Alcazar told *Hispanic.* "He realized that he wanted to be a boxer, and each year I work with him I see him progressing."

FAMILY AFFAIR

De La Hoya credits his family with his success. "They are always there for me," De La Hoya told *Hispanic.* "If I needed a new pair of gloves because they were too old or worn out, my uncle would give me money to buy some. All my uncles would get together and buy me stuff because they saw my potential and believed that I could be somebody in boxing."

De La Hoya's left is a vicious weapon.

BIGGEST FAN. A personal tragedy caused De La Hoya an even more difficult adjustment. His mother Cecilia died after suffering from breast cancer. Cecilia De La Hoya was her son's biggest fan. "My mother would get mad at me when I didn't want to go to the gym because I wanted to be with my friends," De La Hoya told *Hispanic*. "She would say, 'No, you go to the gym because you are going to be a champion.'"

After his mother's death, De La Hoya dedicated every victory to her. "It's like telling her, 'Here's another one for you,'" he told *Sports Illustrated*. Before she died, Cecilia De La Hoya asked her son to win the Olympic gold medal for her. "That is my motivation," De La Hoya explained to the same magazine before the Olympics.

OLYMPIC CHAMP. De La Hoya won the right to represent the United States at the 1992 Summer Olympics by winning a decision over Patrice Brooks at the Olympic Boxoffs in Phoenix, Arizona. Some experts worried that he did not knock out his opponent, but De La Hoya was not concerned. "I was concentrating more on landing clean punches than I was in knocking anybody down because it was more important to make the team than to have the ego trip of putting somebody on the canvas," De La Hoya explained in the *Sporting News.* "When I get to Spain, I'll show people my power."

De La Hoya was the favorite to win the lightweight gold medal at the 1992 Summer Olympics in Barcelona, Spain. "The kid has all the tools," said Pat Nappi, former U.S. national boxing team coach, in *Sports Illustrated.* "Right now, based on what I've seen, he has the gold medal." De La Hoya tried to not get overconfident, though. "I've just got to keep my focus," he explained in the same magazine.

In the end, De La Hoya was the only U.S. boxer to win an Olympic gold medal, defeating Marco Randolph of Germany in the gold medal bout. He celebrated his victory by carrying a U.S. flag in one hand and a Mexican flag in the other. "I went up with the Mexican flag and the American flag," he recalled in *Hispanic.* "If I'd had enough arms I would have gone up with all the flags of the world!" After returning home, De La Hoya paid tribute to his mother by laying his medal on her grave. "I won the medal for mom," De La Hoya admitted in *Sports Illustrated.*

TURNS PRO. De La Hoya's amateur record now stood at 223 wins, 5 losses, and 153 knockouts. His Olympic victory won De La Hoya the nickname "Golden Boy." Having reached his goal of winning the gold medal, he decided to turn professional. This was a difficult choice for De La Hoya since his mother had not wanted him to fight for money. "I started to realize that I had to think about my future," De La Hoya admitted in *Hispanic.* "I had to think about if she were here, how she would want my life to progress. I started to receive commercial deals, and then I thought maybe if I win world titles, continued training, get more endorsements, then I could set my family financially so my father wouldn't have to work. I had to think about all the people who helped me, so I could pay them back and pay myself back for all the hard work I did."

De La Hoya made his professional debut in November 1992, knocking out Lamar Williams in the first round in Los Angeles. He won his first title, the World Boxing Organization (WBO) junior lightweight championship, in March 1994. De La Hoya knocked out title holder Jimmi Bredhal of Denmark in only his twelfth professional fight. He added his second title, the WBO lightweight title, in July 1994 by knocking out Jorge Paez in the second round.

THE PROFESSOR. On February 18, 1995, De La Hoya fought John Molina, the International Boxing Federation (IBF) junior lightweight champion. De La Hoya won the fight, but struggled with Molina's tough style. "I thought I was invincible," De La Hoya admitted in the *Philadelphia Daily News*. "I thought I knew all I had to know." The fight made De La Hoya realize that he needed a more experienced trainer than his father's friend, Robert Alcazar.

De La Hoya hired Jesus "The Professor" Rivero to be his new cornerman. Rivero—who previously trained former WBC flyweight (a professional boxer weighing no more than 112 pounds) champion Miguel Canto—had a unique way of preparing a boxer. He stressed the development of the whole person, inside the ring and out. In addition to working on his boxing, Rivero encouraged De La Hoya to read great works of literature and listen to classical music. "Oscar realizes it is to his benefit to have knowledge of life, to have culture," Rivero told the *Philadelphia Daily News*. "Does it help him as a fighter? Of course. It gives him a more panoramic [complete] view of his profession. I am not only teaching him boxing, but other values: history, geography, classical music. I want Oscar to know there are other things to boxing than money, fame and glory."

"The 'Old Man' is like a gift from God," De La Hoya stated in the *Philadelphia Daily News*. "He has taught me so much about boxing, and about life. He is helping me achieve my goal of becoming a great champion and a better person." Rivero also showed De La Hoya tapes of Willie Pep, a great former boxing champion who used his skill to keep opponents from hitting him.

In May 1995, De La Hoya knocked out Rafael Ruelas in less than five minutes. He sent Ruelas to the canvas twice in the second round before referee Richard Steele stepped in to stop the fight. "He's quick," Ruelas told *Sport Illustrated* after the fight. "That left hook? I didn't see it." The victory added the IBF lightweight championship to De La Hoya's WBO belt and raised De La Hoya's record to 18-0. In September 1995 De La Hoya scored a technical knock out against Genaro Hernandez, handing the boxer his first defeat in 34 fights.

ROLE MODEL

De La Hoya often returns to his old neighborhood to speak to kids about their education and their futures. "I go to schools to speak to kids about their futures," De La Hoya told *Hispanic*. "Just because they are Hispanic, they shouldn't feel left out or below someone else—we should all feel equal. I grew up without having anything in life; I had to struggle, so I can relate to them. The key for all Latinos is to stick together—there is so much jealousy. If we are jealous of each other we are going to destroy ourselves and make ourselves look bad."

TOUGH ENOUGH? Despite his success, some critics said De La Hoya had not fought enough quality opponents. "It's early on in my career and we're not in any rush at all because I'm still young and have many more fights ahead of me," De La Hoya told *Sport*. Many boxing fans, especially in the knowledgeable Hispanic community, thought De La Hoya was not tough enough to be a champion. "I'm a fighter who doesn't get hit, who doesn't have cuts or bruises, and that's the reason why the fans don't appreciate my boxing," De La Hoya explained in the *Fort-Worth Star Telegram*. "If I was cut up— if I was all beat up and looked like a 'fighter'—they would appreciate me more because I would look like a warrior."

Because of his success, some people felt De La Hoya would turn his back on his community. He, however, said nothing could be further from the truth. "I donate money to churches in my old neighborhood, I go to schools, I speak to kids, I make appearances and I sign autographs—I do all these things," De La Hoya told the *Fort Worth Star-Telegram*.

"When I step into that ring, what I'm doing is opening the doors for young Latino fighters or minority fighters or whoever out there who wants to be a boxer. I'm a good role model for kids, and I love doing that."

Superstar

BEATS LEGEND. In June 1996, De La Hoya faced his biggest challenge ever. He was scheduled to fight Julio Cesar Chavez, the World Boxing Council (WBC) super lightweight champion. Chavez was an excellent fighter and a legend in Mexico and among Hispanic fans. He had 99 professional fights and 32 title bouts—an incredible amount of experience—and had lost only one fight in his career. De La Hoya sparred with Chavez as an amateur, and the champion knocked him down.

The crowd at Caesar's Palace in Las Vegas, Nevada, was behind the old warrior Chavez. It soon became clear, however, who the best fighter was that night. De La Hoya marched out of his corner and repeatedly landed stinging blows on Chavez. "I was trying to stop him in his tracks," De La Hoya explained in the *Los Angeles Times*. The young champion kept Chavez away from him with a powerful jab, then pummeled the legendary champion in the fourth round with a six-punch flurry. The fight doctor stepped in at that point, stopping the fight because of a brutal cut above Chavez's left eye.

"I knew if he got injured it would be a big problem for him," De La Hoya stated in the *Philadelphia Inquirer*. "He's a true warrior but when I cut his eye and broke his nose with a left hook I knew I had him." Despite his victory, De La Hoya realized he still needed to improve. "I need many more fights to learn, many more years to become a complete champion," De La Hoya told *Sports Illustrated*.

OUT OF THE RING. De La Hoya is single and lives in Montebello, a mountain resort town near Los Angeles. He has an older brother, Joel, Jr., and a younger sister, Ceci. De La Hoya wants to study to be an architect, and helped design his own home. His house has a boxing gym, bowling alley, and golf course. "I love golf," De La Hoya told *Hispanic*. "I think I am the only boxer who plays golf." De La Hoya is very outgoing and makes money outside the ring from several endorsements.

De La Hoya says there are many similarities between boxing and architecture. "Boxing is an art form," he explained in *Hispanic*. "You have to be really good at it to know what you are doing. You have to create your game plan in your mind and work at it. When I draw a house plan, I think about it, visualize it as I do in boxing and it becomes beautiful. The ring is my canvas, because if I had paint under my feet I would create this beautiful picture; it would be like a Picasso."

De La Hoya wants boxing fans to remember him as one of the greatest fighters ever. "I want to beat what [Thomas] Hearns had done," he told *Sports Illustrated,* referring to the five titles in different weight classes won by the former boxing great. De La Hoya has already won titles in three different weight classes. "If Oscar continues the same way he has been doing these last twelve years, he's going to be one of the biggest in boxing history," Alcazar, told *Hispanic*.

De La Hoya plans to fight for a few more years, then retire. "I want this to be a short career, different than all the other boxers," he admitted in *Sports Illustrated*. "I'll fight 30, 40 times, but I'll fight the best, won't duck anybody. At 26, I'll be happily retired and in architecture school." De La Hoya explained to *Hispanic* that he fights "first for my mother, then my family, then myself, then for all the people who support me—the Mexican people, all Hispanic people. I fight for the whole world."

Sources

Bazaar, June 1996.
Business Week, February 15, 1993.
Dallas Morning News, June 9, 1996.
Hispanic, October 1995.
Los Angeles Times, May 7, 1995; September 10, 1995; December 15, 1995; June 8, 1996.
Philadelphia Inquirer, June 8, 1996.
San Diego Union-Tribune, May 7, 1995.
Sport, October 1995.
Sporting News, July 6, 1992.

Sports Illustrated, October 21, 1991; December 7, 1992; December 20, 1993; May 15, 1995; June 10, 1996; June 17, 1996.

Additional information provided by United States Amateur Boxing.

WHERE TO WRITE:

C/O WORLD BOXING COUNCIL,
GENOVA 33, OFICINA 503,
COLONIA JUAREZ, CUAUHTEMOC,
0600 MEXICO CITY, DF, MEXICO.

Todd Eldredge

1971—

In 1992, Todd Eldredge thought his figure skating career had ended. He had won back-to-back men's titles at the U.S. Figure Skating Championships (1990—91), but a back injury and a string of disappointing performances made him consider giving up the sport he loved. Fortunately, Eldredge—a fierce competitor—decided to prove that he was not finished at the age of 21. With renewed determination, he returned in 1996 to give the greatest performance of his life. Eldredge won the men's title at the World Figure Skating Championships in Edmonton, Alberta, Canada. Because he did not quit, Eldredge is the best in the world.

"All I know is, whether I ever win an Olympic medal or not, skating has still been worth it."—Todd Eldredge.

Growing Up

FISHERMAN'S SON. Todd Eldredge was born August 28, 1971, in Chatham, Massachusetts. His father, John, was a fisherman, and his mother, Ruth, was a nurse. John Eldredge owned a 42-foot boat and fished on Nantucket Sound, leaving

WON MEN'S TITLE AT 1996 WORLD
FIGURE SKATING CHAMPIONSHIPS
IN EDMONTON, ALBERTA, CANADA.

WON THREE MEN'S TITLES
AT THE U.S. FIGURE SKATING
CHAMPIONSHIPS (1990, 1991,
AND 1995).

WON BRONZE MEDAL (1991) AND
SILVER MEDAL (1995) AT WORLD
FIGURE SKATING CHAMPIONSHIPS.

ELDREDGE OVERCAME A
SERIOUS BACK INJURY AND HIS
OWN DOUBTS TO BECOME
THE BEST MALE FIGURE SKATER
IN THE WORLD.

the house most days before the sun came up. Eldredge and his father did not spend much time together, since John Eldredge did not like figure skating, and his son never learned to swim and suffered from seasickness.

FIRST LOVE. Eldredge first fell in love with figure skating when he was five years old. His parents took him to a public ice rink to try out his new hockey skates. "I remember watching the figure skaters in the middle of the rink, spinning and jumping, and I thought it was so cool," Eldredge recalled in the *Detroit Free Press*. "I told my parents I wanted to learn to do that, so they bought me a pair of figure skates."

LEAVES HOME. When Eldredge was ten years old he wanted to move to Philadelphia, Pennsylvania, to train with coach Richard Callaghan. He had met Callaghan at a summer camp and thought the coach could help him become a better skater. Eldredge's parents agreed to let him spend a summer at Callaghan's skater's boardinghouse. "We never thought he'd last down there," Ruth Eldredge told the *Detroit Free Press*. "We figured he'd be homesick in a couple of weeks. But he loved it. He was very self-driven, and he was determined to be the best skater he could be."

Eldredge went to live and train full time with Callaghan and quickly began moving up the ladder of U.S. figure skating. In 1985, Eldredge won the novice (beginner) national championship, then captured the national junior title two years later. He became the best male junior figure skater in the world when he won the gold medal at the 1988 World Junior Figure Skating Championships. "He was talented, there was no question, but also, you could tell he wanted to be the best," Callaghan recalled in the *Detroit Free Press*. "He was dying for a lesson, would go out there and come back for more."

ON THE ROAD AGAIN. In 1987, Callaghan decided to move from Philadelphia to a rink in Colorado Springs, Colorado. Eldredge and his mother made a tough decision. They moved to Colorado with Callaghan, leaving the rest of their family in Massachusetts. The family only got together on holidays and special occasions. Callaghan moved again two years later—this time to San Diego, California—and the Eldredges followed.

NATIONAL CHAMPION. Eldredge began entering senior competitions in 1988, finishing eighth at the U.S. Figure Skating Championships. He moved up to fifth in 1989, and in 1990 was one of the favorites for the men's title. Eldredge got a big break when the 1989 champion, Christopher Bowman, withdrew from the competition with a back injury. In a big upset, Eldredge, still only 18, won the men's title, becoming the youngest men's champion in 24 years. In his first appearance at the World Figure Skating Championships, Eldredge finished a respectable fifth in 1990.

BACK-TO-BACK. Eldredge eventually faced Bowman at the 1991 U.S. Figure Skating Championships in Minneapolis, Minnesota, in an effort to defend his title. Bowman won the short, or required program, with Eldredge second. (In the short program, skaters must successfully complete required jumps and other maneuvers.) In the long program—which counts for two-thirds of the final score—Eldredge showed his skill. (In the long—or free-skating—program, the skater designs his own routine.)

Bowman skated his long program first and made no errors. Then Eldredge took the ice. He landed a triple axel-triple toe jump combination, and the move gave him confidence. He landed seven triple jumps in his program without an error. For the second year in a row, Eldredge won the U.S. men's championship.

An emotional Eldredge gives a winning performance.

THIRD IN THE WORLD. Eldredge then headed to the 1991 World Figure Skating Championships in Munich, Germany. Skating last in the long program, he needed a perfect performance to move from fourth place and into third. Eldredge delivered, and the crowd responded. "I feel it was the best I've skated, and it sounded like the audience got into it, too," Eldredge stated in *Sports Illustrated*. Kurt Browning of Canada won his third straight world title, with Viktor Petrenko of the Ukraine finishing second.

BAD BACK. After two years of success, Eldredge looked forward to competing in the 1992 Winter Olympics in Albertville, France. Unfortunately, in the fall of 1991 his back began to hurt. Doctors discovered that one of his legs was shorter than the other, causing problems in a joint in his back, especially when he landed after jumping. The injury forced Eldredge to withdraw from the 1992 U.S. Figure Skating Championships in Orlando, Florida, but the U.S. Figure Skating Association placed him on the Olympic team because of his past performances.

Eldredge struggled with the decision about whether to participate in the Olympics or to let a healthier Mark Mitchell—the third-place finisher at the U.S. championships—go in his place. He finally decided to go to Albertville, but the injury still bothered him. Eldredge's Olympic experience was a disaster. He failed to complete a double axel in his short program and fell out of contention, finishing tenth overall.

His Olympic performance made Eldredge begin to doubt himself. "I thought I deserved to be at the Olympics after what I'd done the year before," he explained in the *Boston Globe*. "But after the way I skated, I did question whether or not I should have been there. And people were saying that they should have sent somebody who was healthier. That added to the doubt that I already had in my mind."

HARD TIMES. The back injury and his poor Olympic performance made Eldredge doubt himself. He competed at the 1993 U.S. Figure Skating Championships in Phoenix, Arizona, but his heart was not in his performance. Eldredge finished sixth, a disappointing performance for a former champion.

The pressure of being national champion was hard on Eldredge. "I was feeling pressure and I let it get to me," Eldredge admitted in the *Boston Globe*. "I shouldn't have, but that's the way it worked." Callaghan agreed. "Winning those titles at 18 and 19 was a good thing, and I'm glad he did it," Callaghan told the same newspaper. "But the responsibilities that went along with it are difficult. Maybe it was a young age to tolerate those responsibilities."

BIG DECISION. Eldredge had to decide whether he wanted to continue to skate. He quit for three months to try to get his thoughts together. "I told Todd to take as much time off as he needed," Callaghan explained in the *Boston Globe*. "Get out of the rink for a while and reassess what he wanted to do. He could leave the sport and feel good about himself. But if he wanted to continue, I felt he had to learn how to love to skate again and clear his mind of everything else that was in there."

After three months Eldredge returned to the rink and followed Callaghan to the Detroit Skating Club in West Bloomfield, Michigan. He discovered that he wanted to skate again, and that winning was not a matter of life and death. Before his time off Eldredge got mad at himself when he did not skate well. "I can accept when I don't skate well better now than I could a few years ago," Eldredge explained in the *Boston Globe*. "I used to dwell on things that I missed in my program. Now I'll say, 'I'll do it tomorrow.' Or 'I'll do it next time.'"

COMEBACK. Eldredge won a silver medal at the 1994 Goodwill Games, finishing second behind Alexei Urmanov, the 1994 Olympic gold medalist. He felt he was ready for a comeback at the 1994 U.S. Figure Skating Championships in Detroit, Michigan. "I feel like I'm on the road back to where I was," Eldredge told the *Detroit Free Press*. "With every event, I'm feeling more comfortable. There were times I thought about quitting, but the pure love of the sport kept me going. I don't feel I've done all I can do. I have a lot more to offer."

The top two finishers at the U.S. championships would qualify for the 1994 Winter Olympics in Lillehammer, Norway. Two days before the competition began, however, Eldredge came down with the flu, which gave him a temperature of 104 degrees and caused him to faint. Despite the illness, he competed and finished third behind national champion Scott Davis and former Olympic champion Brian Boitano.

Coming up just short of making the Olympic team disappointed Eldredge. But unlike before, he did not let his disappointment slow him down. "I knew in my heart that there was nothing I could have done about what happened at nationals,"

Eldredge confessed in the *Detroit Free Press*. "The whole experience just inspired me to come back and show I can still compete."

Superstar

BACK ON TOP. The 1995 U.S. Figure Skating Championships were held in Providence, Rhode Island. Skating experts made two-time defending champion Scott Davis the favorite, but Eldredge had been skating well and beat Davis three times in competitions in the previous year. "Scott is the defending champion, so he's still the guy to beat, but I'm not a total underdog because I won two titles before and I've had a good season so far this year," Eldredge explained in the *Detroit Free Press*. "Anything can happen."

Eldredge wanted to win back his national championship very badly. "Todd almost wanted the title too much," Callaghan confessed in the *Boston Globe*. "I thought he'd try too hard." Davis led after the short program, but Eldredge was close behind. When Eldredge took the ice for his long program, the competitive fire was burning in his eyes. "Yeah, I saw it," Callaghan recalled in the *Philadelphia Inquirer*. "It said, 'Move over.' He was determined."

Skating to music from the movie "Gettysburg," Eldredge blew away the competition. He almost fell on one jump, catching himself by putting his hands down on the ice. Instead of getting angry about his mistake, Eldredge threw in an unplanned triple jump combination at the end of his program to make up for the mistake. "I wasn't concerned that I had lost the competition when I had that problem," Eldredge explained in the *Philadelphia Inquirer*. "I was concerned that I had done it. I was just determined to keep it clean the rest of the way and see what happened with Scott."

Davis skated after Eldredge and several mistakes took away his concentration. When the final scores were posted, every judge voted for Eldredge. "I can't think of anything I've wanted as much as this," Eldredge confessed in the *Atlanta*

Journal—Constitution. With the win Eldredge became the oldest U.S. men's champion since Charles Tucker won in 1980 at age 26.

Eldredge also became the first male skater to regain the national championship after not winning a medal at the U.S. championships for three years. "It's been a while since I've been up on the podium," he stated in the *Boston Globe.* "But I've had a good year and this caps it all off." Eldredge was the first man to win three U.S. titles since former Olympic champion Brian Boitano won four (1985—88).

SO CLOSE. After regaining his U.S. title, Eldredge wanted to win the 1995 World Figure Skating Championships in Birmingham, England. The defending champion, Elvis Stojko of Canada, injured his ankle before the Canadian Figure Skating Championships. Despite eight weeks of rest, the ankle still caused him a lot of pain, but Stojko decided to compete. Eldredge was glad to hear of Stojko's decision. "You want to go up against the world champion at the world championships and try to dethrone him," Eldredge explained in the *Detroit Free Press.*

Eldredge jumped into the lead in the short program, with Stojko close behind in second. In the free skating final, Eldredge skated before Stojko. He fell on a triple axel, but made up for the mistake by adding another triple jump late in his program. The judges rewarded Eldredge with high scores, moving the American into first place.

The pressure was on Stojko, and like a true champion he produced a remarkable performance. The defending world title holder skated a nearly perfect routine, showing no sign of pain. The final scores showed that the judges favored Stojko, 6 to 3, giving him the title. "I wanted to win, obviously, but it happened that tonight, Elvis skated better, and he should have won," Eldredge told the *Calgary Herald.*

UPSET. In the fall of 1995, Eldredge accepted an invitation to perform in "The Nutcracker on Ice," a figure skating tour. He made $80,000 on the tour, but could not practice to defend his title at the 1995 U.S. Figure Skating Championships in San

Jose, California. As a result, Eldredge finished second to Rudy Galindo, a 26-year-old skater who had never won a medal at the national championships before.

Eldredge worked hard to not let the loss set him back. He trained four hours a day and passed up $100,000 in performance fees to work out in preparation for the 1996 World Figure Skating Championships in Edmonton, Alberta, Canada. "I have to thank Rudy for beating me at [the] nationals," Eldredge admitted in *Sports Illustrated*. "It made me go back and train and get my act together."

REMATCH. The men's competition at the world championships featured a rematch between Eldredge and Stojko. The short program produced a shock when Stojko fell on his triple axel, dropping him to seventh place. Teenager Ilia Kulilk of Russia—the European champion—won the short program, but Eldredge was close behind in second place. Urmanov took third place and Galindo stood fourth.

WORLD CHAMPION. Eldredge had the look of a champion when he took the ice for his long program. He landed eight triple jumps in his routine and had the best performance of his life. Moving quickly around the ice, Eldredge left no doubt that he was the best skater in the competition and the judges agreed, awarding him the championship over Kulilk. After three years of hard work, Eldredge was the best in the world. "I had to believe that someday it would happen," he confessed in *Sports Illustrated* after the competition. "That's the best I've ever skated."

Galindo won the bronze medal, marking the first time since 1981 that two American men had won medals at the world championships. (Scott Hamilton and David Santee finished in first and second place in 1981.) When Michelle Kwan won the women's championship, it marked the first time since 1986—when Brian Boitano and Debbie Thomas won—that the United States won both the men's and women's world championships.

After receiving his medal, Eldredge placed it around his mother's neck. "It was a tremendous feeling to stand on that

FAMILY AFFAIR

Skating has put a tremendous strain on the Eldredge family. To pay for coaching, skates, and costumes, the family took out loans and new mortgages on their home. His parents never told Eldredge how much they spent on his skating. "We didn't want Todd to think about money," Ruth Eldredge explained in the *Detroit Free Press*. "We wanted him to enjoy the sport he loved so much. If he had any idea how much money we're in debt because of skating, he'd probably be surprised. But in a way, the struggles made our family closer. If we were rich people, his success wouldn't be as meaningful. Our situation is unique and was a true lesson in humanity and the strength of family."

When the bills became more than the family could pay, the people of Chatham held celebrity clambakes and Christmas dinners to raise money. They raised as much as $15,000 per year for their hometown hero. Now that figure skaters are allowed to accept money from competitions and ice shows, Eldredge can begin to pay back those who have supported him. "It's a lot easier now to stay in training, because of all the opportunities available to us," Eldredge told the *Detroit Free Press*. "My family sacrificed a lot, so it's nice to be able to pay my own way for a change."

podium and catch my parents eye in the stands," Eldredge confessed in the *Detroit Free Press*. "It made all the sacrifices worth it. I plan to pay them back for all they did."

OFF THE ICE. Eldredge lives in Bloomfield Hills, Michigan and is a spokesperson for Speedo sportswear. Eldredge likes to play golf, tennis, and poker. Always a big sports fan, he has followed the Boston Celtics and the Boston Red Sox since childhood.

Eldredge is committed to training through the 1998 Winter Olympics in Nagono, Japan. "The pinnacle of our sport is the Olympics," Eldredge explained in the *Boston Globe*. "I competed there once and I didn't do as well as I would have liked to. I'd like another chance to make up for what happened in 1992."

Eldredge has learned to keep his skating in perspective, as he told the *Detroit Free Press:* "All I know is, whether I ever win an Olympic medal or not, skating has still been worth it."

Sources

Atlanta Journal, February 12, 1995.
Boston Globe, February 10, 1995; February 12, 1995.
Calgary Herald, March 10, 1995.
Chicago Tribune, February 12, 1995.
Detroit Free Press, January 3, 1994; January 6, 1994; October 29, 1994; December 1, 1994; February 7, 1995; February 8, 1995; February 9, 1995; February 10, 1995; March 6, 1995; March 7, 1995; March 9, 1995; March 10, 1995; October 24, 1995; October 26, 1995; October 27, 1995; October 30, 1995; January 15, 1996; January 16, 1996; January 19, 1996; March 21, 1996; March 22, 1996; March 23, 1996.
Oregonian, February 12, 1995.
Philadelphia Inquirer, February 11, 1995.
San Francisco Examiner, January 15, 1996.

San Jose Mercury News, January 21, 1996.
Sporting News, January 20, 1992.
Sports Illustrated, February 25, 1991; March 25, 1991; April 1, 1996.
Time, February 27, 1995.
Toronto Star, March 22, 1996.
Additional information provided by Reuters News Service and U.S. Figure
    Skating Association.

WHERE TO WRITE:

C/O U.S. FIGURE SKATING ASSOCIATION,
20 FIRST STREET,
COLORADO SPRINGS, CO 80906-3697.

Lisa Fernandez

1971—

"I live for the opportunity to get the game-winning [run batted in] RBI or make the diving play with the bases loaded."—Lisa Fernandez.

Pitcher Lisa Fernandez can throw a softball 75 miles per hour. She can dip, rise, and spin the ball, making her pitches almost unhittable. During the 1996 Summer Olympics in Atlanta, Georgia, Fernandez was nearly perfect. She won the game that sent the United States into the first-ever women's softball gold-medal game against China, then came on to save the championship game for the Americans against the same team. A four-time All-American at the University of California—Los Angeles (UCLA), Fernandez may be the best all-around female softball player in the world.

Growing Up

BASEBALL IN BLOOD. Lisa Fernandez was born February 22, 1971. Her father, Antonio, was a semi-pro third baseman in Cuba, living under the communist government of Fidel Castro. He escaped from Cuba and came to the United States, leaving with nothing but the clothes he was wearing. Fernandez's mother, Emelia, was a third baseman on the Puerto Rican women's softball team. "If someone asked me what my heritage is, I would say I'm Cuban and Puerto Rican, but the U.S. is my home," Fernandez said.

Fernandez's parents met in Los Angeles and then settled in nearby Long Beach. She is an only child, and her parents gave her their love of softball. "My dad was my first coach, and my mom was my first catcher," Fernandez recalled in *Women's Sports and Fitness*. Fernandez began to play softball at an early age. "All I knew was softball," she stated in *USA Today*. We were always playing. I was the batgirl for my mom's slow-pitch team. When I was old enough, I started playing."

Fernandez dove around the family living room at the age of four, trying to catch rolled up socks her parents threw just out of her reach. In her first pitching appearance—at age eight—Fernandez lost 28-0 and walked 20 batters. "I remember thinking to myself, 'This isn't fun,'" she confessed in *Women's Sports and Fitness*. Fernandez did not let her rough start get her down, however. "I just resolved that I would do better the next time out, and gradually I became better," she explained in *Sports Illustrated*.

ARMS TOO SHORT? Fernandez tried out for a team for 13 to 15-year-olds when she was 12. The coach of the team told her that she would never be a champion pitcher because her arms were too short. "He said I wouldn't be able to really compete past the age of 16," Fernandez recalled in *Women's Sports and Fitness*.

Fernandez was crushed because she really wanted to pitch. When she thought about quitting, her mother gave her a good piece of advice. "Don't ever let someone take away your dreams," Emelia Fernandez advised her daughter, according to *Sports Illustrated for Kids*.

SCOREBOARD

SAVED FINAL GAME IN THE WOMEN'S SOFTBALL TOURNAMENT AT THE 1996 SUMMER OLYMPICS IN ATLANTA, GEORGIA, TO ASSURE THE U.S. TEAM OF FIRST-EVER GOLD MEDAL.

FOUR-TIME ALL-AMERICAN (1990—93) AT UNIVERSITY OF CALIFORNIA—LOS ANGELES (UCLA).

ONLY PLAYER TO LEAD THE NATION IN BATTING (.510) AND ERA (0.25) IN THE SAME SEASON, A FEAT SHE ACCOMPLISHED DURING HER SENIOR YEAR AT UCLA.

FERNANDEZ IS A STAR ON THE MOUND, AT THE PLATE, AND IN THE FIELD.

Fernandez celebrates on the mound after the United States wins the gold during the 1996 Summer Olympics.

Fernandez made the team as an infielder, but every chance she got she worked on her pitching. Finally her coach let her pitch in a game. Against the best team in the league, Fernandez gave up only one run. Recognizing talent when he saw it, the coach of the team she faced asked her to switch teams. Fernandez became a starting pitcher on her new team. By the time she was 15, she could throw 75 miles per hour.

Her mother always pushed Fernandez to excel. "My mom didn't allow me on a team I could dominate," she explained in *USA Today.* "She didn't want me to be a big fish in a little pond. So I always played on teams where there were better players, where I had to work hard to get better."

HIGH SCHOOL HURLER. Fernandez was a sensation at St. Joseph's High School in Long Beach. She threw 69 shutouts (the other teams didn't score any runs), 37 no-hitters, and 12 perfect games in high school and is listed in 20 categories in the California Interscholastic Federation (CIF) record book. (A pitcher pitches a perfect game when no batters from the opposing team reach base.) Fernandez's earned-run-average (ERA) was 0.07. She earned high school All-American honors four straight years.

BRUIN BLASTER. College recruiters from around the United States wanted Fernandez to attend their schools, but she chose nearby University of California—Los Angeles (UCLA). She went 11-1 with a 0.25 ERA and batted .310 as a third baseman to lead the Bruins to the 1990 Women's College World Series championship in her freshman season.

In the 1992 Women's College World Series, Fernandez started five of UCLA's six games as the Bruins won their second national crown. She threw shutouts in every game she pitched and set a tournament record with 35 consecutive scoreless innings. Fernandez ended the season 29-0 with a 0.14 ERA while batting .401.

In her senior season (1993) Fernandez had one of the most remarkable years ever. She became the only player to ever lead the nation in batting average (.510) and ERA (0.25) during the same season. Fernandez struck out 348 batters in 249 innings on her way to a 33-3 record on the mound. At the end of the year Fernandez became the first softball player to win the prestigious Honda-Broderick Cup, given annually to the nation's best female collegiate athlete.

RECORD BREAKER. During her four years at UCLA, Fernandez was the best collegiate player in the United States, and maybe the best of all time. Three years in a row (1991—93) she won the Honda Award, given to the nation's best softball player. The Amateur Softball Association (ASA) named Fernandez SportWoman of the Year in 1991 and 1992 and she won most valuable player honors in 1991 and 1992 at the Women's Major Fast Pitch National Championship.

Fernandez led UCLA to two Women's College World Series national championships during her career (1990 and 1992) and two second-place finishes (1991 and 1993). Four times she earned All-American honors. As a pitcher, she compiled a 93-7 record at UCLA, including 42 consecutive victories (second all-time), and set National Collegiate Athletic Association (NCAA) records with her 93 wins and .930 winning percentage. Fernandez pitched 97 consecutive scoreless innings (second all-time), had 74 shutouts, 11 no-hitters, and compiled a career ERA of 0.22 (second all-time).

During her career, Fernandez also excelled at the plate, batting .382 and setting UCLA career records for singles (225), runs scored (142), walks (65), and hits (287). "Lisa Fernandez is the best all-around softball player in the history of the sport," UCLA coach Sharron Backus said. "If you try to compare her to a Major League Baseball player, she has no equal. There is no one who can pitch, hit, and field like Lisa in the major leagues, nor has there been an equal in collegiate softball."

TAKES ON THE WORLD. Fernandez quickly became a vital part of the U.S. women's national team. In 1990, she helped the American team win the gold medal at the Women's World Championship in Normal, Illinois. At the 1991 Pan American Games, held in Indianapolis, Indiana, Fernandez participated on the United States squad that took the gold medal. The U.S. repeated as world champions in 1994 in St. John's, Newfoundland, Canada.

LEFT OUT. With her impressive record in international play, Fernandez felt she was a sure thing to make the U.S. team for the 1995 Pan American Games. Surprisingly, she failed to make the squad when the final roster was announced. "It was a wake up call to what life is all about," Fernandez said, admitting that she was not playing up to her usual standards. "You can't take anything for granted. [You] just have to give your best and as long as you can live with yourself, that's all that matters."

MAKES TEAM. With the Olympics only one year away, Fernandez rededicated herself to training. The hard work paid off, as she earned one of the 15 spots on the first ever U.S. Olympic women's softball team announced in September 1995. Softball would be an official Olympic sport for the first time at the 1996 Summer Olympics in Atlanta, Georgia. "To be selected as one of the top 15 players is a great honor," Fernandez said. "There are, by far, a great deal of athletes that deserve to be in this position. I'm just one of the fortunate ones."

Fernandez was the best pitcher for the United States on their pre-Olympic tour, with an ERA of 0.08. The Americans dominated their competition, going 60-1 on the tour. After the United States lost its only game—at the hands of China in the Superball Classic '95 that ended the team's 106-game winning streak—Fernandez pitched the Americans to the championship of the same tournament with an 8-0, one-hitter, over the same Chinese team.

FAB FIVE. Entering the Olympics, the United States boasted the strongest pitching rotation in the world. "It's no secret that our game is dominated at the mound," Fernandez told the *Sacramento Bee*. The fab five included Fernandez, Christa Williams, Lori Harrigan, Michele Granger, and Michele Smith. Having five quality pitchers posed a difficult problem for the opposition. "Whether it's myself in the middle of the circle or Smith or Granger or Harrigan or Williams, it doesn't matter," Fernandez explained in the *Milwaukee Journal Sentinel*. "When you have the five best pitchers in the world possibly, you can't go wrong. We rely on each other. If someone is struggling, we can talk. We realize our common goal. We want to come out with the gold medal."

Superstar

OLYMPIC HISTORY. Fernandez played third base the first five games of the Olympics. In the first-ever Olympic women's softball game—played at Golden Park in nearby Columbus, Georgia—the United States defeated Puerto Rico 10-0. "We wanted to take no prisoners," Fernandez stated in *USA Today*. "You've got to put people away when you have the chance. There's always going to be a next time, and they're not going to hesitate to come right back at you."

Fernandez knocked in the first run for the United States, had two hits, and scored three times. "This was an important game for us," she admitted in *USA Today*. "It gave us a chance to wet our feet and let people see just what the USA has after hearing all this talk. Words can only go so far. For those other countries who thought they had a chance, they know now they've got something to reckon with." The United States won their first four games by a combined score of 29-1.

ALMOST PERFECT. Fernandez suffered a slight right ankle sprain in a 6-1 win over Japan. She was scheduled to pitch against Canada, but the injury delayed her first start. Fernandez refused to let the injury slow her down. "We're in the Olympics," she told the *Detroit Free Press*. "Nothing can stop me. I'll play with a broken leg."

Fernandez got her first start of the Olympics against the strong team from Australia. The game was scoreless in the fifth inning, when U.S. third baseman Dani Tyler hit a home run to centerfield, seemingly giving the United States a 1-0 lead. "Dani's ball goes over the fence and I think, if I do my job, we'll win," Fernandez explained in *Newsday*.

In her excitement, however, Tyler did not touch home plate. The umpires called her out, taking away the run. "I can't imagine missing any of the plate trotting, but I was so excited I don't remember positively touching it," Tyler admitted in *USA Today*. "I can't really tell you for sure." Replays showed that Tyler did, in fact, miss the plate.

Fernandez tried not to let the mistake bother her. "You have to suck it up," she told *Newsday*. "I can't ask Dani to do more for me than she did." For nine innings the Australian team failed to have a single batter reach base—no hits, no walks, and no errors by the American team. Unfortunately, Tanya Harding of Australia was equally tough, holding the United States scoreless. Harding also attended UCLA and led the Bruins to an NCAA title in 1995.

International rules say that after teams play two extra innings (nine total innings) and the score is still tied, each team starts with a runner on second base. In the top of the tenth inning, Sheila Cornell of the United States singled to center field to drive in the go-ahead run. Now all Fernandez had to do was protect this 1-0 lead and the Americans would win.

BAD PITCH. In the bottom of the tenth, Fernandez struck out the first batter she faced, then got a groundout to shortstop. Only Joanne Brown stood between her and a perfect game. The first pitch to Brown was a ball, but then Fernandez blew two strikes past the Aussie batter. She was one strike away from victory.

The next pitch Fernandez threw was the worst the U.S. hurler had made all game—a rise ball that hung over the plate. She knew right away that she had made a mistake, and Brown took advantage of the bad pitch and hit it hard. "If it wasn't gone, it was going to knock the fence down," Fernandez explained in *USA Today*. "I gave it everything I had, and I probably overthrew it more than I underthrew it. It flattened out over the middle of the plate, and she jumped on it."

The ball was gone, and Australia won the game 2-1. It was Fernandez's first loss in international play in six years. She took the blame for the defeat, despite her brilliant pitching. "I lost," Fernandez admitted in *Newsday*. "I gave up the home run. Of course I can pitch better." She struck out 15 batters in the game.

ANOTHER NAILBITER. Despite the lost, the United States still led their division and earned a spot in the semifinals. There they faced their old rival, the team from the People's Republic of China. Coach Ralph Raymond needed his best pitcher, and Fernandez once again took the mound. "I'm sure Lisa will be ready," Raymond stated in *USA Today*. "She'll want to come back strong. She's a gamer and the one I want to be in a situation like this."

The game was a pitcher's duel, with neither team able to score. Four times the United States got their lead-off (first) batter on base, but could not come up with the big hit. Fernandez retired the first 18 Chinese hitters she faced, then faltered in the seventh inning. Zhang Chunfang hit a bloop single to break up her perfect game. With runners on first and third with two out, Fernandez got one of China's top hitters, Tao Hua, to pop up to end the inning. "I knew this was do or die, and I was going to keep fighting," she told the Gannett News Service. "I was going to show the tenacity [determination] we needed. All the team's emotion starts on the mound."

The game continued in a scoreless tie into the tenth inning. Fernandez retired the side in the Chinese half of the inning and showed no signs of fatigue. "My tank is never empty," she stated in the *Los Angeles Times*. The United States loaded the bases with no one out in the bottom of the tenth. Sheila Cornell then stroked a single to drive in shortstop **Dot Richardson,** giving the United States a 1-0 win.

Fernandez got her first win of the Olympics after giving up 3 hits and striking out 13 batters. "I've never seen her throw better in all the years I've known her," Raymond said. Fernandez also had two hits in the game. "We had some misfortunes," she admitted in the *Los Angeles Times*. "But we fought back."

GOLD-MEDAL CLASH. With the win in the semifinals the United States earned a spot in the gold medal championship game. China defeated Australia to claim the right to a rematch with the Americans. Granger started the game for the United States, but Fernandez was ready to pitch if needed.

The gold-medal game was a classic played before a full house of 8750 fans at Golden Park. Richardson hit a two-run home run in the third inning. The ball landed in foul territory, but curved around the foul pole in the air. The Chinese argued the call—claiming the ball was foul—but video replays showed that it was a fair ball. The United States added another run in the inning to take a commanding 3-0 lead.

TO THE RESCUE. Granger began to struggle in the sixth inning. She gave up a single and a double to put runners on first and second with two outs. With the game in the balance, Raymond called on his ace. In came Fernandez from the bullpen. "We all couldn't wait," U.S. designated hitter Smith explained in *Newsday*. "We knew Lisa was going to get it, we just didn't know how."

"I didn't really expect to go in to pitch because Granger was doing a great job," Fernandez recalled to the Gannett News Service. "But we make a good combination out there because we throw differently." Catcher Gillian Boxx missed the first pitch Fernandez threw, allowing a run to score on a passed ball. Fernandez bore down and struck out Wang Ying for the third out of the inning. The Americans were one inning away from victory.

GOOD AS GOLD. Fernandez was untouchable in the seventh inning. "The look was in her eyes, I knew she was going to do it," Boxx told the Gannett News Service. Tao Hua grounded out to Richardson at shortstop. Then Fernandez struck out both Chen Hong and Xu Jian to seal the U.S. victory. She threw her glove into the air and was mobbed on the mound by her teammates. "You couldn't ask for a better finish as a pitcher," Fernandez said. "You think about ending a game in grand fashion."

Fernandez finished the Olympics with an ERA of 0.33 with 31 strikeouts in 21 innings. "You start out with a challenge, it's a year ahead of you, but you chip away and finally realize your goal," Fernandez told the *Los Angeles Times*. "It wasn't pretty, but we won, and that's what it's all about."

WHY SO GOOD? Fernandez can make the ball break in and out, up and down, and she throws an incredible changeup. She can throw six different pitches, with the best being her rise ball. The pitch jumps almost a foot as it passes through the strike zone. "Repetition is everything," Fernandez declared in the *Los Angeles Times*. "If you can throw a ball over the plate 9 times out of 10, you've got to keep trying for 10 out of 10."

Fernandez has a fierce glare and bounces from foot to foot on the mound. Pitchers throw from 40 feet, and many pitchers are only 35 feet away by the time they release the ball. Because women's softball is such a low-scoring game, the pitcher is a very important player. "There's a lot of pressure that goes along with it [being a pitcher]," Fernandez said. "But that's part of the responsibility you have to the sport. I chose to be a pitcher because the ball is in your hand and it's up to you to perform at the top of your game always."

Fernandez will never stop trying to improve. "God didn't give me that many physical talents," she admitted in *USA Today*. "But one thing He did give me was a lot of heart and a lot of tenacity. I always tell myself never to be satisfied."

OFF THE FIELD. Fernandez lives in the Los Angeles area. She is an assistant coach at UCLA. Louisville Slugger has released a Lisa Fernandez signature bat and the hard-throwing righthander is also a spokesperson for Reebok and Bausch & Lomb.

Fernandez runs softball clinics for teenagers around the United States. She also participates in Reebok women's Sport Training Challenge Camps. Someday, Fernandez would like to open a softball academy and help design equipment made for female players.

Fernandez is considering whether to pitch in the newly formed Women's Professional Fastpitch League (WPL) that is scheduled to begin in 1997. "The new pro league is taking the sport to a whole new level," she explained in *USA Today.* "But no one's really committed yet. People are interested. But we have to take into consideration what's going to happen in 2000 and whether we can maintain our amateur status."

The International Olympic Committee decided to retain women's softball as a regular event at the 2000 Summer Olympics in Sydney, Australia. Fernandez wants to compete at least until that time. "There is still a lot for Lisa Fernandez to improve upon," she said. "In this game there is always room for improvement. The player you see in 2000 will be much improved from the player you saw in 1996."

Fernandez gets her biggest thrills on the softball diamond, as she told *Sports Illustrated for Kids:* "I live for the opportunity to get the game-winning RBI or make the diving play with the bases loaded."

Sources

Daily Oklahoman, September 5, 1995.
Los Angeles Times, July 30, 1996; July 31, 1996.
Milwaukee Journal Sentinel, July 9, 1996.
Newsday, July 27, 1996; July 31, 1996.
People Weekly, August 19, 1996.
Sacramento Bee, April 28, 1996.
San Jose Mercury News, July 27, 1995.
Sports Illustrated, May 24, 1993.
Sports Illustrated for Kids, April 1995; July 1996.
USA Today, July 22, 1996; July 27, 1996; July 29, 1996; July 31, 1996;
    November 5, 1996.
Women's Sports and Fitness, October 1996.

Additional information provided by the Amateur Softball Association of America, the Gannett News Service, and UCLA.

WHERE TO WRITE:

C/O AMATEUR SOFTBALL FEDERATION,
2801 NE 50TH STREET,
OKLAHOMA CITY, OK 73111.

Peter Forsberg

1973—

P eter Forsberg is used to moving. Before he ever played a game in the National Hockey League (NHL), the big center was traded from the Philadelphia Flyers to the Quebec Nordiques as part of a deal for center Eric Lindros. Forsberg then traveled to Norway, where he scored the winning goal for his native Sweden in the gold medal game of the 1994 Winter Olympic hockey tournament. During the 1994—95 NHL season, he arrived in North America, earning the Calder Trophy as the league's rookie of the year for the Nordiques. In what he hopes is his final move, Forsberg packed his bags and led the Colorado Avalanche to the 1996 Stanley Cup championship.

Growing Up

COACH DAD. Peter Forsberg was born July 20, 1973, in Ornskoldsvik, Sweden. The town is in the northernmost part of the country, not far from the Artic Circle. Forsberg's father,

*"[Forsberg is] the best player in the league right now, no question."
—Mike Milbury, New York Islanders coach and general manager.*

Kent, was a hockey coach, and the youngster grew up with the game. "I had a rink right by my house; the school had an outdoor rink," Forsberg recalled in the *Rocky Mountain News*. "My dad was coach of my older brother's team, and it was natural for me to get out there with them. I loved the game since I started to play." Over the years the Forsberg family moved up through the ranks of Swedish hockey together. Eventually Kent Forsberg became coach of the Swedish National Team.

By the time he was 10 years old, Forsberg already showed a great deal of potential. "I thought he had lots of talent and skill in ice hockey—technique with the puck, good skating, and he sees the ice well," Kent Forsberg stated in the *Rocky Mountain News*. "When he was young, it was ice hockey six, seven hours every day. He was in school, come home only to change [clothes] so he can go out and skate and play hockey."

Forsberg never dreamed of playing in the NHL. "I didn't even think about the NHL when I grew up," he admitted in the *Rocky Mountain News*. "I just tried to work hard and do my best in every practice. That's the way I see hockey—you work hard and then you become better. I didn't set goals."

TOO TOUGH? Forsberg tried out for the MoDo team of the Swedish Elite League, the equivalent of the NHL in his homeland, when he was 17 years old. Kent Forsberg coached the team and told his son he was too small to play with the best players in the country. Forsberg took his father's advice and went to the gym to lift weights and bulk up.

In November 1990, Forsberg finally joined the MoDo team. He scored 7 goals and added 7 assists for 14 points in 25 games. Some hockey experts in Sweden criticized Forsberg for being too rough. European hockey is much less physical than in North America and players rely more on speed and passing skills.

"Peter always played with older guys, and he wanted to show them he could give a hit and take a hit," Kent Forsberg explained in *Sport Illustrated*. "Sometimes, he was a little too physical." The criticism hurt Forsberg. "In the beginning, I didn't like it [the criticism] at all," he admitted in the *Ottawa Citizen*. "Everything was bad in the newspapers. Then it changed. They started to write good things."

BIG TRADE. Forsberg's play in Sweden began to attract the attention of NHL scouts. He was so highly regarded that the Philadelphia Flyers chose him with the sixth overall pick in the 1991 NHL Draft. The number one pick in that draft was Eric Lindros, a player most hockey experts considered the next NHL superstar, chosen by the Quebec Nordiques.

Lindros refused to sign a contract with Quebec, saying he did not want to play for Nordiques owner Marcel Aubut. He was still unsigned a year after Quebec drafted him and he demanded a trade to another team. The Nordiques finally reached an agreement with the Philadelphia Flyers. The Flyers traded Forsberg—plus five players, two first-round draft picks and $15 million—to Quebec for the rights to Lindros. (In addition to Forsberg, Quebec received Ron Hextall, Steve Duchesne, Kerry Huffman, Mike Ricci, and Chris Simon.)

The fans in Quebec opposed the trade, saying the Nordiques should not have given up a player as good as Lindros. Nordiques general manager Pierre Page called Forsberg and told him about the trade. "It felt funny to be traded even before I had played a game in the NHL, but when I heard Eric Lindros, I knew it was a big deal," Forsberg recalled in the *Sporting News*. "I had heard about Lindros in Sweden almost as much as Wayne Gretzky."

Quebec knew, however, that Forsberg had the potential to be a future star. "[We] were being told by Swedish hockey observers, who can be very conservative in their assessments of young players, that this was the best player ever to come

Forsberg (left) makes a break for the puck.

out of Sweden," Page explained in *Sports Illustrated*. "I won't say Peter will be a Lindros, but I don't think this franchise is ever going to kick itself for making the trade."

TAKES OFF. Forsberg used his playmaking and speed at the 1993 World Junior Ice Hockey Championships in Gavle, Sweden. "Forsberg dominated every shift at the World Juniors," Detroit assistant general manager Doug MacLean told *USA Today.* "He's an unbelievable stickhandler."

In seven games, Forsberg had 7 goals and 24 assists and his line scored 14 power-play goals. His 31 total points set a tournament record. Sweden finished second in the tournament, losing 5-4 to Canada, despite 1 goal and 3 assists by Forsberg in that game. Despite the fact that his team finished second, Forsberg won tournament most valuable players honors.

Forsberg returned from the junior championships to dominate the Swedish Elite League with the MoDo team. He became the first teenager to win the league's most valuable player award, beating out 33-year-old Hakan Loob, a former member of the Calgary Flames.

OLYMPIC STAR. Sweden entered the 1994 Winter Olympics in Lillehammer, Norway, as a medal favorite. Forsberg could have signed a contract with Quebec before the Olympics, but he decided to play for Sweden. "We figured he was ready [this season] to come to the NHL," Page told *USA Today*. "But the Olympics is a dream-come-true for him. One more year won't hurt him."

The fans in his home country wanted their best player to represent them in the Olympics. "There was a lot of pressure on me to stay on and play in the Olympics," Forsberg admitted in *USA Today*. "Everyone is expecting us to win. There is not a lot of pressure, at least not any more than usual."

SHOOTOUT! Sweden lived up to everyone's expectations, reaching the gold-medal game against Canada. Forsberg assisted on both Swedish goals as the two teams skated to a 2-2 tie after regulation. When the game was still tied after a ten-minute sudden-death overtime, the game went to the shootout phase. In a shootout, each team picks five players to take breakaway shots on the other team's goalie. The team that scores the most goals in the shootout wins the game.

Peter Nedved and **Paul Kariya** of Canada scored in the shootout to make the score 2-0 for Canada. Sweden came back, and when Forsberg beat Canadian goalie Corey Hirsch he tied the shootout 2-2 after both team had five shots. That meant the game would be decided by a sudden-death shootout. The first time one team scored and the other team did not, the game would be over.

Magnus Svensson missed on Sweden's first attempt, but so did Nedved of Canada. The next shooter was Forsberg. He cut left, went almost past the net, then reached back with his right hand and slid a backhand shot barely past the glove of Hirsch.

"Not too many players go for that kind of move," Nedved explained in *USA Today.* Forsberg had tried the move three times before, and had failed to score every time. When goalie Tommy Salo stopped Kariya, Sweden captured the gold medal, 3-2. It was the first-ever hockey gold medal for Sweden.

Superstar

NHL BOUND. Forsberg signed a $5 million, four-year deal with Quebec following his Olympic success. The most he ever made in Sweden was $80,000. "Peter's going to be a great player for us for a long, long time," Quebec coach Marc Crawford stated in the *Sporting News.* "He sees the whole ice the way the great playmakers do. I think you will hear a lot about Peter Forsberg as this season goes on."

Forsberg made his NHL debut during the 1994—95 season. The season was shortened to 47 games due to a contract dispute caused by a disagreement between NHL owners and their players. Once the season began, Forsberg got off to a slow start. "I'm feeling more comfortable all the time," he admitted in the *Sporting News.* "It was difficult to get used to the bigger players and smaller ice surface in the NHL. But I think I'm ready to make a big contribution to the Nordiques."

The Swedish star had a hard time adjusting to life in Quebec. Although he knew English, French is the official language in this Canadian Province. "I'd go home and watch TV, it was in French," Forsberg recalled in the *Rocky Mountain*

News. "You'd go to a restaurant, it was in French. You'd go to a movie, it's in French. I didn't understand a thing. You're sitting there and you can't call home because it's a six-hour [time] difference. It was kind of boring there for a while, but I got to know the guys on the team, and it got better."

ROOKIE OF THE YEAR. Unlike many other European players, Forsberg showed early on that he could give and take a hit. "[He's] strong on his skates and the toughest European I've ever seen," teammate Mike Keane told *Sports Illustrated.* Forsberg led all rookies in assists (35) and points (50). He also scored 15 goals. His playmaking helped linemate Owen Nolan lead the NHL in goals with 29. "From the beginning of the year to now, it's night and day," Nolan stated in the *Detroit Free Press* near the end of the season. "I can't see anybody touching him."

Forsberg won the 1994—95 Calder Memorial Trophy as the NHL rookie of the year. "I see him try new moves almost every night, which shows me he's still learning," Crawford told the *Sporting News.* "He's already very, very good, and he's going to keep getting better."

MOUNTAIN MOVES. Quebec won the Northeast Division championship during the 1994—95 season, but lost in the first round of the playoffs to the New Jersey Devils, the eventual Stanley Cup champions. In June 1995, the Nordiques ownership decided to move the team to Denver, Colorado. The team's new name is the Colorado Avalanche. Denver had had an NHL franchise before—the Colorado Rockies—but the team moved to New Jersey and became the Devils.

Prior to the 1995—96 season the Avalanche signed free-agent winger Claude Lemieux. Lemieux had won the Conn Smythe Trophy as the most valuable player in the Stanley Cup playoffs the previous year with the New Jersey Devils. Soon after the season began, Colorado added what they thought was the final piece of their championship puzzle when they received Patrick Roy in a trade with the Montreal Canadiens. Roy had twice led the Canadiens to the Stanley Cup and was considered the best pressure goalie in the NHL.

MAGNUM FORSBERG. Forsberg became a force in the NHL in his first full season (1995—96). He scored 30 goals and passed off for 86 assists (fourth in the NHL) for 116 total points (fifth in the league). Forsberg centered Lemieux and Valerí Kamensky to form one of the highest scoring units in the NHL. His line scored 107 goals and 272 points during the regular season. "That kid makes plays no one else in the league can imagine," Avalanche general manager Pierre Lacroix told *Sports Illustrated.*

Forsberg had a special moment when he scored his first NHL hat trick against Lindros and the Flyers. (A hat trick is when one player scores three goals in the same game.) "It's a little special," he confessed in the *Detroit Free Press.* "Those guys drafted me, but they traded me."

PLAYOFF AVALANCHE. Colorado won the Pacific Division and compiled the second-best record in the NHL for the second straight season. In the first two rounds of the NHL playoffs, Colorado defeated the Calgary Flames and the Chicago Blackhawks. They now would face the record-setting Detroit Red Wings in the Western Conference Finals. The Red Wings had won an NHL-record 62 games during the regular season.

Surprisingly, Colorado won the first two games of the series on the road at Joe Louis Arena in Detroit. The Red Wings came back to win Game Three in Colorado, but the Avalanche took Game Four to gain a commanding 3-1 lead in the best-of-seven series. Forsberg worked hard against the Red Wings to shut down high-scoring center Sergei Fedorov. "I haven't gotten that many good [scoring] chances in this series," he explained in the *Detroit Free Press.* "That's why I've tried to help the team in other areas. Part of my responsibility is staying close to Fedorov. Stay as close to him as he's staying close to me."

Forsberg's two-way play did not surprise his coach. "It's no surprise to any of us because we've known that Peter is excellent at both [offensive and defensive] ends of the ice," Crawford told the *Detroit Free Press.* "But I'm sure there are plenty of people who may be seeing us for the first time who are surprised by Peter's defense."

Forsberg also threw a number of big hits, disrupting the powerful Red Wings attack. "I don't think I have a reputation of being a physical player," he declared in the *Detroit Free Press*. "It's just that I haven't been scoring much lately, so I needed to find a way to contribute. I've been trying to do a better job of finishing my checks. You have to be physical against a talented team like Detroit. You just need to play smart and intelligent so you're not taking any bad penalties."

Detroit won Game Five at home, 5-2, keeping their hopes alive. The Avalanche finally eliminated the Red Wings with a 4-1 win in Game Six when Forsberg made Colorado's final goal of the game and his second of the series. For the first time in team history, Colorado would play in the Stanley Cup Finals. "Talent is maybe not the most important thing in the playoffs, where you're coming back night after night," Forsberg told the *Denver Post*. "I think what is most important is the will to win."

STANLEY CUP SWEEP. The Avalanche would face the Eastern Conference champions, the Florida Panthers, for the Stanley Cup. Colorado won Game One against the Panthers, then Forsberg took over in Game Two. He scored a hat trick in the first period against Florida—becoming only the sixth player in finals history to record all three goals in one period of action. "When you're in the game, you don't think about it," Forsberg admitted in the *Detroit Free Press*. "But if you look, not that many have done it. It feels pretty good." Colorado went on to win the game 8-1, taking a 2-0 lead in the series.

The Avalanche traveled to Florida and won Game Three, 3-2. They were now on the verge of a sweep. The Panthers would not roll over and die, however, and played a tough defensive game in Game Four. The contest was tied 0-0 after regulation and two overtime periods. Finally Colorado defenseman Uwe Krupp drove a slap shot from the left point to beat Florida goalie John Vanbiesbrouck at 4:31 of the third overtime. The game—the third-longest in Stanley Cup Finals history—ended at 1:05 a.m. eastern time.

The Avalanche, in their first season in Denver, were Stanley Cup champions. The last time an overtime goal decided the Stanley Cup was in 1980 when Bob Nystrom of the New York Islanders scored the game winner in Game Six. Forsberg scored 10 goals and 21 assists in the playoffs, good for 31 points (fifth in NHL playoff scoring). Avalanche captain Joe Sakic won the Conn Smythe Trophy as the most valuable player of the NHL playoffs.

TEAMMATES. Forsberg may be the best player in the NHL, but he centers Colorado's second line. Sakic leads the first unit, but each player has a unique talent. Sakic is quick and has the most lethal wrist shot in the game, a shot he can release from any angle without warning. Forsberg, meanwhile, is creative and tough, a player who makes his linemates better. "He can shift on a dime and find the open man with the same incredible sixth sense [Wayne] Gretzky has always had," Edmonton Oilers general manager Glen Sather told the *Sporting News.*

The Avalanche pair of centers is probably the best on one team since the Edmonton Oilers had Wayne Gretzky and Mark Messier. The two players are competitive, but not with each other. "You go to different teams and you might find the top guys kind of competing, but we don't have that here," Sakic explained in the *Rocky Mountain News.* "That's what any team would want from their top guys. We're not out there to get the attention or the limelight. We're just out there to win hockey games."

Crawford feels that for Forsberg to improve he has to be more selfish and shoot the puck more often. "He's the type of guy that, if he shot the puck a little bit more, I think he'd be even a greater goal scorer that he already is," Crawford explained in the *Detroit Free Press*. "He's learning that he has to change things up. Sometimes you have to shoot to keep the goaltenders honest."

OFF THE ICE. Forsberg lives in Ornskoldsvik, Sweden, during the off-season, and in Aurora, Colorado while the Avalanche is playing. When not playing hockey, he likes to play golf. Each player on the Colorado team was allowed to take the Stanley Cup home for a short time, and Forsberg took the famous trophy with him to Sweden. It was the first time the Stanley Cup had been in the country, and Forsberg invited his friends over for a picnic to see it. He is very popular in his home country and has been called the "Michael Jordan of Sweden."

Despite his strong start in the NHL, Forsberg has not been able to convince his toughest critic: his father. "I don't know that he is special," Kent Forsburg told *Sports Illustrated*. "He's only been in this league one and a half years. When he's been around four or five years, then we'll know if he's a star."

Hockey News rated Forsberg as the fifth best player in the NHL, behind Mario Lemieux and Jamomir Jagr of the Pittsburgh Penguins, Lindros, and teammate Roy. Despite the recognition he receives, the young star still feels a need to improve. "I've got to be a better skater, better shooter, better passer, work a little harder on the ice, be more consistent," Forsberg stated in the *Rocky Mountain News*. "You always have to improve, and can improve in everything."

Forsberg has convinced Mike Milbury, coach and general manager of the New York Islanders, who told *Sports Illustrated* that: "[Forsburg is] the best player in the league right now, no question."

Sources

Denver Post, October 7, 1996.
Detroit Free Press, February 28, 1994; April 15, 1995; February 13, 1996; May 21, 1996; May 28, 1996; May 30, 1996; June 7, 1996.
Hockey News, November 29, 1996.
Miami Herald, June 11, 1996.
Ottawa Citizen, April 11, 1995.

Rocky Mountain News, May 30, 1996; September 29, 1996.
Sporting News, March 27, 1995; March 25, 1996.
Sports Illustrated, February 7, 1994.
USA Today, February 28, 1994; February 10, 1994.

 WHERE TO WRITE:

C/O COLORADO AVALANCHE,
1635 CLAY STREET,
DENVER, CO 80204.

Jim Harbaugh

1963—

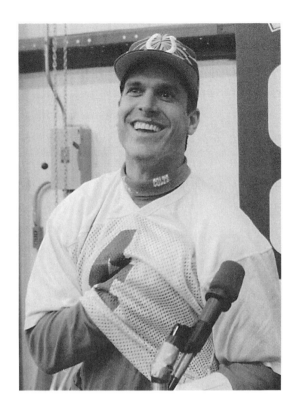

Quarterback Jim Harbaugh knows the meaning of the word comeback. After seven seasons with the Chicago Bears, the team released him. With his career at a crossroads, Harbaugh signed to play with the Indianapolis Colts, but could not earn the starting job. He did not quit, however, and he not only became the Colts starter but also led the National Football League (NFL) in passing in 1995 and took Indianapolis to the brink of the Super Bowl. His play earned Harbaugh the title "Captain Comeback" and made him one of the top players in the league.

"I have an ugly style. I'm always stumbling, diving for first downs. It's past ugly."—Jim Harbaugh.

Growing Up

TRAVELING FAMILY. James Joseph Harbaugh was born December 23, 1963, in Toledo, Ohio. His father, Jack, is a football coach, and his mother, Jackie, was a teacher who became a homemaker after her children were born. The Harbaugh family moved 12 times as his father got new coaching

LED NFL IN PASSING DURING
THE 1995 SEASON.

ELECTED TO PRO BOWL
ALL-STAR GAME FOLLOWING
THE 1995 SEASON.

BIG TEN PLAYER-OF-THE-YEAR
IN 1986 AT THE
UNIVERSITY OF MICHIGAN.

"CAPTAIN COMEBACK" CAME BACK
FROM BEING RELEASED TO TAKE
HIS PLACE AS ONE OF THE BEST
QUARTERBACKS IN THE NFL.

jobs. All the moving around made the family close. "The greatest blessing of my life is my family," Harbaugh confessed in the *Indianapolis Business Journal.*

SPORTS NUT. Harbaugh lived to play sports as a child. "All I cared about was playing sports," he recalled in *Sports Illustrated for Kids.* "It didn't matter if it was wrestling, running track, or playing hockey, soccer, basketball, or football. I remember wanting to play Little League so bad that I'd cry if our game got rained out."

Harbaugh played with his older brother, John, and other kids in the neighborhood. He learned to play sports alone when there was no one else around. Harbaugh often went with his father to school and made up games using the football team's tackling dummies. "He was one of the world's greatest daydreamers," Jack Harbaugh told *Sports Illustrated.* "He'd spend hours throwing a tennis ball against the back wall of the grocery store. When he got home we'd say, 'Where have you been?' and he'd say, 'Doubleheader against the Cleveland Indians. I pitched both ends. We won 'em both.'"

SORE LOSER. Harbaugh always wanted to win very badly. "I was always very competitive," he admitted in *Sports Illustrated for Kids.* "Winning meant everything to me. When I didn't win, I would get very depressed."

Harbaugh's competitiveness sometimes got out of control, however. "I hurt a lot of other kids' feelings," he confessed in *Sports Illustrated for Kids.* "I would blame them for losing the game just because they made a mistake." Because Harbaugh hurt their feelings, he had a hard time getting along with other children. "When I was in seventh grade, I didn't have any friends," he recalled in *Sports Illustrated.*

WOLVERINE QB. Harbaugh earned all-league honors in baseball, basketball, and football at Palo Alto High School in California. Although he was not highly recruit-ed to play football, he did receive one offer from the University of Michigan. Jack Harbaugh had earlier worked as an assistant coach for Bo Schembechler at the school. One assistant coach hurt Harbaugh's feelings by telling him the only reason he was given a scholarship to Michigan was because of his father.

Harbaugh worked his way up the ranks of Michigan quarterbacks and earned the starting job as a sophomore. During his career with the Worlverines, he became the greatest quarterback to play at that school up until that time. Harbaugh set school records for completions (387) and passing yardage (5449). He also threw 31 touchdown passes, fourth best in school history.

In 1986, Harbaugh earned Big Ten Player-of-the-Year and All-American honors as a senior when he set Michigan single-season records for completions (180), attempts (277), and yards (2729). He also set a school single-game record for completion percentage (92.3 percent). Harbaugh became the first quarterback from the Big Ten Conference to lead the nation in passing. He led Michigan to a 27-23 victory in the 1986 Fiesta Bowl over Nebraska and a number-two final season national ranking. Also a star in the classroom, Harbaugh made the Academic All-Big Ten team and graduated with a degree in communications.

CHICAGO'S CHOICE. The Chicago Bears used the twenty-sixth pick in the first round of the 1987 NFL Draft to choose Harbaugh. He played sparingly his first three seasons, serving as a backup to Jim McMahon and Mike Tomczak. Harbaugh became the team's starter in 1990 and led the Bears to an 11-5 record and the National Football Conference (NFC) Central Division title. He completed 160 of 312 passes for 2178 yards and 10 touchdowns. Unfortunately, Harbaugh separated his

WINNING IS NOT EVERYTHING

Even though winning is fun, Harbaugh has come to realize that it is not everything.

"Living is more important than winning," he explained in *Sports Illustrated for Kids.* "I was obsessed with winning when I was a kid. I learned that who you are as a person and having good friends and a strong family mean more than anything. I later learned that winning as a team is better than anything. It's great to share success. So now I focus on helping my teammates be the best they can be."

shoulder on December 19 and missed the rest of the season and the playoffs.

Harbaugh entered the 1991 season as the undisputed leader for Chicago, starting every game for his team. He once again led the Bears to an 11-5 record and had the best statistics of his career. Harbaugh threw for 3121 yards (the second most in Bears history) and 15 touchdowns, and ran for 338 more yards. He also set Bears single-season records for completions (275) and attempts (478). Harbaugh got his first taste of NFL playoff action as the Bears lost 17-13 in the first round to the Dallas Cowboys. He completed 22 of 44 passes for 218 yards and 1 touchdown in the game.

REBUILDING BEARS. Chicago was forced to start a rebuilding process in 1992. The Bears finished 5-11 that season and coach Mike Ditka lost his job. The low-point for Harbaugh occurred in October 1992. Ditka reprimanded his quarterback on the sidelines during a Monday night game on national television. Harbaugh had changed a play and his poor throw resulted in an interception by the Minnesota Vikings that was returned for a touchdown. The Vikings won the game 21-20. "People have been yelling at me for years," Harbaugh said, "and 95 percent of the time I deserved it."

WORST SEASON. The 1993 season was brutal on Harbaugh. The Bears finished 7-9 under new coach Dave Wannstedt, and the quarterback was sacked (tackled before throwing the ball) an incredible 43 times. "I don't think anybody could've flourished—Troy Aikman included," Harbaugh explained in *USA Today.* "The coaches figured it out once and said I was getting hit once every 2.5 times I threw the ball. And I mean drilled. [But] I don't think I was shell-shocked." Harbaugh lost the ball on fumbles 7 times, the most of any NFL quarterback.

Harbaugh took the blame for Chicago's poor season. He passed for only 2002 yards, his fewest since becoming the

team's starter in 1990, threw only 7 touchdown passes, and was picked off (intercepted) 11 times. Harbaugh's lack of arm strength prevented him from throwing deep passes, and other teams' defenses shut down the Bear's short passing attack.

Bears fans turned on Harbaugh. On talk radio and at games the fans made it clear they were unhappy with their quarterback. "To go to the ballgame and listen to the fans, well, it

Harbaugh rifles a pass down the field.

was just cruel and brutal," Jack Harbaugh told *USA Today.* One time the booing was so bad the Harbaugh's mother, Jackie, broke out in tears. "I had taken all the criticisms for any faults the team had," Harbaugh explained in the same newspaper "It got to be a joke. The constant booing. I always felt I could turn it around, but the coach has to make a commitment to say, 'This is my guy, and we're going to ride it out.'"

Chicago lost their last four games to fall out of a tie for the Central Division lead and miss the playoffs. Harbaugh failed to throw a touchdown pass in his last three-and-a-half games. The Bears had the worst offense in the league and Wannstedt decided to shake things up. During the offseason, the Bears signed free-agent quarterback Erik Kramer, who had previously played for the Detroit Lions, to a three-year, $8.1 million contract.

Harbaugh requested that the Bears release him, and the team agreed. The decision was hard on him since he had wanted to spend his entire career with one team. "Jim was the scapegoat," Chicago wide receiver Tom Waddle told *Sports Illustrated.* "He had to bear the brunt of the fact that our offense [was terrible]." Harbaugh started for the Bears for four seasons. He held the team records for passing attempts (1759) and completions (1023), and completion percentage (58 percent). Harbaugh passed for 11,567 yards, second in Bears history to Hall-of-Fame quarterback Sid Luckman.

COLT SIGNAL CALLER. Luckily for Harbaugh, the Indianapolis Colts were shopping for a starting quarterback. During the off-season the Colts traded their starter, Jeff George, to the Atlanta Falcons. Colts' operations chief Bill Tobin had drafted Harbaugh for the Bears in 1987, and he jumped at the chance to sign him for Indianapolis. "They piled all the garbage on his doorstep in Chicago," Tobin stated in *USA Today.*

Harbaugh did not let the 1993 season get him down. "I feel real good about myself as a player and as a person," he explained to *USA Today.* "Last year is in the rear-view mirror now." The Colts were a young team and had drafted running back Marshall Faulk from San Diego State University to help their rushing attack.

BENCHED AGAIN. Harbaugh started nine games for Indianapolis, but lost his starting assignment to Don Majikowski. Coach Ted Marchibroda told him the reason for his demotion was that Harbaugh was not playing well in the fourth quarter. "I've hurried myself a little bit," Harbaugh confessed to the Gannett News Service. "I've run maybe when I shouldn't have, trying to make big plays and make something happen. I have to stay in there and throw and give the other guys a chance to do their jobs."

The Colts offense was terrible in 1994. They ranked twenty-seventh in total yards and twenty-eighth in passing. Harbaugh struggled, throwing for only 1440 yards, his lowest total since becoming a starting quarterback. During the off-season following the 1994 season, Indianapolis traded first- and fourth-round draft picks to the Tampa Bay Buccaneers to acquire quarterback Craig Erickson. Marchibroda told Harbaugh he would be the backup.

Superstar

NEW OFFENSE. During the off-season Indianapolis hired Lindy Infante as their offensive coordinator. Formerly the head coach of the Green Bay Packers, Infante had a reputation for developing quality passing attacks. Harbaugh liked the new system Infante installed. "It's a quarterback-friendly offense," he explained to the Gannett News Service.

Erickson started the first two games of the 1995 season, but he played poorly in each game. In the season opener, against the Cincinnati Bengals, Erickson threw three interceptions and fumbled a snap that resulted in a two-point safety for the Bengals. Harbaugh relieved Erickson in the fourth quarter and almost pulled the game out for the Colts. He threw for a touchdown with seven seconds left in the game and then threw for the two-point conversion that tied the game. The Colts lost in overtime, however.

RELIEF PITCHER. Harbaugh came on in relief of Erickson again in the second game of the season with the Colts trailing the New York Jets 24-3 at halftime. He completed two fourth quarter touchdown passes, again forcing an overtime. This time, Harbaugh threw a 24-yard pass to wide receiver Sean Dawkins to set up the game-winning field goal.

After his heroics in the first two games of the season, Marchibroda made Harbaugh the starter for the Colts' third game, against the Buffalo Bills. "When I made the change to start him against Buffalo the last time, I said, 'Jim, do you want to start?'" Marchibroda revealed to the Gannett News Service. "'Yes, I love to start, but coach I'm having a lot of success coming off the bench,' and I said, 'Why is that Jim? What's the difference?' and he said, 'I'm playing wide-open football. I'm in a no lose situation.' I said, 'Well if you start, just continue to do that,' and that's what he's done. He's playing the best football of his career."

The Colts lost to Buffalo, 20-14, but Harbaugh was now the starter. "Jim typifies a lot of what we stand for," defensive end Trev Alberts told the Gannett News Service. "He went through a difficult season last year, where people were writing nasty things about him. He kept fighting and kept fighting and came back, and that's kind of what this team is all about. Jim is playing with an awful lot of confidence, and the guys are really responding to him."

SQUASHING THE FISH. Harbaugh had his most impressive comeback against the undefeated Miami Dolphins. Miami led the Colts by 21 points, 24-3, at halftime on their home field—Joe Robbie Stadium. Miami quarterback Dan Marino broke the career record for most completions for an NFL quarterback (3687) in the first half and everything was going the Dolphins' way. "I'd say Miami was feeling pretty good," Harbaugh explained in *Sports Illustrated*. "You know—make Harbaugh beat you, and who's he? It's a pretty good strategy."

Harbaugh did not quit, however. He threw three second-half touchdowns to bring his team back and tie the game 24-24. Cary Blanchard then kicked a 27-yard field goal and won the game for Indianapolis in overtime. "Dan's [Marino] known for his comebacks, and he's great at it," Harbaugh told the Gannett News Service. "Nobody really has that high an opinion of me as a quarterback. I have an ugly style. I'm always stumbling, diving for first downs. It's past ugly."

The next week the Colts came from behind to beat the defending Super Bowl champions, the San Francisco 49ers, 18-17. "These guys have the kind of faith in Jim that the Cowboys have in Troy Aikman, that the Dolphins have in Dan Marino, that the Steelers had in Terry Bradshaw," Tobin explained in *Sports Illustrated*. "They get in the huddle and know something good is going to happen."

"CAPTAIN COMEBACK." Harbaugh earned the nickname "Captain Comeback" by leading the Colts to three come-from-behind victories during the 1995 season. The Colts earned a playoff berth and Harbaugh finished the year as the league's highest ranked quarterback. He completed 200 of 314 passes (63.7 percent) for 2575 yards and 17 touchdowns. Opposing teams only intercepted five Harbaugh passes. He finished with a 100.7 rating in the NFL's complicated quarterback efficiency system, the best in the league.

Fans, coaches, and his fellow players elected Harbaugh to his first Pro Bowl all-star game. "Sure, I'm pleased to have the top rating," he admitted to the Gannett News Service. "But I know who I am. I'm not Dan Marino, who is headed to the Hall of Fame. I'm just a guy who loves to win, and is willing to give my body to be a winner."

Harbaugh credited Infante with helping him become a better quarterback. Infante impressed on his quarterback that he had to think pass first, run second. "He'll scramble, but he keeps looking upfield while scrambling," Infante explained to *Sports Illustrated*. "He finally understands that quarterbacks in this league are not here to run."

PLAYOFF RUN. Harbaugh won his first playoff game as the Colts defeated the defending AFC champion San Diego Chargers in the first round of the NFL postseason. Faulk missed the game with an injury, but Zack Crockett gained 147 yards and 2 touchdowns as his replacement. Indianapolis now had to travel to Kansas City to face the Chiefs, the team with the best regular-season record in the NFL.

The wind chill at kickoff was minus nine degrees. "The conditions made it tough for anybody to move the ball," Harbaugh admitted in *Newsday*. "Sometimes the best plays were the ones you had to improvise." Throughout the game Harbaugh kept drives alive with third-down scrambles. On the Colts' only touchdown drive they converted five times on third down and once on fourth down. Harbaugh finished off the 77-yard, 18-play drive with a 5-yard pass to Floyd Turner. "We were just winging it the whole drive," Harbaugh explained in *Newsday*. "Nothing special."

Chiefs' quarterback Steve Bono threw three costly interceptions and Kansas City kicker Lin Elliot missed three field goals, including a 42-yarder with 42 seconds left that would have tied the game. In a shocking upset, Indianapolis won the game, 10-7. Harbaugh completed 12 of 27 passes for 112 yards and ran for 112 more. "Jimmy did what he was supposed to do," Marchibroda told *Newsday*. "Jimmy made the big plays."

HAIL MARY. The Colts were in the AFC Championship Game for the first time in 24 seasons and the first time since the franchise moved from Baltimore to Indianapolis. The game against the Pittsburgh Steelers was a classic, with each team making comebacks. The Steelers scored to take a 20-16 lead and Indianapolis was 84 yards away from victory with only 1:30 left in the game and one timeout.

"Captain Comeback" would not give up, though. Harbaugh completed 4 of 8 passes for 26 yards and ran for 9 more yards on his team's last drive. He played the last 5 plays of the drive with a dislocated middle finger on his throwing hand after running into Steelers lineman Brentson Buckner. "He was clearly our leader today," Colts running back Lamont Warren stated in *Newsday*. "He kept his poise in adverse situations."

Indianapolis had one last chance to win the game from the Pittsburgh 29-yard line. Harbaugh threw up a "Hail Mary" pass. (A "Hail Mary" pass occurs when the offensive team sends several receivers to one spot in the end zone. The quarterback throws the football high in the air. The offensive team hopes that either one of their wide receivers can catch the ball in the air or on a rebound, or that a defensive player is called for pass interference.) The ball bounced around from player to player. It appeared at first glance that Indianapolis wide receiver Aaron Bailey caught the ball.

"On the field, I thought he caught it," Harbaugh told *Newsday*. "When I saw the replay, I thought he caught it. When I saw the replay about the third time, I saw the ball hit the ground." Harbaugh completed 21 of 33 passes for 267 yards and 1 touchdown in the game and also rushed 6 times for 29 yards. "I believed the whole time that we would win," he revealed in *Newsday*. "I believed it before the game. I believed it in my heart. All we had to do was play with courage and the guys did that. You can't come any closer. We were right there."

Harbaugh was proud of himself and his Colts teammates. "It was a great season," he explained to *Newsday*. "We came close to making the Super Bowl. All we do is try and give ourselves a chance to win. We try to fight for 60 minutes. You saw that today. That was a 60-minute fight. If you do that, you can look up at the scoreboard afterward."

FRANCHISE PLAYER. Harbaugh could have left Indianapolis after the 1995 season, but the Colts named him their franchise player, meaning that Harbaugh could not leave the team as a free-agent. He signed a four-year contract extension in August 1996. Marchibroda was not as lucky, as he was fired during the off-season. Indianapolis promoted Infante to the head coaching position.

The Colts lost four offensive line starters to free agency prior to the 1996 season. The biggest loss was left tackle Will Wolford. In addition to these free-agent loses, Indianapolis suffered several key injuries, losing Faulk, defensive ends Tony Bennett and Ellis Johnson, and linebacker Trev Alberts.

Harbaugh also missed several games with injuries and was sacked 36 times.

REMATCH. Despite their setbacks, the Colts finished the season 9-7 and made the playoffs for the second straight year. "I don't know if I've ever been around a team where so many different guys have stepped in and contributed," Harbaugh told the *Sporting News*. "Guys get their shots and they make the most of it. That's what this team is all about." Harbaugh finished the season with 2630 yards passing and 13 touchdown passes.

Indianapolis returned to Pittsburgh for a playoff rematch with the Steelers. This time, however, the game was not close. The Steelers won the game big, 42-14, shutting down the Colts' offense. "We knew they had a great defense," Harbaugh explained to the Associated Press. "They're number two in the NFL, you know." Harbaugh completed only 12 of 32 passes for 134 yards in the game, but he was constantly under pressure. He suffered a gash on his jaw and a chipped tooth against the Steelers.

OFF THE FIELD. Harbaugh lives in Orlando, Florida, in the off-season, with his wife, Miah, and their two children. He has an older brother, John, and a younger sister, Joanie. Harbaugh gives motivational speeches, trying to pass on his winning attitude to others.

Harbaugh is still close to his family and makes phone calls to help his father recruit at Western Kentucky University. He has held auctions to raise money for the program and donated $17,000 to buy jerseys and pants.

Harbaugh does not let success go to his head, because he knows how quickly things can change. "It's nice to have people pat you on the back, but you can't pay that much attention to it," he admitted in *Sports Illustrated*. "You can have fun with it, though, and I am—because I've been on the other side."

Sources

Indianapolis Business Journal, May 6, 1996.

Newsday, January 8, 1996; January 15, 1996.
Sporting News, May 2, 1994; September 23, 1996.
Sports Illustrated, October 16, 1995; May 20, 1996.
Sports Illustrated for Kids, November 1996.
USA Today, July 28, 1994.
Additional information provided by the Gannett News Service, the National
    Football League, and the University of Michigan.

WHERE TO WRITE:

C/O INDIANAPOLIS COLTS,
PO BOX 535000,
INDIANAPOLIS, IN 46253.

John Harkes

1967—

"Seems like people with negative views will keep on trying to put soccer down. But the game is here to stay, so they might as well sit back and enjoy it. It's coming and it's coming strong."—John Harkes.

There is no place like home, especially for soccer player John Harkes. The University of Virginia star traveled to England to take on the finest soccer talent in the world. After becoming the best American ever to play in Europe, Harkes returned to the United States in 1994 to lead the American World Cup team to a surprise victory over soccer power Colombia. In 1996, he joined the Washington D.C. United team of Major League Soccer (MLS), the new U.S. professional soccer circuit. In a successful homecoming, Harkes led his team to the first-ever MLS championship.

Growing Up

SOCCERTOWN, USA. John Harkes was born March 8, 1967, in Kearny, New Jersey. His parents, Jim and Jessie Harkes, are both Scottish immigrants. Jim Harkes played soccer with other Scots in Kearny, a mill town. He had also played the game in Scotland for the Dundee Junior team. Harkes spent every other summer and two entire years in Scotland as a child.

The city of Kearny had a large youth soccer program. The sport was popular because many of the town's residents came from Scotland, where soccer is the only game. "Where I grew up, we all played soccer in the streets," Harkes recalled in the *Detroit Free Press*. "We thought all American kids were doing that. It wasn't until later that I found out most kids were playing baseball and basketball."

TOO SMALL? Harkes began tapping the ball around with his brother, Jimmy, when he was four and joined a youth-league team when he was four-and-a-half years old. Most of his teammates were three years older. Jim Harkes was the team's coach, and he thought his son was too young to play with the bigger children. "I said, 'You're just too wee, son,'" Jim Harkes told *Sports Illustrated for Kids*. "But he stuck with it and did well."

Two of Harkes friends as a child were goalie Tony Meola and midfielder Tab Ramos. "In Kearny, you weren't cool if you didn't play soccer," Meola declared in *Sports Illustrated for Kids*. The friends would later play together for the U.S. national team. As children, Meola and Harkes both acted as ballboys for the New York Cosmos of the North American Soccer League (NASL), the last major American outdoor soccer league. The great Brazilian player Pele was on the Cosmos.

CAVALIER KICKER. Harkes captained the soccer team at Kearny High School where he earned all-state honors his last three seasons. As a senior, *Parade* magazine named him the best high school player in the United States after he scored 24 goals, passed off for 17 assists, and led his team to a 24-0 record and the state title. A highly recruited player by college soccer powers, Harkes chose the University of Virginia.

Harkes played at Virginia for three years (1985—87). "John is the blood and guts of a team," his coach at Virginia, Bruce Arena, told *Sports Illustrated for Kids*. "John has a lot of heart and a lot of fight and has been able to get big goals in big games." Harkes earned Missouri Athletic Club Player of the Year honors as the best college player in the country in 1987 after leading the Cavaliers in scoring with 15 goals and 4 assists in 18 games. Eight times he scored the game-winning goal for Virginia. Harkes first made the U.S. national team that same year and has been a member of the squad ever since. He also played for the United States in the 1988 Olympics.

AN AMERICAN IN ENGLAND. Harkes made an important decision in January 1990. He wanted to earn money from soccer and test his talents against the best players in the world. Harkes and his old friend Meola traveled to England to tryout for the Sheffield Wednesday team. Neither player made the team, but Harkes's play impressed Sheffield Wednesday's manager, Ron Atkinson.

Harkes and Meola came back to the United States and earned spots on the 1990 U.S. World Cup team. Harkes, however, was determined to return to England. "I was thinking World Cup then, that it would be better for me to train with the U.S. team," Harkes explained in *Sports Illustrated*. "But after being here [in England] for a while and seeing how I've improved as a player, seeing the speed of the real game, the one-touch passing, I'm sorry I didn't stay. If you make it here, you can play anywhere in the world. It toughens you mentally, it makes you a pro."

WORLD CUP I. The 1990 World Cup was played in Italy. The Americans—surprised to even be in the biggest soccer tournament in the world—were overwhelmed by the experience. "We were just happy to be there," Harkes told the *Detroit Free Press*. "When I stepped out on the field for the first game against Czechoslovakia, I didn't even know how to warm up. I was busy looking for my family in the stands. Then, we went out and played them like it was a friendly Sunday afternoon game, and we learned a lesson very quickly with a 5-0

loss." The Americans lost all three games they played by a combined score of 8-2 and finished twenty-third among twenty-four teams.

The experience in the World Cup opened up opportunities for Harkes. "Playing in the Cup gave European teams a chance to see the top Americans, and that's what opened the door for me," he explained in the *Detroit Free Press*.

In October 1990, Harkes joined the Sheffield Wednesday reserve team. Sheffield Wednesday played in the Premier

"HARKSEY"

Harkes's big goal made him a fan favorite in England. At Sheffield Wednesday's next game the fans began calling him "Harksey," and the support was important to the American player. "I thought it was going to be really mean and tough [playing in England]," he admitted in *Sports Illustrated.* "I thought I might even get hounded. People yelling at me, 'Go home, Yank.' The guys on the team were great, too. I was warned, 'You're going over there, taking somebody's job.' But I experienced no hint of that. Once I proved to them I could play the game, I had no problems." Harkes became so comfortable that he developed a British accent.

The British teen magazine *Mizz* named him one of the "10 most gorgeous" players and *People Weekly* listed him as one of its 50 most interesting people. Harkes received bags of mail and fans chased him for his autograph. The British gave him the nickname "The American Express."

Division, the major leagues of English soccer. Harkes got his chance to play for the big club when its regular right back, Roland Nillson, tore ligaments in his right leg. Atkinson called Harkes up to replace the injured player.

Harkes had a hard decision to make. He and Nillson were friends, having met at the 1988 Olympics where Nillson played for Sweden. "Roland used to give me a lot of advice," Harkes admitted in *Sports Illustrated.* In addition, Harkes had never played right back before. He finally decided that he could not pass up the chance to play in the elite English league.

BIG GOAL. In Harkes's third game, Sheffield Wednesday played their traditional rival, Derby. The team had not won at Derby since 1956. The game was tied 0-0 in the thirty-second minute of play when Harkes got the ball. "The ball got switched over to me from the left midfield, and I pushed it ahead," he recalled in *Sports Illustrated.* "Now, usually, in this league, somebody will cut you up, stop you somehow. But suddenly nobody was near me and I told myself, 'I'm gonna put my head down and crack it.' And that ball just took off, 35 yards into the far corner of the net. Then there were all these guys chasing me down the field yelling, 'Jeez, what a peach that was! Brilliant!' It meant so much to me."

Harkes did not realize it at the time, but the shot would be voted British television's Goal of the Year. "To do that against one of the great keepers is marvelous," Atkinson stated in *Sports Illustrated.* "There was no element of fluke to it. The shot was unstoppable. And it was his first goal for the team!" Harkes later set up the game-winning goal in a 2-1 victory, passing the ball to striker Paul Williams. "I scored one of the best goals I'll ever score in my life," he told his wife, Cindi, over the phone, according to *Sports Illustrated for Kids*.

In 1991, Harkes led Sheffield Wednesday to a League Cup championship over Manchester United at Wembley Stadium in London. He was the first American to play a major match in this soccer shrine. "I've dreamed of going to Wembley since I was a kid," Harkes confessed in *Sports Illustrated*. He was now the best-known American player in Europe. "The last American to hear such roars of approval in Wembley Stadium was [singer] Bruce Springsteen," a British soccer columnist wrote.

Harkes scored 7 goals in 82 games for Sheffield Wednesday. When he could not reach agreement with the team on a new contract in 1993, Derby County purchased his rights for $1.5 million. Harkes became the first American to score in Wembley Stadium in a game that same season. He also became the first American player to play in the FA Cup Final, the Super Bowl of English soccer. Harkes played two full seasons with Derby County before moving to West Ham United for the 1995—96 season.

Superstar

WORLD CUP II. Most of the best American players returned to play for their country in the 1994 World Cup, the first ever held in the United States. Despite being able to put their best team on the field, the Americans were a big underdog in the 24-team tournament. Harkes said there were just three things on his mind, according to *People Weekly:* "World Cup, World Cup, World Cup."

"There is pressure on us to bring soccer to this country," Harkes declared in the *Detroit Free Press*. "But I hope the interest in soccer isn't just based on how we do. Soccer is the most beautiful game in the world, and that's why Americans should give it a chance. I hear from the guys in England that we're a joke. We have to prove these skeptics wrong. This is the highest stage in our sport. If we don't do it now, we never will."

The Americans were more businesslike than in 1990. "This time, we're not tourists," Harkes told the *Detroit Free Press*. "I started counting down, saying, 'This guy has played in Europe; this guy has played in Europe.' It makes all the difference. No matter how brief their careers might have been, they've had a taste of soccer at the highest level. The professionalism on this outfit is a lot better than in '90. Back then, we were all just learning."

UPSET. The U.S. team opened the tournament with a tie against Switzerland. They then faced the powerful Colombian team in the Rose Bowl in Pasadena, California. The night before the game Harkes called a players-only meeting. "We talked about what an incredible thing it would be if we could beat Colombia, what it would mean for U.S. soccer, and we walked out feeling really good about ourselves," Harkes revealed in the *Detroit Free Press*.

Harkes was credited with the first goal for the United States when Colombian defender Andres Escobar accidently kicked in a ball the American intended to center to his teammate Ernie Stewart. "After that first goal, you could sense that they [the Colombians] were frustrated," he explained in the *Detroit Free Press*. "We were closing up all their options, and they were running out of ideas. You can just tell when you're in control of a match, and we were." Stewart added a second goal for the United States, and they held on for a 2-1 victory. It was the first win for the United States in the World Cup since 1950.

SUSPENDED. Harkes played every minute of the first three first-round games for the United States. The Americans suffered a disappointing 1-0 loss against Romania, forcing them to play pre-tournament favorite Brazil in a do-or-die match. Harkes had the best scoring chance for the United States against the Romanians, knocking a shot off the left post.

The American team advanced to the second round of the World Cup for the first time in 64 years. Unfortunately, Harkes could not play in the game against Brazil because of a suspension given him for two yellow cards he received for rule infractions. "This is very bad for us," teammate Tab Ramos told the *Detroit Free Press*. "You can't replace John Harkes. There's only one on our team."

Harkes was angry because he said he did not know the correct rules regarding yellow cards. "You can't imagine how depressed I am," he admitted in the *Detroit Free Press*. "It's a shattered dream. It's a dream to play Brazil in the World Cup, and I can't be part of it. All I can do is keep my spirits up, and hopefully we'll upset them and I'll get another chance in the quarterfinals." Harkes missed his chance when the United States lost to Brazil, 1-0, eliminating the Americans from the tournament.

MOVING UP. The U.S. national team continued to earn respect when they won the 1995 U.S. Cup, defeating Nigeria and Mexico and earning a tie with Colombia. "Finally, we're starting to arrive and get the respect of the other national teams, Harkes stated in the *Detroit Free Press*. "It's been a long time coming. It's been a lot of hard work."

The United States had one of their best international tournaments ever at the 1995 Copa America, the world's oldest soccer tournament. The Americans had not won a game in the 1993 Copa America tournament. Harkes captained the U.S. team that defeated the mighty teams from Argentina (3-0) and Mexico (4-1) and reached the semifinals. The United States lost to Brazil once again 1-0 in the semifinals, but they earned the respect of the defending World Cup champions. The last time the United States had made the semifinals of a major international tournament was at the 1930 World Cup.

Harkes was named co-most valuable player of the tournament. "A lot of people were talking about the last time we were in Copa America and didn't win a game," Harkes explained in the *Detroit Free Press*. "For us to come this far as a team together—the full squad, everyone pulling together—it's one of the biggest triumphs ever for the U.S. squad. People talk about the World Cup—but to win successfully like we have and go this far in the Copa American is unreal."

MLS BEGINS. In order to host the World Cup, American soccer officials had to promise that they would start a major outdoor soccer league in the United States. In 1996, the United States had a major outdoor soccer league for the first time since 1985. Major League Soccer (MLS) kicked off in the spring with 10 teams. The league signed contracts with ESPN to televise 35 regular-season games and ABC agreed to televise the league's championship game. "This country has been crying out for something like this for a long time," Harkes stated in *Sports Illustrated for Kids*.

At first Harkes said he would not leave England to play in the MLS. "We'd love to be here [in the United States], playing in our country, but I can't see how," Harkes explained to the *Detroit Free Press*. "Not until the MLS has top players, top salaries and sold-out stadiums. It would be nice if I could play here in America and raise my family here, but right now, that isn't possible. My experience in England has been wonderful. I've learned so much over there. I want soccer to take off in this country, really, I do. But do I take a chance and leave top-quality soccer in Europe? What if the league fails after one year, then what? I didn't want to leave America in the first place, but now I'm torn."

Harkes changed his mind, however, and in 1996 he returned to play for the Washington D.C. United team of MLS, coached by his college coach, Bruce Arena. "I've done everything I can," he explained to the *Detroit Free Press*. "I've played six times at Wembley [Stadium], got a League Cup winner's medal, scored the 'Goal of the Year.' Now I want to come back. Kids need heroes to look up to."

The new American league featured Harkes and other U.S. stars such as Ramos, Eric Wynalda, Alexi Lalas, and

Cobi Jones, as well as international stars such as Carlos Valderrama of Columbia and Jorge Campos of Mexico. "Everyone was asking me what kind of league we were going to have," Harkes said. "And I didn't know."

Harkes was named to the first-ever MLS All-Star Game on July 14 in Giants Stadium in East Rutherford, New Jersey, but a pulled left hamstring caused him to miss the game. For the season he scored two goals and assisted on six others, but his job was acting as the glue that held together the team's offense and defense. Harkes plays midfield, which he says is like a quarterback in football. "The midfielder controls the play," he told *Sports Illustrated for Kids*. "He's the important link between the defense and the offense."

MLS CUP '96. D.C. United overcame an early season slump to earn the right to play the Los Angeles Galaxy—featuring Jones—in the 1996 MLS Cup at Foxboro Stadium in Foxboro, Massachusetts. "For me, coming back to the States was a challenge, to build this league and see it grow," Harkes explained in *Newsday*. "The players all are very excited with soccer finally being on the map in this country. So this game is just as important, if not more important, than those big tournaments I've played in—the World Cup, the [English] FA Cup—because we're not only going out to do our best for our club but for soccer in general in the United States. I don't have any doubt now that this league will go very far."

Weather on game day was horrible. Rain and high winds made conditions nearly impossible for the players and the 36,643 fans. D.C. United fell behind 2-0 but rallied for a 3-2 sudden-death victory. Midfielder Marco Etcheverry won most valuable player honors after setting up all three D.C. United goals. Defender Eddie Pope scored on a header from a corner kick by Etcheverry four minutes into overtime to win the game. "The fever [for soccer] is alive in the U.S.," Harkes told the Gannett News Service. "We put it on the map today."

STAYS HOME. Harkes has decided to continue to play in the MLS. Although soccer is more popular in England, he does not regret his decision. "Everyone talks about it being a tough choice in terms of what I left behind," Harkes said after the first MLS season. "It was incredible there. But what we've done in the past six months is incredible as well. I don't have any doubt this league is going to do very well. It's an exciting time right now for soccer in the United States. And everybody knows that."

OFF THE FIELD. Harkes lives with his wife, Cindi, and his son, Ian Andrew. Cindi Harkes is also a former player at the University of Virginia who trained with the U.S. women's national team in 1994.

One of Harkes's goals is for soccer to grow in the United States, and he hopes he can be a role model for younger players. "So many kids are interested in the game today," he told *Sports Illustrated for Kids.* "I think it's important for the kids to have somebody to look up to."

Harkes hopes the MLS and soccer with take off in his home country. "Seems like people with negative views will keep on trying to put soccer down," he confessed in *Sports Illustrated.* "But the game is here to stay, so they might as well sit back and enjoy it. It's coming and it's coming strong."

Sources

Boston Globe, July 20, 1995.
Cincinnati Enquirer, July 18, 1995.
Detroit Free Press, June 3, 1994; June 7, 1994; June 15, 1994; June 16, 1994; June 17, 1994; June 23, 1994; June 27, 1994; June 28, 1994; June 30, 1994; July 2, 1994; July 6, 1994; June 26, 1995.
Miami Herald, July 22, 1995.
Newsday, October 20, 1996.
People Weekly, May 19, 1994; June 6, 1994.
Sport, July 18, 1994.
Sports Illustrated, April 22, 1991.
Sports Illustrated for Kids, May 1996.
USA Today, August 21, 1996.
Additional information provided by D.C. United, the Gannett News Service, Major League Soccer, and the Reuters News Service.

WHERE TO WRITE:
C/O WASHINGTON D.C. UNITED,
13832 REDSKIN DRIVE,
HERNDON, VA 22071.

Juwan Howard

1973—

Juwan Howard believes in keeping his promises. Before signing to play for the University of Michigan as part of the famous "Fab Five" team, he promised his grandmother that he would get his college degree. Despite leaving Michigan after only three years, Howard remembered his promise. During his first season with the Washington Bullets of the National Basketball Association (NBA), Howard became the first basketball player to leave school early and still complete his degree on time. He shows the same dedication on the court, where he became an NBA all-star in only his second season. As the leader of a young Bullets team, Howard promises he will lead the team to the NBA championship.

"I love the game of basketball. This is my dream. My livelihood. And I take it very seriously. I want to be the best."— Juwan Howard.

Growing Up

RAISED BY GRANDMA. Juwan Antonio Howard was born February 7, 1973, in Chicago, Illinois. His mother, Thelma, was only 17 years old when Howard was born, and his father,

Leroy Watson Jr., left the family when his son was only a baby. Thelma Howard was so poor she could not afford a crib for her new baby, so he spent the first week of his life sleeping in a dresser drawer.

Realizing she was too young to raise her son, his mother sent Howard to live with his grandmother. Jennie Mae Howard raised him and two of his cousins in an apartment on Chicago's South Side, one of the poorest areas in the United States. "My parents were very young when they had me, and so my grandmother took on a lot of the responsibility of raising me," Howard explained in *Jet*. "She gave me direction."

Howard's grandmother encouraged him to read and get a good education. "My grandmother was solid," he told *Sports Illustrated*. Even though gangs ruled his neighborhood and shootings frequently occurred around his home, Howard stayed out of trouble and always came home by nightfall.

GROWTH SPURT. Howard played many sports as a child, but baseball was his favorite. He pitched and played first base. By the time Howard turned 12, he had already grown to over 6-feet-tall. He joined a youth league team and started to play basketball. "I loved the fancy passing and dribbling," Howard recalled in *Sports Illustrated for Kids*.

It took time and practice for Howard to improve as a basketball player. "My grandmother always told me that if you work hard, you'll see progress," he explained in *Sports Illustrated for Kids*. Howard watched professional players and tried to copy their moves. His favorite player was the legendary Julius "Dr. J" Erving. Howard even has a Dr. J tattoo on his left arm.

HIGH SCHOOL HOOPS. By the time Howard entered the ninth grade at Chicago Vocational High School, he had grown to 6-feet-6-inches tall. He was still clumsy as a basketball player, but the hard work had started to pay off. Vocational High School was poor, and the team often practiced in an unheated gym. "We didn't even have a locker room—we dressed for home games in a history classroom," Howard recalled in *Sports Illustrated*.

By his senior year in high school, Howard had grown to nearly 7-feet-tall and developed into one of the top-rated centers in the United States. He averaged 27 points and 12 rebounds a game in his senior high school season, good enough to earn him the Player of the Year award for the state of Illinois. "He was dedicated, he was goal-oriented, and he had a lot of pride," Howard's high school coach Dick Cook told the *Baltimore Sun*. "Juwan never wanted to be outplayed. He never missed a practice, and when that was over he was always staying after to work on his fundamentals: the short shots, the jump hooks. You get to coach a kid like that maybe once in your life. I've come across kids who have been as talented, but never anyone as dedicated." Howard worked hard in the classroom, too, graduating with a B average.

TRAGEDY STRIKES. College coaches made Howard one of the most highly recruited basketball players in the United States. During his senior season he accepted a scholarship to the University of Michigan. Howard held a press conference to announce his decision, on what should have been the greatest day of his life.

When Howard arrived home, however, neighbors told him that his grandmother had died of a heart attack. He cried and cried that night. Jennie Mae Howard had been the most important person in his life, so important that Howard tattooed Jennie Mae in a valentine over his heart. "I wanted to do something really special for her," he explained in *Sports Illustrated*. Howard still talks to his grandmother in his thoughts, and visits her gravesite regularly. "I always tell her how my season is going," he told the same magazine. Since his grandmother's death, Howard has become closer to other members of his family, including his mother.

"FAB FIVE." Entering the University of Michigan, Howard was the first member of one of the most famous recruiting

Howard (center) battles for a rebound.

classes ever. The "Fab Five," as sportswriters called them, included Howard, Chris Webber (now Howard's teammate on the Bullets), Jalen Rose (now with the Indiana Pacers), Ray Jackson, and Jimmy King. The team was known for its flashy play and uniforms. The "Fab Five" made baggy shorts standard equipment for college basketball players around the United States.

Unfortunately, the "Fab Five" also received a reputation as trash-talkers (athletes who excessively brag and celebrate) who tried to intimidate and embarrass their opponents. Howard thinks the criticism the team received was unfair. "They made us to be a bunch of gangsters and we really were just a bunch of 18-year-old kids having fun," he said. "I didn't think some critics were fair to us."

TOURNAMENT TIME. The "Fab Five" became one of the first set of all freshmen to all start at the college level. Howard got off to a strong start, averaging 11.1 points and 6.2 rebounds during his first year. Michigan struggled throughout the regular season, but still qualified for the 1992 National Collegiate Athletic Association (NCAA) Tournament. Despite their talent, experts did not expect the University of Michigan Wolverines to be contenders for the national title.

Surprising everyone but themselves, however, Michigan beat four straight tournament opponents to reach the NCAA Final Four in Minneapolis, Minnesota. The Wolverines then polished off the Cincinnati Bearcats in the semifinals to earn a spot in the national championship game. There they faced the defending NCAA champions, the Duke University Blue Devils. Although Duke ended the "Fab Five's" dream season with a 71-51 victory, the future looked bright for the Wolverines.

TITLE GAME II. The Wolverines clawed their way back to the 1993 NCAA Final Four in Howard's sophomore season. There they faced the powerful Kentucky Wildcats. The game was a classic, going back and forth until the very end. Michigan won the game, 81-78, in overtime. The Wolverines would play the University of North Carolina Tar Heels in the championship game, and this time experts made the "Fab Five" the favorite.

Michigan and North Carolina met in April 1993, at the Superdome in New Orleans, Louisiana. North Carolina led by two points with eleven seconds left on the clock. A basket would tie the game and force overtime, but Wolverine captain Webber called a timeout so that his team could set up a play. Unfortunately, Michigan had used all its timeouts, and the referee called Webber for a technical foul. The call awarded North Carolina two free throws and possession of the ball. The Tar Heels won the game and the national championship, 77-71.

"FAB FIVE" MINUS ONE. Webber decided to turn professional after his sophomore season at Michigan, breaking up the "Fab Five." The loss of Webber, however, did not destroy the Wolverines. Michigan coach Steve Fischer told *Sports Illustrated* that Howard was the glue that held the team together. His teammates elected him the team's cocaptain. "We knew that in order for us to win, some people had to sacrifice, and I didn't mind sacrificing a part of my game," Howard explained in the *Fort Worth Star-Telegram.* "Egos and jealousies were definitely not going to get us anywhere, and we all knew that."

Howard posted the best numbers of his career as a junior—20.8 points and 8.9 rebounds per game—and became a leader on the court and off. He powered the Wolverines to the Elite Eight of the 1994 NCAA Tournament, where they fell in the Midwest Region Final to the eventual national champion, the Arkansas Razorbacks. Howard scored 30 points and pulled down 13 rebounds against Arkansas, but it was not enough. In four tournament games, Howard averaged 29 points and 12.8 rebounds, earning Most Outstanding Player of the Midwest Regional honors.

Superstar

BULLET BOUND. Following his junior year, Howard decided he was ready to enter the NBA. In his career at Michigan, he averaged 15.3 points and 7.5 rebounds per game and was 1 of only 5 players in school history to score over 1500 career points (1526) and grab more than 700 rebounds (745). Howard ranked ninth in career NCAA tournament scoring (280 points). He also made an impression off the court, visiting hospitals as part of the From the Heart program.

The Washington Bullets selected Howard with the fifth pick in the 1994 NBA Draft. Unfortunately, he had a difficult time agreeing on a contract with the Bullets. At one point the negotiations became so frustrating, Howard broke down and cried. "It was very depressing," he recalled in the *Baltimore Sun.* "But what happens with negotiations is a business, and I understand that." Howard finally signed a $36.6 million contract. The fight over his contract made him determined to show the Bullets that he was worth every penny.

REUNION. On the same day that Howard signed his contract, the Bullets traded with the Golden State Warriors for Webber, the NBA Rookie of the Year the previous season (1993—94). The trade reunited the two college teammates and friends. "The two of us together, we can be one of those one-two punches like with Scottie [Pippen] and Michael [Jordan], Hakeem [Olajuwon] and Clyde [Drexler]," Howard explained in the *Baltimore Sun*. "We've talked about it and we feel we can dominate this league just like we did in college."

Despite missing training camp and the first seven games of the season, Howard made an immediate impact in the NBA during the 1994—95 campaign. He averaged 17 points per game (third among NBA rookies) and 8.4 rebounds (first among NBA rookies). "I proved a lot of people wrong," Howard said after the season. "A lot of people questioned my talent. Some thought it would take me longer. But what I accomplished as a rookie didn't surprise me at all. I have confidence that I'm better than any other player out there on the floor. I knew it wouldn't take long to learn the NBA style of play. Once I got that down pat, it worked like clockwork."

BACK TO SCHOOL. Before signing with Michigan, Howard promised his grandmother he would complete his college degree. He worked hard in his spare time to complete his degree during his rookie season with the Bullets. Howard took classes by mail, often doing his homework on the team plane. "My teammates were surprised," he admitted in *Sports Illustrated for Kids*. "They saw I was serious about my studies."

Through hard work and determination, Howard became the first NBA player to leave school early but still graduate on time. "This was something that was very important to my grandmother and I know she is watching me and smiling and crying right now," he told the *Washington Post*. "And just like she inspired me, I want this to stand not just as an example now, but as an example for my own kids."

THE WIZARDS

In 1996, the owner of the Bullets, Abe Pollin, decided to change the name of the team. He felt the name was too violent. Pollin had been a friend of prime minister Yitzak Rabin of Israel, who was shot to death by a Jewish extremist opposing Rabin's Middle East peace plan. The new name—the Wizards—will go into effect at the start of the 1997—98 season. That season the Wizards will also play in a new arena, the MCI Center.

Howard earned his degree in communications and attended graduation ceremonies with his "Fab Five" teammates Ray Jackson and Jimmy King and the other students from the class of 1995. "Graduating was one of the best feelings of my life," Howard recalled in *Sports Illustrated for Kids*. "I'll never forget that day." He was the first member of his family to graduate from college, a fact he is very proud of.

ALL-STAR. Howard opened his second season as an NBA star. He averaged 22.1 points (tenth in the NBA) and 8.1 rebounds per game. Eastern Conference coaches named Howard to his first NBA All-Star Game, where he scored 2 points and pulled down 7 rebounds. "I never thought I would be here in my second year in the league," Howard admitted in the *Baltimore Sun.* "But I'll say this: I'm going to stop being so modest. I worked all summer to prepare myself to be one of the best players in the league. And I've done it." At the end of the season, Howard earned third-team All-NBA honors. (The NBA chooses three All-NBA teams at the end of the season made up of the best players from the league. As a member of the third team, Howard was chosen as the third best player at his position.)

BIG PAYDAY. Howard became a free agent after the 1995—96 season. This meant he could sign with any other NBA team. The Miami Heat—coached by the legendary Pat Riley—signed Howard to a $100 million contract. The NBA, however, said that the contract put the Heat over their salary cap, the limit on how much a team can spend on players for their team. In the end, Howard resigned with the Bullets for $105 million.

TEAM LEADER. Now that his contract problems are behind him, Howard wants to lead the Bullets into the playoffs. "By my standards, he was a leader the first time he walked into the gym," Bullets assistant coach Derek Smith said. "We're taking more notice of Juwan, too, because we're asking him to do more, and that showcases his leadership." The undisputed team leader, Howard often carries the Bullets on his shoulders. "He's mature beyond his years," Bullets coach Jim Lynam said. "I probably lean on him more than I should. But if you see the game sliding, you have no choice. He's someone you can depend on."

The last time the Bullets made the playoffs was 1988, but the past does not matter to Howard. "This is the '90s now," he told *Sports Illustrated*. "I know this: I'm not going to be satisfied until I get a [championship] ring." Howard is glad to be teamed up again with his old friend Webber for the 1996—97 season. "I appreciate having a true friend around like Chris," Howard explained in *Sports Illustrated for Kids*. "We feel you'll never see two other forwards who play so well together."

WHY SO GOOD? Howard practices two hours a day, four days a week, in the off-season, working on his shooting and his moves. "I want to be one of the best ever to play this game," Howard told *Sports Illustrated for Kids*. "For that to happen, I need to work hard." Howard has great moves in the low post (playing close to the basket) and can shoot outside. He also is an excellent defender and passer, and runs the floor very well for a big man. "Juwan is an outstanding player," New York Knicks center Patrick Ewing told the same magazine. "You can tell he spends a lot of time working on his game."

OFF THE COURT. Howard lives in Washington, DC, during the season, and returns home to Chicago during the summer. He likes to watch football, play baseball and pool, waterski, and swim. His favorite athlete is Michael Jordan. Howard also enjoys listening to the music of Boyz II Men. He got a big

GOOD SPORT

Howard is very active off the court to help children and those in need. He is the NBA spokesman for Reading Is Fundamental (RIF), a program that donates more than 11 million books to kids every year. In February 1995, Howard established the Juwan Howard Foundation, which has given 1,000 winter coats to needy kids in Washington, DC. That same year, *Sports Illustrated for Kids* awarded Howard its Good Sport Award. He understands his position as a role model for children. "Growing up in a household with no parents, I know how it is for kids who look up to athletes," Howard explained in *Sports Illustrated*. He is also opening three Juwan Howard Learning Centers, providing kids with after-school homework help.

thrill when he was chosen to carry the Olympic torch through the streets of Washington in 1996.

Howard wants to be one of the best of all time. "I don't want to be one of those guys who take the money and don't care about anything else," he explained in *Sports Illustrated*. "It bugs me when you read the paper and some of the NBA veterans are saying, 'These young guys, they're messing up the league.' Well, I'm one of those young guys. And I don't only care about the money. I love the game of basketball. This is my dream. My livelihood. And I take it very seriously. I want to be the best."

Sources

Baltimore Sun, February 11, 1996.
Fort Worth Star-Telegram, January 23, 1996.
Jet, May 22, 1995.
Milwaukee Journal Sentinel, February 16, 1996.
Sporting News, November 28, 1994.
Sports Illustrated, November 25, 1991; December 23, 1991; February 26, 1996.
Sports Illustrated for Kids, December 1995; November 1996.
Washington Post, August 15, 1996; October 27, 1996.
Additional information provided by the University of Michigan and the Washington Bullets.

WHERE TO WRITE:

C/O WASHINGTON BULLETS,
USAIR ARENA,
LANDOVER, MD 20785.

Paul Kariya

1974—

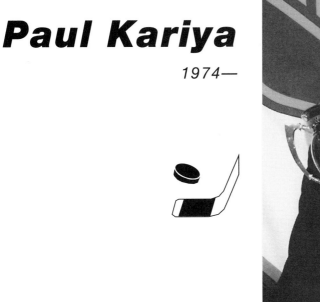

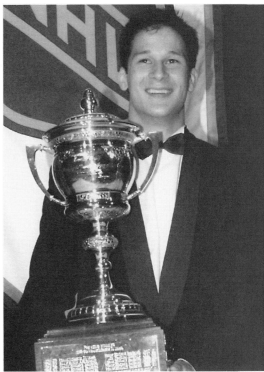

Education has always been important to left-winger Paul Kariya of the Anaheim Mighty Ducks. His parents are both school teachers and Kariya is a student of hockey. He studied one of the best professors in the game, the "Great One," Wayne Gretzky. As a child Kariya studied films of Gretzky and used the lessons he learned to become a rising star in the National Hockey League (NHL). Scoring 50 goals in his first full professional season, Kariya hopes to live up to the title some hockey experts have given him: The Next Gretzky.

"[The] heir apparent to Gretzky is Kariya. He's just sweet to watch."—Ron MacLean, host of Hockey Night in Canada.

Growing Up

LEARNS FROM PARENTS. Paul Tetsuhiko Kariya (ka-REE-ya) was born October 16, 1974, in West Vancouver, British Columbia, Canada. He is the second oldest of five children of Tetsuhiko, a Japanese-Canadian, and Sharon Kariya. Kariya's father is a math and computer science teacher at Argyle Secondary School, and his mother is also a school teacher.

"School was very important in our household," Kariya explained in *Sports Illustrated for Kids*. "We didn't watch much TV because we were doing homework or playing sports."

Tetsuhiko Kariya played for the Canadian National Rugby Team, and his son played several sports growing up. He liked lacrosse, tennis, golf, soccer, swimming, and basketball. "At one time, I dreamed about playing in the [National Basketball Association] NBA," Kariya admitted in *Sports Illustrated for Kids*. "I had a pretty good three-point shot."

GROWS UP WITH GRETZKY. Kariya's best sport, however, was hockey. He began to skate at the age of four and first played hockey when he was six years old. When he was nine, Kariya played in a league with fourteen-year-old players. And by the time he turned fifteen, he decided he wanted to play in the NHL.

Even though he grew up in Vancouver, Kariya was an Edmonton Oilers fan. His hero was the "Great One," Wayne Gretzky. "[Gretzky is] a person I greatly admire," Kariya explained in *Sports Illustrated for Kids*. "He did things with style, with class. I want to do things in a similar way."

Kariya tried to pattern his game after Gretzky. "I enjoyed watching the [Oilers' style of play], and I tried to incorporate some of what Wayne does into my game, the way he uses his teammates and finds open people," Kariya told *Sports Illustrated*. "The game seems to slow down when he has the puck."

BIG DECISION. When he was 15 Kariya played Junior A hockey for Penticton, British Columbia, scoring 132 points (45 goals and 87 assists) in 41 games. The league named him the player of the year for 1992. Kariya needed to make a decision after graduating from Penticton High School. His parents wanted him to attend college in the United States, but profes-

Beating his opponents to the puck, Kariya (left) moves it down the ice.

sional teams wanted him to sign with them. The Tri-City Americans of the Western Hockey League offered Kariya $200,000, but he decided to go to college. "I've always thought college hockey was a great place to learn the game," he explained in *Sports Illustrated.*

College hockey powers like Harvard University and Boston University recruited Kariya, but he chose the University of Maine Black Bears. Maine had a strong program, holding the number-one ranking for most of the 1991—92 season.

Orono, Maine—the home of the University of Maine—reminded Kariya of his home. The Black Bears were the only game in Maine, and had a strong fan following in the state. "Ever see that movie *Hoosiers,* where the whole community gets behind the high school basketball team?" Black Bear defenseman Chris Imes asked in *Sports Illustrated*. "Well, that's the way it is with hockey at Maine, except it's not just one town. It's the whole state."

BEST BEAR. Kariya—nicknamed "The Kid" by his teammates—scored 93 points (24 goals and 69 assists) in 36 games during his freshman season at Maine, setting a National Collegiate Athletic Association (NCAA) record of 2.6 points per game. With linemates Jim Montgomery (32 goals) and Cal Ingraham (NCAA-leading 46 goals), the number-one line was the most dangerous in the country. In honor of his incredible first year, Kariya became the first freshman to win the Hobey Baker Award as the nation's top college player.

Kariya earned the title "The Wayne Gretzky of college hockey," after NHL coach Mike Keenan compared him to the great player. "He's as creative and electrifying as any player I've witnessed in quite some time," Maine coach Shawn Walsh told the *Sporting News*. "What really sets him apart is his ability to focus and keep an even keel on all situations. He's electrifying—that's the best word for it. He's quick and he's creative. He's got that special sense. The game is played in front of his eyes at a lot slower pace than a normal person. He can read everything before it's happening."

Maine entered the NCAA Hockey Tournament as a favorite, and they played their way to the Final Four at the Bradley Center in Milwaukee, Wisconsin. In the national semifinals, Maine defeated the University of Michigan, 4-3, in overtime. The victory earned the Black Bears a trip to the national championship game.

There Maine faced defending NCAA champion Lake Superior State from Michigan. The Black Bears' hopes for the title seemed dim after two periods, as they trailed the Lakers, 4-2. At that point Kariya took over. Three times he set up Montgomery for goals, with the game winner coming on a pretty pass across the crease.

"When those guys come at you at about 100 miles-an-hour, there's not a lot you can do," Lake Superior State coach

Jeff Jackson explained in *Sports Illustrated*. Maine led 5-4, then held on. Laker forward Sean Tallaire hit the crossbar of Maine's net with only a minute left. When the final buzzer sounded, the Black Bears had the game and the national championship. It was the first national championship of any kind for Maine, who finished their dream season with a 42-1-2 record.

TOP PICK. In January 1993 Kariya earned all-tournament team honors at the World Junior Ice Hockey Championships in Sweden, where he helped lead Canada to the gold medal. The expansion Anaheim Mighty Ducks used their first-ever first-round draft choice—the fourth pick overall—to pick Kariya in 1993. Three teams passed on drafting Kariya because they thought he would be too small—at 5 feet, 11 inches and 165 pounds—to play in the NHL.

Kariya had to decide whether to sign with the Ducks or play for Canada in the 1994 Winter Olympics in Lillehammer, Norway. "A lot will depend on when I feel I'm ready for an 84-game schedule, physically and mentally," Kariya explained in *Sports Illustrated*. "Right now I'm thinking there's no way I'll be ready for the NHL next year."

SO CLOSE. Instead of signing with Anaheim, Kariya split the 1993—94 season between the University of Maine (8 goals and 16 assists in 12 games) and the Canadian Olympic team. He was the best player for the Canadian Olympic hockey team, scoring 3 goals and 4 assists in 8 games. "He thinks and plays at a better speed than anybody else," Canadian Olympic coach Tom Renney told the *Detroit Free Press*.

The Canadians reached the gold-medal game in the Olympic hockey competition against Sweden. The game went into overtime, and was decided in a shootout. (In a shootout, five players from each team take penalty shots on the other team's goalie. The team that scores the most goals in the shootout wins the game.) Sweden's **Peter Forsberg** beat Canadian goalie Corey Hirsch to give his team a one-goal lead in the shootout. Kariya—who scored one of Canada's goals in regulation and also scored earlier in the shootout—

was the last hope to tie the game. When he did not score on goalie Tommy Salo, Sweden won the gold medal, and Canada earned the silver.

WORLD CHAMPS. Later in the year Kariya joined the Canadian team competing at the World Ice Hockey Championships. On a squad loaded with NHL veterans, he led the team in scoring with 5 goals and 7 assists in 8 games. Canada faced Finland in the finals, and like the Olympics, a shootout decided the championship. The two teams tied, 1-1, at the end of regulation and one overtime period. Luc Robitaille of the Los Angeles Kings scored the game-winning goal, giving Canada a 3-2 win. It was Canada's first world championship victory since 1961.

MIGHTIEST DUCK. After 14 months of contract negotiations, Kariya signed a three-year, $6.51-million deal with the Mighty Ducks. Anaheim fans were excited to see their new star. More than 9000 fans showed up for Kariya's first practice.

Playing in the NHL was an adjustment for Kariya. "Everything is different," he admitted in the *Detroit Free Press*. "It's a constant learning process, what it takes to succeed here. Everyone knows what you do. So you're constantly trying to adjust your game."

A contract dispute caused by a disagreement between players and owners delayed the start of Kariya's first season (1994—95). When it did begin, he led all NHL rookies in scoring with 18 goals in 47 games and added 21 assists. The NHL made Kariya a finalist for the Calder Trophy, awarded to the league's best rookie. (Peter Forsberg of the Quebec Nordiques won the award.)

The Ducks played a tough defensive game but did not have a high-powered offense. Kariya had to slow down his fast-paced style to help his team. "I've been pretty happy with the way things are both for the team and myself," Kariya confessed in the *Detroit Free Press*. "We don't have the type of offense here to put up big numbers. You expect that going into the game. If you're not scoring any goals, you're not going to win games. But I think our effort has been there for the team and myself personally. I've been getting a lot of chances."

Superstar

ALL-STAR. Kariya became an NHL star in his first full season (1995—96). He scored 50 goals, 9 of them game-winners, with 3 in overtime. Kariya started for the Western Conference at the 1996 NHL All-Star Game where he scored a goal. After the season, he won the Lady Byng Trophy for good sportsmanship and earned a spot on the NHL first-team all-star team. (The all-star first-team is made up of the league's best players at each position.)

The Ducks finished with 35 wins and 78 points, barely missing the playoffs. Late in the season, Anaheim traded with the Winnipeg Jets for high-scoring winger Teemu Selanne, who took some of the offensive pressure off Kariya. "Now that Teemu is here, when we're coming up the ice, passing back and forth, no one knows what we're going to do," Kariya explained in *Sports Illustrated for Kids*.

Because Anaheim missed the playoffs, Kariya was available to play for Canada in the 1996 World Ice Hockey Championships in Vienna, Austria. He scored a 3-goal hat trick to lead Canada past the United States, 5-1, in the quarterfinals, then scored one goal in a penalty shootout to help Canada past Russia, 3-2, in the semifinals. The Czech Republic ended Canada's run with a 4-2 victory in the championship game.

OFF THE ICE. Kariya is single and lives in Tustin Ranch, California, during the season, and returns to Vancouver when the Ducks' season ends. When not playing hockey, he likes to play tennis, golf, and basketball. Kariya eats pasta and vegetables before every game. His younger brother, Steve, plays hockey for the University of Maine.

MICKEY MOUSE OPERATION

The Walt Disney Corporation owns the Mighty Ducks. Playing for Disney has benefits for Kariya. He gets all the free passes he wants to Disneyland, can get into Disney movies free, and even played himself in the Disney film *Mighty Ducks 3*. "Being in the movie was fun," Kariya admitted in *Sports Illustrated for Kids*. "But I'm no actor. I'd better not give up my hockey career."

WHY SO GOOD?

Kariya is one of the fastest skaters in the NHL. "I know I'd hate to be a defenseman that has to face him one on one," Wilson admitted in the *Sporting News*. "He is capable of embarrassing you with his speed."

Kariya can also handle the puck and make beautiful passes to waiting teammates. A team player, he looks to pass first, shoot second. "He's an unbelievable passer," veteran winger Jari Kurri told *Sports Illustrated for Kids*. "To me, he's one of the top five players in the NHL."

Kariya learned a lot from Wayne Gretzky, his idol. Like Gretzky, Kariya likes to set up behind the opponent's net and feed the puck to teammates. Also like the "Great One," Kariya continually studies hockey and opposing players to get an advantage. "My parents were school teachers, and they told me that nothing comes easy, you have to work hard for everything," he explained in the *Sporting News*. "Maybe that's why I try to watch every player in the league when I'm on the bench. You never know when you can pick up a move, or see the tendency of an opponent that might help you."

Kariya likes to read. He studied business administration at Maine—where he made the Dean's list—and he hopes to go into business when his hockey career is over. "So much of business is like sports," Kariya told *Sports Illustrated*. "Teamwork, dedication, work ethic, competitiveness."

In order to improve his hand-eye coordination Kariya took up juggling. "I had a book, *Lessons from the Art of Juggling*." he recalled in *Sports Illustrated*. "I can do the one where you take the bite out of the apple as it comes by. If it gives you just that split second more of coordination, it's something you have."

Ron MacLean, host of Hockey Night in Canada, gave Kariya the highest compliment he could when he told *Maclean's:* "[The] heir apparent to Gretzky is Kariya. He's just sweet to watch."

Sources

Calgary Herald, April 30, 1996.
Detroit Free Press, February 24, 1994; February 28, 1994; March 1, 1994; April 27, 1994; May 6, 1994; May 9, 1994; February 4, 1995; March 10, 1995; July 7, 1995; January 22, 1996; March 26, 1996; April 29, 1996; May 4, 1996; May 6. 1996; June 20, 1996; August 9, 1996.
Maclean's, April 8, 1996.
Sporting News, February 14, 1994; February 13, 1995.
Sports Illustrated, February 22, 1993; April 12, 1993; February 13, 1995.
Sports Illustrated for Kids, February 1994; November 1996.

WHERE TO WRITE:
C/O MIGHTY DUCKS OF ANAHEIM,
2695 KATTELLA AVENUE,
P.O. BOX 61077,
ANAHEIM, CA 92803-6177.

Tonia Kwiatkowski

1971—

Tonia Kwiatkowski, the 26-year-old figure skater, is called the "Grand Old Lady" of the sport. In 1996 she finished second at the U.S. Figure Skating Championships, earning a trip to the World Figure Skating Championships in Edmonton, Alberta, Canada. In a sport dominated by teenagers, Kwiatkowski has proven that it is never too late to achieve your dream.

Growing Up

LOVED TO SKATE. Tonia Kwiatkowski was born February 12, 1971, in Cleveland, Ohio. She is the only child of Phil Kwiatkowski, a heavy-machine operator, and his wife, Corinne, a homemaker. Kwiatkowski began to skate at the age of five, taking lessons at the Greenbriar Ice Rink in Parma Heights, Ohio. She participated in the "Learn to Skate" program, where she learned how to stand on her skates, bend her knees correctly, and get back up after a fall.

"I look at myself as the Cal Ripken of figure skating. I just keep coming back and giving the audience more."—Tonia Kwiatkowski.

When she was seven, Kwiatkowski began private lessons with Carole Gatti. Within just a year, she finished second in the Cleveland Invitational Championships, her first competition. Kwiatkowski impressed skating coach Carol Heiss Jenkins while competing in the tournament. Jenkins won the Olympic figure skating gold medal at the 1960 Winter Olympics in Squaw Valley, California, and also captured five world championships (1956—60). She recognized that Kwiatkowski enjoyed her sport. "She loved to skate," Jenkins recalled in *People Weekly*. "That's what was so wonderful."

When she decided to take up skating full time, Kwiatkowski had to give up gymnastics, another sport she enjoyed. When she was nine she tried out for a junior gymnastics team and made it, becoming the youngest gymnast on the team. Kwiatkowski tried to compete in both sports, but soon her mother told to pick the one she liked best. She chose skating. "I just enjoyed the skating so much more, and I thought I was better at it," Kwiatkowski admitted to ESPN *SportsZone*.

Kwiatkowski made steady progress under Jenkins's watchful eye. In 1981, the two moved to the Winterhurst Ice Arena in Lakewood, Ohio, where they could have more ice time. In 1986 she also began working with choreographer Glyn Watts at Winterhurst Ice Arena. (A choreographer is a person who designs a skating program, including the music and costumes.) Watts was a three-time European and World Championship medalist in ice-dancing.

HARD WORK. Training to be a champion skater was hard. Kwiatkowski skated five hours a day, five days a week. She got up every weekday morning at 5:30 a.m., skated until 8

Leaping in the air, Kwiatkowski gives one of her stellar performances.. ▶

a.m., then went to school. After school, Kwiatkowski returned to the rink for more practice. She also took ballet classes two nights a week. Kwiatkowski had to change middle schools because she needed a more flexible schedule.

Kwiatkowski attended Lakewood High School. She was a good student, earning membership in the National Honor Society in her junior and senior years. Because she did not skate on weekends, Kwiatkowski was able to attend football and basketball games with other students.

Unlike other skaters, Kwiatkowski did not have to move away from her parents to train. "I've been lucky because I didn't have to move away from home to get good coaching," she wrote for ESPN SportsZone. "There are plenty of examples of skaters who haven't been so lucky. I was able to be home for all these years of skating." Kwiatkowski's parents encouraged, but never pushed, their daughter.

WINS MEDAL. Kwiatkowski won the 1987 Midwestern Junior championship and took third in the national junior championships. She made her first appearance in the senior division at the U.S. Figure Skating Championships in 1990, where she finished sixth. The next two years she finished fourth and fifth.

Kwiatkowski finally earned a medal at the 1993 U.S. Figure Skating Championships in Phoenix, Arizona, taking third place behind champion Nancy Kerrigan. Her finish qualified her to travel to the World Figure Skating Championships in Prague, Czech Republic. Because Kwiatkowski had not qualified for the world championships the year before, she had to skate in a preliminary qualifying competition to reach the finals.

Unfortunately, Kwiatkowski fell early in her qualifying program. She let the fall bother her and destroy her confidence. As her program progressed Kwiatkowski fell several more times. When the final scores were posted, she stood in sixteenth place in her group, not good enough to qualify for the finals.

"I'd been practicing well, had a great warmup," Kwiatkowski recalled for ESPN *SportsZone*. "Then I went out and skated the worst program of my life. It was like a dream—a really bad dream. When I'm asked what happened, I still can't really tell people. I guess I just kind of flipped out. All I know is, after all the hard work, I didn't qualify for the finals."

CONSIDERS QUITTING. Her disappointing performance at the world championships destroyed Kwiatkowski's confidence. After finishing fourth at the 1994 U.S. Figure Skating Championships in Detroit, Michigan, and missing the American Winter Olympic team, she considered giving up skating.

Jenkins told her pupil to seriously think about her decision. "I told her, 'You have to make the decision so that at 40, you don't have any should-haves, would-haves, could-haves,'" Jenkins recalled in the *Detroit Free Press.* "I told her to take off a month, two months, whatever. Two weeks later, she was back. She said, 'I'm here to train. I'm in the next session, ready to start.'"

Kwiatkowski spent two weeks of her break from skating relaxing and hanging out with her friends. Soon she realized she missed the sport she loved. "I went to the gym to work out, and I thought, 'I don't want to do this. If I'm going to come here, I might as well skate,'" she told the *San Francisco Examiner.*

BACK IN THE MEDALS. With her degree in hand, Kwiatkowski could devote herself full time to her training. She also began working with a sports psychologist to help her deal with her nervousness. Kwiatkowski entered the 1995 U.S. Figure Skating Champi-

DEGREE OF SUCCESS

Kwiatkowski, unlike many other skaters, did not let skating keep her from attending college. She decided to attend Baldwin-Wallace College, just ten minutes away from the Winterhurst Ice Arena. Even though going to college may have interfered with her skating, Kwiatkowski feels she made the right decision. "I think interacting with people your age and with older people—like teachers and professors—is important," she explained to ESPN *SportsZone.* "You learn communications skills by being around other people. And not going to school may mean not having many friends or important experiences. Then, when your skating career is over, what do you do? It's purely an individual decision—each person has to make up their own mind. But I'm glad I did what I did."

In June 1994, Kwiatkowski graduated from Baldwin-Wallace with a bachelor's degree in psychology and communications. Because of her skating, the four-year degree took her five years to achieve. "Having graduated from college and knowing there's so many other things I can do, I think that's helped my confidence, as well," Kwiatkowski explained in the *San Francisco Examiner.* Kwiatkowski is a member of Pi Gamma Mu, the International Honor Society in Social Sciences.

onships in Providence, Rhode Island, with renewed confidence in her ability, despite stiff competition from Nicole Bobek and Michelle Kwan. "It started after nationals last year," Jenkins told the *Los Angeles Times* about her star pupil's new attitude. "Everybody said, 'She ought to quit. Let's be honest. This is for young kids.'"

Kwiatkowski started strong, winning the short program over Bobek and Kwan after completing every jump perfectly. (In the short program, each skater must successfully complete required jumps and maneuvers.) Kwan wobbled on the landing of one of her jumps and Bobek landed on two feet after one of her spinning leaps. The long program, worth two-thirds of the final score, would decide the championship. (In the long program, skaters design their own individual routine.)

THIRD AGAIN. None of the top-three contenders skated well in the long program. Bobek touched her hand to the ice on the landing of a triple-toe loop and Kwan fell on one jump and landed another on two feet. Kwiatkowski fell on her triple flip and attempted only three triple jumps, one fewer than Bobek and two fewer than Kwan. When the final scores were posted, she finished third, behind Bobek, the new national champion, and Kwan.

Kwiatkowski's third-place finish was not good enough for her to earn a trip to the 1995 World Figure Skating Championships in Birmingham, England. Despite her poor performance in the long program, Kwiatkowski was pleased with her comeback. "People had pretty much written me off," she stated in *People Weekly.* "I guess I showed them."

Superstar

GRAND OLD LADY. Kwiatkowski turned down an opportunity to skate in the national ice tour of "The Nutcracker" in order to train for the 1996 U.S. Figure Skating Championships in San Jose, California. Kwiatkowski entered the competition as the "Grand Old Lady' of U.S. amateur skating at one month shy of her twenty-fifth birthday. Her main competition were all teenagers: Bobek, Kwan, and 13-year-old **Tara Lipinski.** "I don't feel that old," Kwiatkowski complained in the *San Francisco Examiner.* (Kathaleen Kelly Cutone, a 28-year-old lawyer from Massachusetts, was actually the oldest competitor.)

Kwiatkowski knew that if she wanted to contend with her younger competitors, she would have to add more of the difficult triple jumps to her programs. She planned to do six triples in her long program, one more than she did the year before. Kwiatkowski had developed a new long program—set to the music of John Tesh and Vangelis—and also had new costumes.

WINS SILVER. Kwiatkowski got a break when an ankle injury forced Bobek to withdraw from the competition after the short program. She took advantage of her chance, performing beautifully in her long program. Skating last, Kwiatkowski successfully completed six triple jumps and two combinations, a triple Lutz-double toe and a triple-toe-double toe. She received second-place marks from every judge, her best ever performance in nine national championships. "I always knew I could do it, and I proved today I could do it," an excited Kwiatkowski told the *Detroit Free Press.*

TAKES ON THE WORLD. Achieving her major goal, Kwiatkowski joined gold medal-winner Kwan and third-place finisher Lipinski on the U.S. team that would travel to Edmonton, Alberta, Canada, to compete in the 1996 World Figure Skating Championships. "Making worlds was one of my goals for this year, and I was on cloud nine

TOO OLD?

Making a joke out of the way reporters always talked about her age, Kwiatkowski came to the post-competition news conference at the 1996 U.S. Figure Skating Championships using a walker. Even though she tries to have a sense of humor about her age, she does not understand why people make such a big deal out of it. "I get a bit tired of it because I think I've done well for my age—considering everyone thinks I'm so old," Kwiatkowski explained in the *Edmonton Journal.* "I'm not that old. I don't understand why they keep saying this. So after the long program I went into the press conference with a walker, just to say, look I'm really not that old. I would think that after skating so well and proving myself they would let it drop. But they don't."

Kwiatkowski thinks her age gives her an advantage over younger skaters. "I think I have an advantage just with maturity," she explained to the *San Jose Mercury-News.* "As far as disadvantages, maybe younger kids have more energy than I do. I train three hours a day with full run-throughs. I don't feel that old." Like a superstar in another sport, Kwiatkowski just wants to compete. "I look at myself as the Cal Ripken of figure skating," she revealed in *People Weekly.* "I just keep coming back and giving the audience more."

as soon as I finished my program," she admitted to ESPN *SportsZone*.

Although she tried not to think about it, Kwiatkowski's poor performance at the 1993 World Championships stuck in her mind. Once again she had to go through the qualifying round, but this time she had much more confidence. "I'm a different person than I was then [in 1993]," Kwiatkowski explained in the *Edmonton Journal*. "I know I can make it through qualifying and I'm going in there with that attitude."

Kwiatkowski easily qualified for the finals this time, finishing fourth in her group despite a fall. "This is redemption," the relieved skater admitted in the *Los Angeles Times*. "I can't say I thought about [1993] every day, but every now and then, that thought came to my mind: 'I could have been in the final round.' This is what I've been training for for the last three years, to get to the qualifying round and to get through it. This feels good, to get some of the anguish out of me." Kwiatkowski and former world champion Midori Ito of Japan (26 years of age) were the two oldest skaters to earn spots in the finals of the competition.

EARNS RESPECT. Kwiatkowski skated well in the short program, but the judges gave her lower scores than she felt she deserved, placing her in ninth place. "You learn that marks are out of your control, so you have to be satisfied by just going out and skating your best, which I did," she explained to ESPN *SportsZone*. "Honestly, I was so happy with the way I skated that I didn't let it affect me at all."

In the long program, Kwiatkowski again did her best and moved up one spot to eighth in the final standings. "I skated about as well as I could have in the long program, and I was pretty happy with my marks," she told ESPN *SportsZone*. "And I know that being the eighth-best skater in the world isn't too bad." Kwiatkowski competed despite a slightly separated shoulder.

OFF THE ICE. Kwiatkowski lives with her parents in Broadview Heights, Ohio, a suburb of Cleveland. "I'm an only child, so I don't think they mind having me around," she told the *San Francisco Examiner.* After her skating career is over, Kwiatkowski would like to coach. She already is working with several young skaters. Kwiatkowski is also interested in a career as a television commentator.

Kwiatkowski plans to skate through the 1998 Winter Olympics in Nagano, Japan. As she told *Newsday:* "I'm just focused on proving to myself that I still can do this. [As] long as I can continue to skate with the top girls, I will."

Sources

Detroit Free Press, February 11, 1995; March 23, 1996.
Edmonton Journal, February 27, 1996.
Los Angles Times, February 11, 1995; February 12, 1995; March 18, 1996;
    March 19, 1996.
Newsday, February 11, 1995.
People Weekly, March 18, 1996.
San Jose Mercury News, January 15, 1996; January 21, 1996.
Additional information provided by ESPN SportsZone.

WHERE TO WRITE:
C/O U.S. FIGURE SKATING ASSOCIATION,
20 FIRST STREET,
COLORADO SPRINGS, CO 80906.

Lisa Leslie

1972—

The road to success has been a long trip for Lisa Leslie. The journey began in the back of a semi-truck, traveling throughout the country with the driver, her mother. Now Leslie is the driver—taking the ball to the basket as a member of the Olympic gold-medal-winning U.S. women's national basketball team. At the 1996 Summer Olympics in Atlanta, Georgia, she led the victorious Americans in scoring as they swept away the best competition in the world. A player who once scored over 100 points in one half during a high school game, Leslie now hopes to be a model—both on the court and in the world of fashion.

Growing Up

TRUCK-DRIVING MOM. Leslie was born on July 7, 1972. Her father left the family when Leslie was four, and she met him just once before he died during her junior high years. Leslie was cared for much of the time by a live-in housekeeper and her aunt because her mother, Christine, worked as a cross-country truck driver. Christine Leslie bought an eighteen-wheel rig in 1982 and was on the road for weeks at a time. The travel was hard, but she needed the money to support her three children.

"There were some sad times," Leslie admitted in *Sports Illustrated*. "Mom had to travel so far and so long. But we understood she had to do it. It made me mature really fast. I had so much to do." During summer vacation Christine Leslie took her two youngest daughters on the road with her. The two girls slept on a bunk bed in the back of the truck. "It was 36 inches wide," Leslie recalled in the same magazine. "All of us would jam in there. We had to hold on to each other. That helps us now. We all hold on to each other in a lot of ways."

CHANGE OF HEART. Leslie had grown to 6 feet tall by the seventh grade. "Fortunately, my mother is 6' 3"," she stated in *People Weekly*. "She raised me to be confident and hold my head up." Because so many people asked her about playing basketball, Leslie became angry and turned against the game. "I hated it," she admitted.

A friend, Sharon Hargrove, finally convinced Leslie to try out for the school team. She soon discovered she loved the sport. "I just changed my whole attitude," Leslie recalled. "I guess it was my destiny, but I never knew it."

Leslie's cousin Craig pushed her to excel. He encouraged his cousin to do push-ups, sit-ups, drills, shoot baskets by herself, and play basketball with boys. Leslie patterned her game after male players. "There weren't that many [female] role models, at least not many that I knew of," she recalled in *Sports Illustrated*. "If, by the way I play, I can be a role model or encourage someone else, that would be great."

SCOREBOARD

LEADING SCORER ON THE 1996 OLYMPIC GOLD-MEDAL-WINNING U.S. WOMEN'S NATIONAL BASKETBALL TEAM (19.5 POINTS PER GAME).

COLLEGE BASKETBALL PLAYER OF THE YEAR IN 1994 AT THE UNIVERSITY OF SOUTHERN CALIFORNIA.

SCORED 101 POINTS IN FIRST HALF OF A HIGH SCHOOL BASKETBALL GAME IN 1990.

A SUPERSTAR AT EVERY LEVEL OF PLAY, LESLIE NOW LOOKS FORWARD TO A CAREER AS A PROFESSIONAL MODEL.

Leslie (right) out jumps her opposition during the tip off of a 1996 Summer Olympic game.

REACHES CENTURY MARK. Leslie attended Morningside High School in Inglewood, California. She first received national attention as a junior in 1989. Leslie averaged 21.7 points, 12.8 rebounds, and 6.2 blocked shots per game. *USA Today* named her a first-team high school All-American.

In February 1990, Leslie had one of the most incredible games in high school basketball history. Facing South Torrance High, she scored 101 points in the first half. "I heard a buzzer and looked up at the scoreboard," Leslie recalled in *Sports Illustrated*. "It showed us up 49-6. I asked, 'Is this the half?'" It was the end of the first quarter and Leslie had scored all of her team's points.

Morningside led 102-24 at the half (teammate Sherrell Young scored the other point). Leslie made 37 field goals and a national high school-record 31 free throws. South Torrance, which had suffered several injuries prior to the game, was left with only four healthy players. Realizing his team could not compete, the South Torrance coach forfeited the second half of the game. Leslie begged the South Torrance coach to continue, but he refused.

The women's national high school record for points in one game is 105, set by the legendary Cheryl Miller, sister of basketball star Reggie Miller of the Indiana Pacers. "Anyone that can count knows that I would have had it [the record]," Leslie explained to *Jet*. "They just shortened the game. I feel that I have the record." Some people thought Leslie was unsportsmanlike to score so many points against an overmatched team. "It wasn't personal," she explained to *Sports Illustrated*. "They knew I was going for the record. I thought knowing that would take some of the hurt away."

PLAYER OF THE YEAR. Leslie led Morningside to the state title in her senior season. She averaged 26.9 points, 15 rebounds, and 6.9 blocked shots per game. In the state championship game against Berkeley High School, Leslie scored 35 points, pulled down 12 rebounds, and blocked 7 shots, despite suffering from chicken pox and a high fever.

During Leslie's high school career Morningside compiled a record of 125-9—including a 28-2 mark in postseason games—and two state titles. Leslie finished her career with 2896 points (second among women in California major high school history, behind Miller) and 1705 rebounds, a new women's state record. She also won 4 letters in volleyball and track. As a senior, Leslie won the state title in the high jump (5 feet, 5 inches) and as a junior she placed third in the triple jump.

Basketball experts unanimously named Leslie the best high school player in the United States in 1990, awarding her the prestigious Naismith Award. (The Naismith is given to both high school and college players.) She also won the Dial Award, as the nation's top high school student-athlete. Leslie maintained a 3.5 grade point average and served as class president her last 3 years at Morningside. She won *Parade* magazine All-American honors in 1989 and 1990.

STAYS HOME. College coaches made Leslie the most highly female recruited player since Miller graduated from high school in 1983. She decided to stay home and attend the University of Southern California (USC), the same school that Miller put on the college basketball map. Miller held the school's scoring record and led the Trojans to two National Collegiate Athletic Association (NCAA) Tournament titles. She also led the U.S. women's national team to the 1984 Olympic gold medal and is considered one of the best female players of all time.

The comparisons to Miller did not scare Leslie. "I don't want this to sound like I'm cocky or anything," she told *Sports Illustrated*. "But by the time I get to my senior year, I think I can be just as good as Cheryl."

Leslie was an instant sensation, earning National Freshman of the Year and Pacific-10 Conference (Pac-10) Freshman of the Year honors. The Pac-10 named her to its first team (a team made of the conference's best players), the first freshman ever to be so honored. Leslie averaged 19.4 points (fourth in the Pac-10) and 10 rebounds per game (second in the Pac-10). She led the nation's freshmen in both categories.

Despite her first-year success, Leslie needed to improve. "I think it was a revelation to Lisa that there were weaknesses in her game that other people could exploit," USC coach Marianne Stanley explained to *Sports Illustrated*. "There's a lot that she's still learning. She's like the colt who wants to get up and go and isn't real secure with all the skills yet." By the time she joined the Trojans, Leslie had grown to 6 feet, 5 inches tall.

Leslie worked hard, and her game improved in each of the next three seasons. During her career she led USC to four NCAA Tournaments and twice the Trojans advanced to the final eight of the tournament (1992 and 1994). Southern California finished with an 89-31 record during her career and won one Pac-10 championship. Leslie earned All-American honors three times (1992, 1993, and 1994) and she was the only player in history to be named to the All-Pac 10 first team four times (1991—94).

PLAYER OF THE YEAR. Leslie had her best year as a senior (1993—94), when she averaged a career-best 21.9 points and 12.3 rebounds per game. She earned the coveted Naismith Award, given annually to the best female college basketball player in the country. "A lot of coaches have said I have the potential to be the kind of player who can help women's basketball reach more people," Leslie stated in *Sports Illustrated.* "I guess you never know when you've fulfilled those expectations. All I can do is try to be the kind of player my team needs, and if that's what women's basketball as a whole needs—great!"

WORLD TRAVELER. Leslie got her first taste of international competition with the 1989 U.S. Women's Junior World Championship team, averaging a team-high 13.3 points and 11.7 rebounds. In 1990, she tried out for the 12-member U.S. women's national team, and the coaches made her the last player cut. A year later, Leslie led the U.S. women's team to a gold medal at the World University Games in Sheffield, England, averaging 13 points and 4.4 rebounds per game.

In 1992, Leslie attended the U.S. Olympic Trials, the youngest player trying out for the women's national team. She failed to make the team, but continued to work on her game. Leslie was named the Female Athlete of the Year by USA

SLAM DUNKING

Leslie brought an added dimension to women's college basketball because she could dunk the basketball. She had been able to dunk since ninth grade, but did not think it was very important. "Dunking is something guys care more about than girls," Leslie explained to *Sports Illustrated.* "There's something about jumping that seems to fascinate guys. Girls are more like, as long as the ball goes in, who cares how you got it there?" The first woman to dunk a basketball in a college game was Georgeann Wells—a 6-feet-7-inch-center at the University of West Virginia—in 1985.

Basketball in 1993, and in 1994 she finally qualified for the U.S. women's national team in 1994. She played for the national team for the first time at the qualifying tournament for the 1994 World Basketball Championships. Leslie averaged 18.4 points and 6.6 rebounds per game as the United States finished first.

BAD TASTE. Leslie led the U.S. women's national team to a gold medal at the 1994 Goodwill Games. She averaged a team-best 18 points per game and pulled down a team-leading 7.3 rebounds per contest. The U.S. women's national team then traveled to Sydney, Australia, for the 1994 World Women's Basketball Championships.

Brazil, the eventual champions, defeated the Americans in the semifinals, 110-107. The loss frustrated Leslie. "That left a bad taste in our mouths," she admitted in the *New York Times*. "Since that loss I have visualized playing them again." The United States won the bronze medal, and Leslie was a major contributor to the team's success. She averaged 10.5 points and 4.8 rebounds per game.

To make a living, Leslie traveled to Italy to play professionally. She spent the 1994—95 season playing for the team in Sicilgesso. For the season, Leslie averaged 22.6 points and 11.7 rebounds per game. The fact that there were no women's professional teams in the U.S. bothered Leslie. "I think we are cheated as a gender," she explained to *Entertainment Weekly*. "No one knows what happens to all the great people in our game. It seems like we're written off."

Superstar

DREAM TEAMER. Leslie received her greatest honor when USA Basketball named her to the 1996 women's basketball "Dream Team" for the 1996 Summer Olympics in Atlanta, Georgia. "Atlanta will be an opportunity for us to go down in history as one of the greatest teams ever," Leslie told *Essence*. "It'll be a showcase for us as role models—not only for girls who play basketball but for women in general."

Tara VanDerveer—the successful coach of the Stanford University Cardinals—put the U.S. Olympic team through a rigorous workout schedule. Players lifted weights, watched films, and traveled. The tough workouts brought the team together. "With [VanDerveer] giving us such hard workouts, we had to pick each other up," Leslie explained in *Sports Illustrated*. "We became so close because, at the beginning, it was the coaches versus the team." The team went 51-0 on their 9-month, 9-country pre-Olympic tour, with Leslie leading the team in scoring at 17.3 points per game.

UNSTOPPABLE. The U.S. women's "Dream Team" lived up to their nickname once Olympic basketball competition began, convincingly sweeping away the best teams in the world. Leslie was glad to be home after the team's long journey. "This is the place we've been trying to get to," Leslie explained in the *New York Times*. "We've been to so many different countries we've never really had a home court. It was nice to finally be home."

In the quarterfinals against Japan, Leslie broke the women's Olympic record with 35 points in a 108-93 U.S. victory. The Americans then blew out the Australian team, 93-71, in the semifinals behind 22 points and 13 rebounds from their star center. The victory against Australia set up a rematch with the defending world champions from Brazil for the Olympic gold medal.

A sellout crowd attended the women's basketball championship game at the Georgia Dome. Before the game, VanDerveer told Leslie to shoot more from the outside. The change in the American strategy threw off the Brazilians. Leslie hit 12 of 14 shots and scored 29 points in a 111-87 U.S. victory. The American point total also set an Olympic gold-medal game record. "That was our best whole game," VanDerveer told *Sports Illustrated*. Australia defeated Ukraine, 66-56, for the bronze medal.

When the U.S. men's "Dream Team" also won the gold medal, it marked the first time since 1984 that the Americans won both the men's and women's basketball championships.

Leslie was the team leader at the Games. She led the team in scoring at 19.5 points per game and was second in rebounding (7.3 per contest). Leslie, an unstoppable force inside the paint, shot an amazing .653 from the floor. "It was very emotional for me," Leslie confessed in the *New York Times.*

OFF THE COURT. Leslie lives in Inglewood, California. Along with Olympic teammates Sheryl Swoopes and Dawn Staley, she starred in a commercial for Nike directed by Spike Lee. Leslie likes to play board games and cards during her spare time.

Leslie studied communications at USC and would someday like to be a sports commentator. Being so tall sometimes makes it difficult for Leslie to find a date. "I normally date guys who play basketball and who are taller than I am," Leslie admitted in *People Weekly.*

Leslie encourages young people to stay in shape. "When you work out, you feel better about yourself," she explained in *Working Woman.* "You feel like you've done something." Following the Olympics, Leslie was not sure if she wanted to continue to play basketball. "I want to pursue something different," she admitted in *People Weekly.* "I played 10 years straight to be an Olympian. I'm tired." Leslie finally decided to continue her career, however, signing a contract to play in the newly formed Women's National Basketball Association (WNBA).

Through her play, Leslie wants to be a role model for children in the future. "I think people do need that one star that even people who aren't that familiar with the game can recognize," she told *Sports Illustrated.* "It not only gets the attention of the public, it gets the attention of the kids who will grow up to be the next superstars."

Sources

Entertainment Weekly, July 19, 1996.

Essence, April 1996.

Jet, February 26, 1990.

New York Times, July 21, 1996; July 24, 1996; July 26, 1996; July 28, 1996; July 30, 1996; August 1, 1996; August 3, 1996; August 5, 1996.

People Weekly, July 8, 1996; August 19, 1996.

Sports Illustrated, February 19, 1990; December 3, 1990; November 25, 1991.

Working Woman, May 1996.

Additional information provided by the University of Southern California and USA Basketball.

WHERE TO WRITE:

C/O USA BASKETBALL,
5465 MARK DABLING BOULEVARD.,
COLORADO SPRINGS, CO 80918-3842.

Tara Lipinski

1982—

"I want to go to the Olympics and win."
—Tara Lipinski.

In 1996, Tara Lipinski arrived as one of the top female figure skaters in the United States. Her third-place finish at the U.S. Figure Skating Championships earned Lipinski a trip to the World Figure Skating Championships. What makes her success so surprising, however, is that Lipinski is only 14 years old. A tremendous jumper, she hopes to win a gold medal at the 1998 Winter Olympics in Nagano, Japan.

Growing Up

BORN TO SKATE. Tara Lipinski was born June 10, 1982, in Philadelphia, Pennsylvania. She is the only child of Jack and Pat Lipinski, who lived in Bayonne, New Jersey, a suburb of Philadelphia. Lipinski began roller skating at the age of three, then took to the ice when she was six. She had many other interests—including horseback riding, playing the piano, baton twirling, and modeling—but skating quickly became her first love.

In 1991, Jack Lipinski accepted a transfer to Houston, Texas, to become a company executive for the Coastal Corporation, a company involved in the energy industry. Lipinski lived in Texas for two years, but needed more intensive coaching than she could receive in the Houston area. To further her career, she and her mother moved to Maryland to work with coach Jeff DiGregorio at the University of Delaware Figure Skating Club. Jack Lipinski stayed in Texas.

BIG WIN. Lipinski moved quickly up the ranks of U.S. junior competition. She won the 1994 Midwestern and Southwestern novice (beginner) competitions, then became a star at the 1994 U.S. Olympic Festival. Lipinski—at the age of 12—became the youngest-ever winner of the Olympic Festival women's skating competition. Previous winners of the competition included future champions like Kristi Yamaguchi, Nancy Kerrigan, and Michelle Kwan. Lipinski's victory earned her the Mary Lou Retton Award.

MOVING UP. Lipinski followed her Olympic Festival win with a fourth-place finish at the 1995 World Junior Championships in Budapest, Hungary. Her international success made her the favorite to win the junior women's competition at the 1995 U.S. Figure Skating Championships in Providence, Rhode Island.

In Rhode Island, Lipinski finished second in the short program, trailing Sydne Vogel, a 15-year-old from Alaska. (In the short program, the skater must successfully perform required jumps, spins, and movements on the ice.) In the long program, Vogel skated first. (In the long program, the skater can design her own routine.) She delivered a strong performance, but fell on a double axel and did not complete another jump. Lipinski had the chance to win.

Lipinski wore pink and had her hair pulled back in a pony tail. She landed six triple jumps in a three-and-one-half-minute program. Surprisingly, the judges placed Lipinski sec-

ond in the long program behind Vogel, even though many observers felt she should have won. Despite completing more impressive jumps, she received lower artistic marks than Vogel. (In figure skating, judges award two sets of scores—one for technical merit and one for artistic impression—that each carry equal weight in the final score.) "I'll beat her next year," Lipinski told the *San Diego Union-Tribune.*

ON THE MOVE AGAIN. After finishing a disappointing fifth at the 1995 World Junior Figure Skating Championships in Brisbane, Australia, the Lipinskis split with DiGregorio. Pat Lipinski argued with DiGregorio over what jumps her daughter should attempt in competition. Over a three-week period, the Lipinskis traveled and interviewed four nationally known coaches. They visited Carol Heiss Jenkins, a former Olympic champion who at the time coached **Tonia Kwiatkowski.** They also visited Kathy Casey, coach of two-time U.S. men's champion Scott Davis, and Galina Zmievskaia, coach of Olympic champions Viktor Petrenko and Oksana Baiul.

The decision was important, because it would affect Lipinski's career and the whole family. Working with a new coach meant that the daughter and mother would have to move again. "I feel bad for Tara," Pat Lipinski admitted in the *San Jose Mercury News.* "I don't think she deserved this disruption."

Lipinski and her mother finally moved to the Detroit, Michigan, area to work with coach Richard Callaghan at the Detroit Skating Club. Callaghan coached 1995 U.S. women's national champion Nicole Bobek and 1995 men's national champion **Todd Eldredge.** "I like Richard and the facilities here in Detroit, and I have friends at the rink, so I'm happy here," Lipinski told the *Detroit Free Press.* Lipinski impressed her new coach. "She's self-disciplined," Callaghan explained to the same newspaper. "She's extremely talented. If things go the way they should, Tara has a great future."

Superstar

SENIORITIS. In 1996, Lipinski decided to skate in the senior division of the U.S. Figure Skating Championships in San Jose,

California. "Even though I'm little, I have to skate like a woman," she stated in the *Detroit Free Press*. "I'm just going to skate the best I can and see what happens. I'm not expecting a medal, but it would be nice."

The favorites in the women's competition included 1995 national champion Bobek, 1995 runner-up, Kwan, and veteran Kwiatkowski. Lipinski tried not to let the pressure of competing at a higher level affect her. "In my short program I'm going to try a triple Lutz [one of the most difficult jumps in figure skating]," she explained in the *San Jose Mercury News* just before the competition. "This year I don't want to have a lot of pressure. I just want to try out some new things and be good. I just have to focus on my skating. I think I'll be fine."

Before the long program began, an ankle injury forced Bobek to withdraw from the competition. Kwan and Kwiatkowski finished first and second in the short program, but Bobek's injury opened the possibility for Lipinski to take the bronze medal. Once again she needed to beat out Vogel for third place.

TAKES THIRD. Lipinski and Vogel battled in their final programs. Vogel entertained the crowd with jumps that sometimes lifted her above the boards along the ice, but she failed to complete several of her attempts. Lipinski, meanwhile, landed six triple jumps in her long program, good enough to place her ahead of Vogel and win the bronze medal.

TAKES ON WORLD. In an unexpected move, the U.S. Figure Skating Association decided not to offer Bobek a spot on the American team for the 1996 World Figure Skating Championships in Edmonton, Alberta, Canada. The decision meant that Lipinski would get a chance to compete against the best skaters in the world. "I'd love to get in the Top 10 at the World Championships—or just skate a clean program," she told *People Weekly*.

In her first ever world championship short program, Lipinski fell once and had to touch her hand to the ice after another jump. These mistakes cost her, as the judges placed the young skater in twenty-third place. "I guess I was a little nervous, but I felt good during the warmup," Lipinski admitted in the *Detroit Free Press*. "I just hope I skate really good in the long [program]."

Lipinski delivered a fine performance in her long program, successfully completing triple jump after triple jump and receiving a standing ovation from the sell-out crowd. Even though she had no chance to win a medal, the performance was good enough to lift Lipinski to fifteenth-place, a respectable showing for a first-time participant.

THE BEST. Lipinski made history at the 1997 U.S. Figure Skating National Championships in Nashville, Tennessee. Although she was thought to be a contender for the title, most people felt it very unlikely. Lipinski was up against Kwan who had won 14 out of 15 competitions since the fall of 1995. As the finals began, everyone expected Kwan to win.

Lipinski was the final skater and Kwan the next-to-last skater. As Kwan took the ice before the sold-out crowd at Nashville Arena she appeared poised and confident. Her program started off solidly when she landed her second-most-difficult element: the triple Lutz-double toe loop combination. However, this is where her superb long performance ended. Kwan stunned the crowd by falling three times during her program. The disbelieving crowd, feeling sorry for Kwan, began cheering and Kwan began to pull herself together. Although, she gave a strong finish to her program, the damage had already been done.

After Kwan's disastrous performance, Lipinski took the ice. She knew that even to beat Kwan on her worst day, she would have to land every jump perfectly. Although the pressure was on, Lipinski delivered a stellar performance. Midway through her performance Lipinski landed what is believed to be the first triple loop-triple loop combination ever done in competition, by a man or a woman. The crowd went wild, and at that point everyone in the arena knew that Lipinski would be crowned the champion. By coming in first place, Lipinski became the youngest U.S. ladies figure skating champion in history. "I'm in shock," Lipinski told *Sports Illustrated for Kids*.

WORLD HISTORY. After her spectacular performance at the Nationals, Lipinski began preparing for her second appearance at the World Figure Skating Championships in Lausanne, Switzerland. Although Lipinski felt confident she could take home the title of world champion, most people still thought it unlikely. Lipinski proved them wrong when on March 22, 1997, she narrowly beat Kwan for the title. By again completing a flawless performance, Lipinski became the youngest woman to win the world figure skating title. Her record will probably be unbeatable since a new rule requires all participants in the world championships to be at least 15 years old.

OFF THE ICE. Lipinski lives in West Bloomfield, Michigan, with her mother. Her favorite athletes are gymnasts Mary Lou Retton and Dominique Moceanu and figure skaters Oksana Baiul and Elvis Stojko. Lipinski enjoys reading, cooking, sewing, and playing tennis. She already knows what she wants to do when her skating career is over. "I want study to be a lawyer, because my dad is a lawyer," Lipinski explained in *Sports Illustrated for Kids*.

Lipinski explained why she loves skating to the *New York Times:* "I would never quit skating. It's really cool that you can skate on one blade and jump. How many people can go out there and land a jump every time and keep doing it?" She expressed her long-term goal to *Current Events:* "I want to go to the Olympics and win."

Sources

Current Events, October 31, 1994.
Detroit Free Press, January 8, 1996; January 22, 1996; January 23, 1996; March 19, 1996; March 23, 1996.
Edmonton Journal, March 14, 1996; March 24, 1996.
New York Times, October 11, 1994; March 23, 1997.
People Weekly, March 18, 1996.
San Diego Union-Tribune, February 10, 1995.
San Jose Mercury News, January 15, 1996; January 21, 1996.
Sports Illustrated for Kids, October 1995.

WHERE TO WRITE:
C/O U.S. FIGURE SKATING ASSOCIATION,
20 FIRST STREET, COLORADO SPRINGS, CO 80906-3697.

Christy Martin

1968—

Christy Martin works hard at her career. She spends hours training and practicing, sharpening her skills in the gym to become the best in her profession. What makes Martin unique, however, is that she is a woman in the male-dominated sport of boxing. After taking up the sport on a dare from her friends, she has become a star and world champion. Along the way, Martin also met the love of her life, her trainer Jim Martin. She has achieved fame after growing up as a coal miner's daughter in rural West Virginia.

"Every time I go out there, I try to do something spectacular."
—Christy Martin.

Growing Up

DADDY'S GIRL. Christy Martin was born June 12, 1968, in Bluefield, West Virginia, but grew up in Mullens, West Virginia. Martin's father, John, was a coal miner, and her mother, Joyce, is a homemaker. Her father and brother, Randy, worked hard in the coal mines, a major industry in West Virginia. Both of Martin's grandfathers died of black lung disease, caused by breathing coal dust while working in the mines.

Martin's father introduced her to sports. "He always had me shooting baskets," she recalled in *People Weekly*. "I would cheat on my piano lessons so I could go outside and dribble." Martin played catcher in Little League baseball and starred on the basketball team at Mullens High School, twice earning all-state honors. She scored 50 points in one half of a high school game.

TOUGH WOMAN. Martin attended Concord College in Athens, West Virginia. She studied physical education and was the main weapon on the basketball team. While a freshman in college, her teammates and friends dared Martin to enter a Toughwoman Contest. The competition required two women to fight each other in a boxing ring.

Martin took the dare, and found she enjoyed boxing. "It was crazy, but the crowd got behind me," she recalled in *People Weekly*. Although Martin won the local contests from 1987 to 89, she did not take boxing seriously as a career. "It was a way to win $1000 and have fun in college," she explained in the *Charlestown Gazette*. "I did it as a dare. I was just having a blast." Besides, Martin told *Time:* "There's not that much to do in southern West Virginia."

FULL-TIME FIGHTER. In 1989, Martin began to fight for promoter Larry Carrier, who called Martin because he wanted an easy opponent for a female fighter he promoted. He got more than he bargained for. Even though she did not have any formal boxing training, Martin earned a draw (tie) with her more experienced opponent. "I only wanted to do this once, but I guess I'm not a good loser," Martin recalled in *Sports Illustrated*. She decided to fight a rematch with the same fighter, and this time she won.

Martin celebrates her victory of the World Women's Boxing Association's lightweight championship.

Martin's parents tried to talk her out of making boxing a full-time career. They wanted her to become a school teacher instead. "My mom would cry, and she didn't want to come to the fights," Martin told the *Fort Worth Star-Telegram.* "My dad said, 'If you're really going to do this, you need to get a trainer who can teach you proper boxing technique.'"

TRAINER AND HUSBAND. Martin impressed Carrier with her toughness. In 1991, he sent her to work on her technique with Jim Martin. A former lightweight boxer and a confessed male chauvinist, Jim Martin did not like the idea of training a woman. "I had it rigged up to have one of my lightweights break a couple of her ribs," Jim Martin admitted in *People Weekly*. "I was expecting her to be wearing combat boots."

When Christy arrived at his gym, Jim Martin realized he was wrong about his new fighter. She came with her mother and carried her dog in her arms. "She was nice," Jim Martin recalled in the *Fort Worth Star-Telegram*. "I couldn't believe she was a fighter." Martin impressed her new trainer even more when she got in the ring. "[S]he worked harder than my men," Jim Martin said. "I said, 'Wow! I could make some money off this woman.'"

WEDDING RING. Soon the relationship between Martin and her trainer became more than professional. "I never thought I'd be kissing one of my fighters," Jim Martin admitted in *People Weekly*. "But after one fight I was so proud of her, I just gave her a hug and a kiss on the cheek." The couple married in 1992. Jim Martin says it is hard to see his wife getting punched. "But I couldn't be married to Christy and stop her from doing what she really wants to do," he explained to the same magazine.

The marriage helped Martin's parents accept her boxing career. "[They] felt more confident," she told the *Fort Worth Star-Telegram*. "They know he's not going to put me in a fight I shouldn't win. He's always looking out for me."

COAL MINER'S DAUGHTER. Despite her talent, Martin had a hard time finding opponents to fight. Most boxing promoters said they did not want to get involved with a woman fighter. "So, I'd tell the promoter," Jim Martin explained in *Sports Illustrated*. "If you want my man fighter, you got to take my woman fighter." Many times Martin had to fight for no money, just to get some exposure.

In order to get her career moving, Martin visited the famous boxing promoter, Don King. "I met him at one of his shows," she recalled in the *Charlestown Gazette*. "[King] had some other people go up to him and say: 'She's a good fighter, exciting and works well with the media. You should take a chance with her.'"

Martin showed King her moves in the ring and impressed the powerful dealmaker. She became the first female boxer to work with a major promoter when she signed a four-year contract with King. "She can be the Muhammad Ali of female fighters," he told *People Weekly*. King promoted Martin as the "Coal Miner's Daughter."

Superstar

WORLD CHAMPION. King gave Martin opportunities to fight in preliminary bouts before the main events of his major boxing promotions. In February 1996, Martin became the first female boxer to appear on national television when Showtime carried her bout against Sue Chase—a former kickboxer. She made the most of the limelight, knocking Chase out in the third round of the fight.

In a bout before the Mike Tyson—Frank Bruno World Boxing Council (WBC) heavyweight fight in March 1996, Martin faced "Dangerous" Deirdre Gogarty, for the WBC women's lightweight championship. The fight was competitive throughout, and Gogarty stung Martin in the second round. The punch caused her to bleed from her nose. "I was concerned she's my wife first, my fighter second," Jim Martin told *Time*. "She told me, 'Don't you dare stop this fight.'" Despite the injury, Martin landed punches with both hands, winning a unanimous six-round decision and the championship.

WHY SO GOOD? Martin is a great technical fighter, whose best punches are a tough jab and a quick hook to the ribs. She is aggressive, coming out at the opening bell looking to knock out her opponents. (Fourteen of her fights have ended in the first round.) Even though she is not as strong as male boxers, Martin has great speed in the ring and has shown great determination to become the best boxer she can be.

One of her sparring partners, Jimmy Maloney, a top-20 rated 140-pound fighter, knows how tough Martin can be in the ring. "She was hitting those pads: Pow! Pow! Pow!," he described to the *Fort Worth Star-Telegram*. "I said, 'I'm not sparring against her.' But my coach kept coaxing me to get into the ring with her. When I did, at first I hesitated to hit her because she was a girl. But she hits hard. I thought, 'If I don't hit, she'll kill me.' All the guys love her because she boxes hard. We have a good time, joke around, you know. But when we get in the ring, we try to kill each other."

Some boxing fans have trouble watching a woman bleeding in the ring, but Martin has proved how tough she is. "Everyone has their opinion," she stated in the *Charlestown Gazette*. "A lot of people say boxing's a manly thing to do. As long as I keep the two separate—keep aggressive and ferocious in the ring and outside the ring, let everyone know I'm a woman—I don't have a problem with it. To be honest, I really don't hear that too much. Most everyone is complimentary of my skills and hard work."

Martin—who wears a pink robe, pink shoes, and pink trunks—does not like people who criticize her for boxing."Women athletes have such a difficult stereotype to overcome," she confessed in *People Weekly*. "It's a tough world for a woman, no matter what you do."

Despite her success, Martin makes only $15,000 per fight, far less than the millions male boxing champions receive. "Whatever you make, you're not satisfied," she admitted in the *Charlestown Gazette*. "You've got to have a winning attitude. Winners are not satisfied with their performance or their money. If the doors of exposure open for me, I should fight for free. The exposure we've received has been tremendous."

Jim Martin told *People Weekly* that "there's not another woman boxer out there like Christy." In fact, Martin has a hard time finding women to fight. Currently there are 100 fighters involved with the Women's World Boxing Association, which was founded in 1992. "There's a long line and the list keeps growing," Martin told the *Charlestown Gazette*.

"We're getting national exposure, so girls are calling from all over the world."

Martin's record is 35-2-2 with 25 knockouts, and she has not lost a bout in the last seven years. Her only two defeats came against Andrea DeShong, whom she has since beaten. In her career, Martin has won three world championships."I never imagined it would lead to this," she confessed in the *Charlestown Gazette*. "It was just my job. I certainly never dreamed I could reach this standard. I really thought I'd have one pro fight, start teaching phys. ed., maybe raise a family. Now all of a sudden, little girls are asking me for my autograph."

OUT OF THE RING. Martin lives in Orlando, Florida. She has appeared on the *Late Show with David Letterman,* the *Today Show,* and *Prime Time Live.* "It's fun, all the media coverage," Martin told the *Fort Worth Star-Telegram.* "It's fun to go into the store and see yourself on the cover of *Sports Illustrated.* But it's a double-edged sword. It's difficult when every day, you have interviews and the media in your house." She is considering several book and movie deals. When not in the ring, Martin likes to shop.

Martin wants to start a family and does not plan to fight for very long. "I may have to put those family plans off for a while," she admitted in *Time*. "Actually, I'm kind of a softie outside of the ring." Until she retires, however, Martin plans on giving boxing everything she has. "I work hard at boxing," she explained in *People Weekly*. "Every time I go out there, I try to do something spectacular."

Sources

Charleston Gazette (West Virginia), April 10, 1996.
Fort Worth Star-Telegram, July 2, 1996.
People Weekly, June 24, 1996.

WOMEN'S WORK?

Despite the fact that she is the first woman to achieve success in the male-dominated sport of boxing, Martin does not want to lead a crusade for woman's boxing. "I'm not a pioneer to women's boxing," she admitted in *People Weekly*. "I'm not trying to make this statement that women should be on every card."

Martin added in the *Fort Worth Star-Telegram:* "I try to prepare myself well, try to go and put on the best show I possibly can for the people. I don't look at it as being a female in a male-dominated sport, because I'm not trying to fight a man. I'm just competing against a woman."

Register/Herald (Beckley, West Virginia), February 10, 1996.
Sports Illustrated, April 15, 1996.
Time, April 1, 1996.

 WHERE TO WRITE:

C/O WORLD BOXING COUNCIL,
GENOVA 33, OFICINA 503, COLONIA JUAREZ,
CUAUHTEMOC, 0600 MEXICO CITY, DF, MEXICO.

Steve McNair

1973—

S teve "Air" McNair has had to overcome doubters his entire football career. After turning in outstanding performances as a high school quarterback, most major college coaches only wanted him to come to their schools if he agreed to play in the defensive backfield. Then, after four record-breaking seasons leading the Alcorn State University Braves, National Football League (NFL) scouts doubted McNair's ability to lead complicated professional offenses because he played for a small college team. Today, after two seasons with the Houston Oilers, no one doubts that McNair has the ability to be one of the best quarterbacks in the NFL for many years to come.

"When I get on the field, I feel unstoppable."
—Steve McNair.

Growing Up

MOUNT OLIVE MCNAIRS. Steve McNair was born February 14, 1973. He shared a bedroom with his three brothers in a small house in Mount Olive, Mississippi. Mount Olive is a small

SET NATIONAL COLLEGIATE
ATHLETIC ASSOCIATION (NCAA)
RECORD FOR CAREER
TOTAL YARDAGE—14,665 YARDS—
IN FOUR SEASONS AT
ALCORN STATE UNIVERSITY.

THREW FOR 4863 YARDS AND 44
TOUCHDOWNS AND ALSO RUSHED
FOR 936 YARDS AND 9 MORE
SCORES IN SENIOR SEASON AT
ALCORN STATE.

DRAFTED HIGHER (THIRD
OVERALL PICK) THAN ANY
AFRICAN AMERICAN
QUARTERBACK IN NFL HISTORY.

MCNAIR HAS ONE GOAL
HE WANTS TO REACH—WINNING
THE SUPER BOWL.

town with a population of only 900 people. McNair's mother, Lucille, was a single parent who had worked in the cotton fields as a child. She raised five children on her own after her husband, Selma—an off-shore oil-rig worker— abandoned the family.

McNair's mother worked an eight-hour shift at Magne-Tek Universal, a fluorescent light manufacturer. "When she was gone, we had to make sure dinner was cooked and the house was clean," McNair recalled in *Newsday*. He credits his mother with any success he has had. "She is my number one fan, my role model, my hero," he admitted in *People Weekly* about his mother.

Lucille McNair taught her children the value of hard work. Each morning, McNair fed the chickens and pigs and the cats and dogs. He also worked in the garden, picking peas, squash, beans, and okra. All this work had to be done before McNair left for school at 8 a.m. "You did it to survive," McNair explained in *Newsday*. "There were a lot of sacrifices that had to be made in order to make it in life." McNair also sang in the choir at the Mount Pleasant C.M.E. Church.

ROLE MODEL. McNair's older brother, Fred, became the male head of the household. "A lot of nights I prayed and cried and wondered how this family could carry on," Lucille McNair admitted in *Sports Illustrated*. "Fred had to become the father in the house. When Fred told [Steve] and the others to jump, they jumped."

MOUNT PLEASANT ARENA. The children in the Mount Olive area played sports in a cow pasture they called Mount Pleasant Arena. The boys would play baseball, basketball, and football all year long. McNair joined the games as a young child and often played with much older players. "I'd say he was around 3 feet tall; he was out there playing along with us," Ronnie Grant, who is 14 years older than McNair, told the Gannett News Service. "He used to get out there and play with us just like the older guys."

AIR I AND II. Fred McNair starred at quarterback for Mount Olive High School. When he graduated and went to play at nearby Alcorn State University, his younger brother took over as Mount Olive's quarterback. He literally followed in his brother's footsteps by painting gold spots on his shoes, the main Alcorn State color, and wearing Fred's number 9.

McNair got his nickname, "Air McNair," from his brother. "One summer we were throwing the ball around, and Monk got this idea that I needed a flashy name," Fred McNair recalled in *Sports Illustrated*. "We thought of Fly and Sky, but we settled on Air. Monk told me, 'You'll be Air and I'll be Air II,' and that just stuck."

It was Fred who taught McNair how to hold and throw a football. "Fred has taught me absolutely everything I know," McNair told *Sports Illustrated*. "I can't thank him enough for giving me a map and then showing me how to take the short road when he's taken the longer one."

Even though he admired his brother, McNair wanted to break all his records. "Steve was a quiet child," Lucille McNair revealed in *People Weekly*. "But he came up to me one day and said, 'Momma, you know everybody is talking about how good Fred is. But I'm going to show them. I'm going to be better.'"

MULTI-SPORT STAR. McNair played both offense and defense at Mount Olive High School. As a defensive back, he tied the state record of 30 interceptions held by Terrell Buckley, now with the Miami Dolphins. McNair led the Pirates to the 1989 Class A state championship.

Escaping a tackle, McNair runs for a touchdown.

McNair also starred on the baseball team. Playing shortstop and pitching, he won all-state honors all four seasons in high school. One time McNair's fastball was once clocked at 90 miles per hour. He also played basketball and participated on the track team.

QB OR BUST! McNair had a difficult decision to make after graduating from high school. He turned down a $5000 signing bonus to become a professional baseball shortstop with the Seattle Mariners organization. McNair also had college scholarship offers to play basketball and run track. His mother and brother Fred talked him into sticking with football.

Major colleges such as Florida State, Miami, Mississippi, Mississippi State, and Southern Mississippi recruited McNair. Unfortunately, these schools wanted him to play defensive back, not quarterback. "Many scouts tried to discourage me from playing quarterback on the college level," McNair told the Gannett News Service. "But I knew what I wanted to do." McNair finally decided to follow his brother to Alcorn State. "I wanted to play quarterback," he told *People Weekly,* explaining his decision. "Alcorn was the only one that would give me a chance."

FOLLOWING FRED. Once again, McNair decided to follow his brother. Fred McNair played receiver at Alcorn State for three years and then took over at quarterback in his final season. He was the fifth-rated quarterback in Division 1-AA in 1989, throwing for 1898 yards and 14 touchdowns. Fred McNair signed as a free agent with the Dallas Cowboys in 1989 and then went on to play in the Canadian Football League, the World League, and the Arena Football League.

"I'll never stop being Fred's little brother totally," McNair stated to the Gannett News Service. "There was a lot of pressure on me because Fred was a great player at Alcorn. When I first got to Alcorn, people said, 'There's Fred,' and it was me. People said we looked alike and dressed alike."

FRESHMAN PHENOM. In his first football scrimmage for Alcorn State, McNair completed 7 of 7 passes. Coach Cardell Jones knew he had a star on his hands. "It's going to be hard to keep this kid on the bench," he recalled thinking in *People Weekly.*

In his first game, McNair played on an injured ankle and led the Braves to a come-from-behind 27-22 victory over Grambling on the road. "He threw for 3 touchdowns and close to 335 yards, and we won the game," Jones told *People Weekly.* "He just has that winning attitude. He's the type of leader that keeps the group together and moves the ball 80 yards down the field with just minutes to play and scores the winning touchdown. It takes a special breed to do that."

BIG DECISION. McNair first gained national attention after his junior season. He threw for 3197 yards and 22 touchdowns and ran for 633 yards. McNair now had a tough decision to make, because he could be a first- or second-round pick in the 1993 NFL Draft. "I am a country guy who is playing and not knowing the value of my life," McNair admitted in the *Sporting News*. "I didn't know I was that good. I was going to leave. We could use the money, and I wanted to help my mom. It was time for me to move on."

McNair's mother and brother tried to talk him into staying is school. "I was hoping he would stay in school," Lucille McNair explained in the *Sporting News*. "I had a hard time without a college education. If anything went wrong with his sports career, I wanted him to have a degree to fall back on. Besides, you don't miss what you don't have. We never have had money, but we've been blessed. So it really was no big decision to have Steve stay. I told him to get his education. I'll live for another year."

McNair decided to return to Alcorn State for his senior season. "I am an Alcornite and will continue to be an Alcornite," he announced in *Jet*. "I want my degree. I signed a four-year commitment to Alcorn and I intend to fulfill it." He took out a $1 million insurance policy to protect him if he was injured.

HEISMAN HOPEFUL. McNair was a pre-season candidate for the prestigious Heisman Trophy, awarded annually to the nation's best college football player. No player from a predominately black college had ever won the award and the fact that Alcorn State played in the small-college Southwest Athletic Conference (SWAC) also hurt McNair's chances. "If the Heisman Trophy is truly about the best player in the country, then it shouldn't matter what division he plays in—the voters should take a serious look at McNair," Tennessee-Chattanooga coach Buddy Green told the Gannett News Service.

McNair tried not to let the Heisman hype bother him. "Sure, I think about winning the Heisman," he explained in *People Weekly.* "But I don't go out every week and say, 'I've got to put up these numbers to win it.' If I win it, that's good. If I don't, it's still good."

Superstar

RECORD BREAKER. McNair put up numbers that made the Heisman Trophy voters take notice in his senior season. He was Alcorn State's best quarterback and the team's leading rusher. McNair threw for 4863 yards and 44 touchdowns and also rushed for 936 yards.

In one game—against Southern—McNair accounted for 649 yards in total offense—a new Division 1-AA single-game record. In the same game he broke the National Collegiate Athletic Association (NCAA) career total yardage mark—held by 1990 Heisman Trophy winner Ty Detmer of Brigham Young—of 14,665 yards. In another contest, against Tennessee-Chattanooga, McNair set the Division 1-AA record with 8 touchdown passes. He also set the NCAA record with 527.2 total yards per game in his final season.

"To be honest, everything has gotten better," McNair told *Sports Illustrated,* explaining his senior-season success. "I'm feeling comfortable with the offense. I know I can take advantage of defenses. I'm better with drop-back passing; I can sit back there as long as I want; I've got a great offensive line, receivers catching the ball. And once you've got those things clicking, it makes things easier. I've matured enough. I've developed into a great quarterback."

During his four years at Alcorn State, McNair compiled 16,823 total yards (rushing and passing yards), equal to 9.56 miles. He threw for 14,496 yards and 119 touchdowns and rushed for 2327 yards and 13 touchdowns. McNair brought his team back to win 28 times, including 11 games with the Braves trailing in the fourth quarter. Alcorn State finished with a 30-10-2 overall record in McNair's career and a 23-4-1 mark in the SWAC. The Braves also beat their main rival, Jackson State, four straight times after having lost to them six consecutive seasons before McNair arrived.

McNair won the SWAC Player of the Year award four straight years and led Alcorn State to two SWAC championships. "He'd take over a game whenever he wanted," linebacker Marlo Perry of Jackson State told the Gannett News Service. "He throws the ball so precisely. And if you got anywhere near him, he'd take off and run and hurt you that way. He could just dominate." McNair finished third in the balloting for the Heisman Trophy, behind winner Rashaan Salaam of Colorado.

McNair was such a hero in his home state that in the final session of Congress in 1994, Representative Bennie G. Thompson of Mississippi honored him by making a speech recognizing his great career. "Because he is widely acclaimed by National Football League scouts for his athletic ability, Steve McNair will most likely join the ranks of many outstanding Mississippians who have played in the NFL," Thompson said, according to *Jet*. "McNair is more than just an exceptional football player. He is an impressive young man who has represented his family, Alcorn and the state with great distinction."

SMALL-TIME? McNair played in the Senior Bowl, an all-star game for the best graduating players in the United States, in an effort to show NFL scouts that he could play with players from major colleges. He completed 8 of 19 passes for 88 yards, with 1 interception in the game, but some scouts still were not convinced. They said McNair could not play in a pro-style offense and that he ran too much to be successful in the NFL.

The criticism bothered McNair. "The thing that bugs me the most is how people make negative comments about the level of competition I faced," he admitted in *Newsday*. "Things of that nature just keep nagging and nagging. I don't doubt myself just because I come from a small school. I really think I'm the best quarterback here [at the Senior Bowl], regardless of what school I came from. If I was at Florida or

Florida State, I'd be the number one player [in the draft], no question about it. There's just something about small schools that people don't like. I just want to be rated as a quarterback. Period."

Many standout professional players had come from the SWAC, including the NFL's all-time leading rusher Walter Payton (Jackson State) and all-time leading receiver Jerry Rice (Mississippi Valley State). "Walter Payton and Jerry Rice grew up in small towns with plenty of competition," McNair explained in *Sports Illustrated*. "They both had the community behind them like I do, and they put down the foundation for me. When I look at what they have done, I say, 'Why not me?'"

AIR OILER. The Houston Oilers—who finished 2-14 in 1994—chose McNair with the third pick in the first round of the 1995 NFL Draft. "A lot of teams that at first wanted me at the end wondered about the level of competition I came from and they slacked off," McNair told the Gannett News Service. "Houston stuck by me from the start." Oilers' owner Bud Adams brought McNair, his brother Fred, and his mother to Houston for a draft-day celebration.

McNair became the highest drafted African American quarterback ever. (Doug Williams of Grambling State was drafted seventeenth overall by the Tampa Bay Buccaneers in 1978 and Andre Ware of the University of Houston was drafted seventh overall in 1990 by the Detroit Lions.) "When I get in the league and learn the offense, the sky's the limit for me," McNair stated in *Newsday*. "I have no negative things about life. I want to go out and win a couple of Super Bowls. Hope-

DOUG WILLIAMS

Doug Williams, a 1977 graduate of Grambling College, is the most successful professional quarterback ever to come from the SWAC. He finished fourth in the 1977 balloting for the Heisman Trophy, behind Earl Campbell of Texas. The Tampa Bay Buccaneers drafted him in the first round of the NFL Draft and in 1988 he won the Super Bowl Most Valuable Player trophy by leading the Washington Redskins to a 42-10 win over the Denver Broncos. Williams is still the only African American quarterback to ever start the Super Bowl.

Williams was a role model for McNair. "He made it easier for the next generation," McNair explained for the Gannett News Service. "Once they saw what he could do, coming from a small school, they began to look back into those college for more guys." Williams gave McNair some good advice, according to the same source. "Don't let anybody tell you that you can't make it. You can make it. You can make it if you set your mind to it."

fully, that dream will come true." McNair signed a $28.7 million contract.

NO PRESSURE. The Oilers did not place pressure on McNair to become their starting quarterback immediately. "Steve is going to be our third quarterback," Houston coach Jeff Fischer told the Associated Press. "Somewhere in the second to third year, he can compete for the starting job. Steve is going to be a franchise player, a franchise quarterback." (A franchise player is one designated by an NFL team that cannot leave the team as a free-agent.)

McNair worked with Houston offensive coordinator Jerry Rhome, who earlier had coached quarterback Troy Aikman in his rookie season in Dallas. "I think it's a great pick and we're going to have a blast with him," Rhome explained to the Associated Press. "He has no limitations. The guy can use sideline to sideline. He has mobility. He can throw on the run. We're going to be able to do a lot of things we normally wouldn't be able to do with an offense."

LION TAMER? McNair spent most of his first season on the sideline, learning by watching starting quarterback Chris Chandler run the offense. He got his first serious playing time near the end of the 1995 season against the Detroit Lions. McNair started the second half in place of Chandler—who was suffering from mononucleosis—and led the Oilers on two touchdown drives, almost bringing Houston back from a 24-3 deficit.

McNair threw for 203 yards, completing 16 of 27 passes. The Oilers lost the game 24-17, but the rookie quarterback impressed the Lions. "He's good and it shocked me," Detroit cornerback Ryan McNeil confessed in the *Sporting News*. "He's got a nice touch on the ball. He doesn't read just one receiver, and the most dangerous thing about him is his mobility."

STARTING QB. With the Oilers out of playoff contention with a 5-9 record, McNair got his first chance to start in the team's second-to-last game, leading Houston to a 23-6 victory over the New York Jets. He threw for 198 yards and 1 touchdown, a 35-yard strike to Haywood Jeffries, that built a 23-0 lead. McNair stood in all day against a fierce Jets blitz designed to rattle the young signal caller. "They blitzed him every single snap," Oilers' general manager Floyd Reese told the *Sporting News*. "He was hit from all directions, all different ways. He saw stuff he had never seen in his life. It didn't rattle him; it didn't bother him."

McNair made his second start in the last game of the 1995 season, against the Buffalo Bills. He directed Houston to a 28-17 win. McNair was 12 of 26 for 168 yards and a touchdown, and enjoyed being the team's leader. "It feels great," he admitted to the Gannett News Service. "I worked well with the other guys. We put it together and made some big plays. There's still a lot for me to learn but I think I'm getting the hang of it now."

STILL LEARNING. Despite having two wins as a starting quarterback under his belt, McNair began the 1996 season as the Oilers' number-two signal caller. He worked hard during the off-season with Rhome, trying to master both the mental and physical requirements of being an NFL quarterback. "I think the importance [of last season] was letting him realize how much he had to learn," Rhome told the *Sporting News*. "In getting in there under an actual battle, he really realized, after those 2½ games, how far away he was and how little he knew."

McNair remained patient about his position as a backup. "That's [starting is] something I really don't worry about," he explained in the *Sporting News*. "I'm just out here trying to do my job and trying to improve and develop into a great quarterback as soon as I can, because you only have so long to play in this league. And once the time comes, I've got to go out there and perform."

FAN FRUSTRATION. The 1996 season was tough for the Oilers. Owner Bud Adams announced the previous season that he wanted to move the franchise to Nashville, Tennessee, and the fans in Houston turned against the team. The Oilers played their home games in front of small crowds that seldom exceeded 30,000 fans. "It's a part of history that we are leaving and it's the true fans that are coming out," McNair explained to the Associated Press. "I feel good about the people who are coming out. It's not a lot we're asking, just to support us."

AIR APPARENT. The Oilers got off to a 5-3 start with Chandler at the helm. McNair got his first start of the year in Game Nine against the Seattle Seahawks, which Chandler missed with a strained groin muscle. "I think he's made a lot of progress," Fischer said about McNair. "I think at this point he's ahead of schedule."

McNair played well against the Seahawks, completing 12 of 18 passes for 225 yards and 1 touchdown, and had Houston in position to win the game with only seconds remaining on the clock. Kicker Al Del Greco attempted a 37-yard field goal to break a 16-16 tie, but Seattle defensive end Michael McCrary blocked the kick. Robert Blackman of the Seahawks picked up the ball and raced 61 yards for the winning touchdown in a 23-16 Seattle victory.

"We had a chance to win," McNair told the Associated Press after the disappointing loss. "Things like that just happen. You've got to keep fighting, keep working and keep preparing. We'll get the breaks sooner or later."

McNair started three of Houston's last four games in 1996, establishing himself as the likely starter for 1997. He had the best game of his career in the season finale against the Baltimore Ravens, completing 19 of 24 passes for 238 yards and a touchdown. He also ran 24 yards for another score in a 24-21 Houston victory. The Oilers finished with an 8-8 record, just missing the playoffs.

McNair completed 61.5 percent of his passes in 1996 (88 of 143) for 1197 yards and 6 touchdowns. He felt he had earned the starting job for the Oilers. "I'm going into the off-season with the idea that I'm the Number One quarterback," McNair admitted to the Associated Press after the season. "If you settle for second, then you're going to be second. I'm ready to step up and take the starting role."

OFF THE FIELD. McNair lives on a 640-acre ranch in Mount Olive. Lucille McNair wanted one thing from her son once he signed a professional contract. "I want a big house—a roomy house," she admitted in *People Weekly.* "So whenever they [her children] come home, there'll be room for all of them." McNair made his mother's dream come true when he bought her a 9000-square-foot house near his ranch.

Despite making millions of dollars, McNair still likes living in Mount Olive. "This is my home," he declared in *Sports Illustrated.* "These are my kin. This place is who I am." McNair is very close to his family. "Every big decision I've made I've made it with my family," he explained in *Jet.* "What's best for me is going to be best for my family. We just keep getting closer and closer. If I'm in the spotlight, my family is going to be in the spotlight."

McNair was in line to be the Oilers' starting quarterback in 1997. He has confidence in his ability to succeed. "When I get on the field, I feel unstoppable," McNair told *Sports Illustrated.* "The field is just a big pasture, and it's just me dodging everybody. I feel those people can't stop me."

Sources

Jet, January 31, 1994; September 26, 1994; November 7, 1994; December 19, 1994; May 8, 1995.
Newsday, January 22, 1995; April 30, 1995.
People Weekly, December 5, 1994.
Sport, November 1994.
Sporting News, May 1, 1995; December 18, 1995; August 12, 1996.
Sports Illustrated, August 30, 1993; September 26, 1994; November 28, 1994; December 18, 1995.
Additional information provided by the Associated Press and the Gannett News Service.

WHERE TO WRITE:

C/O HOUSTON OILERS,
6910 FANNIN STREET, THIRD FLOOR,
HOUSTON, TX 77030.

Dikembe Mutombo

1966—

"When I block a lot of shots, I feel like I'm in charge. I'm The Man. Don't come in here. This is my place."
—Dikembe Mutombo.

Center Dikembe Mutombo of the Atlanta Hawks is the one man in the National Basketball Association (NBA) that shooters least like to see. During his six-year professional career the intimidating defender has led the league in blocked shots four times and was recognized as the 1994—95 NBA Defensive Player of the Year. A three-time NBA all-star as a Denver Nugget, Mutombo has taken his ability to disrupt the opposing team's offense to Atlanta. He is used to moving, as his basketball career has taken him around the world.

Growing Up

FULL HOUSE. Dikembe Mutombo was born June 25, 1966. He was one of seven children—five boys and two girls—of Mukamba and Biamba Mutombo. Mutombo and his family shared a six-bedroom home with up to a dozen cousins. "We believe in big, [extended] families in Africa," Mutombo explained in the *Sporting News*. "And we don't stay away from one another for very long."

Mutombo grew up in Kinshasa—the capital of Zaire—an overpopulated city with a high crime rate. "If you were not tough in Kinshasa, you did not survive," Mutombo recalled in the *Sporting News*. "When you grow up in a country like mine, you have trouble and injustice around you all your life. I never had the freedom to say what I wanted, to always do what I wanted." Mutombo relaxed by raising several pets as a child, including a cat, a dog, and a monkey.

FEELS LIKE SOMEBODY. The Mutombo household was strict. His father was the director of the city's high schools and had attended France's famous university, the Sorbonne. "My father is a very loving man, but he's also very tough-minded and outspoken," Mutombo's brother, Ilo, stated in the *Sporting News*. "He didn't allow any funny business when we were growing up. You had to be well-mannered, clean, and a good student. In fact, education was the only word in our house."

The Mutombo family is a part of the Luba tribe, the group of people who are considered the upper-class in Zaire. "People in Zaire, you know, don't like our tribe very much," Mutombo admitted in the *Sporting News*. "They think we're showoffs. They think we think we're the best at everything. It goes back to colonial times. And, you know, there's some truth to it. I know it's something in my blood. I feel like I am somebody."

The family suffered a great tragedy when Mutombo's brother Kayinda—only 24 years old at the time—died mysteriously while playing in a championship handball match. Because of their son's death, Mutombo's parents did not let their other children play sports for some time after the death. "My parents were so scared that something bad would happen

Mutombo attempts to make two.

again that they said they'd never again let us play sports," Ilo Mutombo recalled in the *Sporting News*. "But that feeling didn't last very long. After a while, they came to the conclusion that [Kayinda's death] was simply God's will and had nothing to do with playing sports."

TOO TALL. Mutombo eventually grew to almost 7-feet tall. Other people treated him differently because of his height. "I didn't want to go to the market after a while," he confessed to *Sports Illustrated.* "People would run away. They thought I was a ghost, from another planet, not a kid from the neighborhood. It would make me sad. We have this belief in African culture that your child should not grow up and look down on your head. Teachers thought I had no respect because of that."

LOVES SPORTS. Mutombo's favorite sport as a child was soccer. He began playing in elementary school and soon developed into a star. Mutombo played goalie, and his height helped him cover the net. "I was the tallest goalkeeper in all of Zaire," he claimed in the *Sporting News.*

Despite his height, Mutombo did not play basketball until his senior year in high school. His brother Ilo played center on Zaire's national team. He and his father convinced Mutombo that because he was so tall he was perfect for the sport. Mutombo had a hard time with his coordination, and tripped and fell—cutting his chin—the first time he ran up the basketball floor.

LONG DISTANCE RECRUIT. Within two years, Mutombo had earned the starting center position on the national team, pushing his brother to power forward. "I traveled to various countries with my national team as a teenager for two years before I came [to the United States]," Mutombo recalled in *Sport.* "I was the youngest on the team, but I was just traveling with them, learning how to play basketball."

Mutombo began to become interested in basketball in the United States and especially liked to follow the careers of NBA stars. He read about the NBA in newspapers posted on the windows of the U.S. Embassy in Kinshasa. Herman Henning—a former high school coach in Chicago working for the U.S. government in Zaire—noticed Mutombo. He told John Thompson, the basketball coach of the Georgetown University Hoyas, about the developing center.

Thompson offered Mutombo an academic scholarship to attend Georgetown, where he originally planned on studying medicine. "I used to be a good student in science, so I always focused on becoming a doctor," Mutombo explained in *Sport.* "[I] came here [to the U.S.] with the idea of going to medical school and then going back home and helping the people in Africa. I ended up changing my mind when I realized there was an opportunity to use my height and play basketball for the school and get a free education."

RISING STAR. Mutombo did not play basketball during his freshman season at Georgetown because he wanted to improve his English. He worked seven hours a day to learn the new language. Mutombo learned so well that he graduated from the university in four years with degrees in both linguistics and diplomacy. "I was so proud of myself," Mutombo told *Sports Illustrated* about earning his diploma.

As a sophomore, Mutombo served as the backup for Alonzo Mourning—now a member of the Miami Heat in the NBA. The Georgetown University Hoyas advanced to the East Regional Final of the National Collegiate Athletic Association (NCAA) tournament, losing to Duke, 85-77. The next season Mutombo led the Hoyas in rebounding and scored 10.7 points per game.

Mutombo was still a raw talent and needed to develop his basketball skills. Coach Thompson brought in Bill Russell, the Hall-of-Fame center of the great Boston Celtics championship teams of the 1960s, to talk to his young player. "Bill Russell told me, 'You can do it,'" Mutombo recalled in *Sports Illustrated*. "He was there for five days. He talked to me for three, four hours a day. The man is so smart. He convinced me I could play." Mutombo still works with Russell during his off-seasons. "I want to be remembered as maybe a guy who could put himself in the same category as Bill Russell," he stated in the same magazine.

By his senior season (1990—91), Mutombo had developed into a legitimate NBA prospect. He led Georgetown in scoring (15.2 points per game) and rebounding (12.2 boards per game). Most importantly, Mutombo was a defensive force, earning Big East Defensive Player of the Year honors.

DIKEMBE TO DENVER. Despite his success at Georgetown, many basketball experts did not think Mutombo should be a high draft choice in the upcoming 1991 NBA Draft. They said it would take years for him to develop into a solid professional. The Denver Nuggets disagreed with this opinion, and chose 25-year-old Mutombo the oldest player in the draft—with the fourth-overall pick.

Mutombo signed a five-year, $13.7 million contract, more money than anyone in his family could have imagined. "When I signed my contract, my father was so happy he had a party for three days," Mutombo recalled in *Sports Illustrated*. "This is something that never has happened in my family before, someone making a lot of money, someone who could help the family. I already have been able to send money to my uncles, to my brothers, to my sisters. And if something happens— someone is there to help. I hear people say, 'You must be proud of yourself,' but that is not the way I feel. I think that you don't feel proud of what you are doing; you feel proud about what people say you are doing."

ROOKIE SUCCESS. Denver was a bad team—they finished 20-62 the previous season—and Mutombo had a hard time adjusting to losing after having so much success at Georgetown. "When I got to Denver, it was a change for me," he admitted in the *Sporting News*. "It was hard for me to accept it [the losing]."

Mutombo brought hope to Nugget fans with his play during his rookie season. He averaged 16.6 points per game— still his career best—and pulled down 12.3 rebounds a contest. Mutombo also established himself as a defensive force, blocking 210 shots. He finished second in the voting for the 1991—92 NBA Rookie of the Year voting, behind Larry Johnson of the Charlotte Hornets, the number-one pick in the draft. "I do not believe this, that I get here," Mutombo confessed in *Sports Illustrated*. "I did not think I would be a professional basketball player."

WHAT'S IN A NAME?

Mutombo's full name is Dikembe Mutombo Mpolondo Mukamba Jean Jacque Wamutombo. "In Africa friends and relatives can come to the hospital and give you a name if they want," he told *Sports Illustrated*, explaining his long name. It is a good thing Mutombo does not have to put his full name on the back of his jersey.

NO RECOGNITION. Mutombo led the NBA in blocked shots during the 1993—94 season with 4.1 per game and also pulled down 11.8 rebounds (sixth in the NBA). His 336 blocks set a team record. Amazingly, the NBA did not name Mutombo to either the first- or second-All Defensive team. "It was sad," Mutombo told *Sport.* "I've been trying to search for an explanation. I broke my team record [for blocked shots]. What didn't I do?"

DREAM COME TRUE. The Nuggets barely made the playoffs, finishing the 1993—94 season with 42 victories. In the first round they faced the powerful Seattle Supersonics. The Sonics earned the best regular season record in the NBA at 63-19. Denver quickly fell behind in the best-of-five series, 0-2, and were on the verge of being swept.

After Game Two Mutombo had an important dream as he slept. He dreamt that Denver won Game Five of the series. "I had seen the game in my sleep and we had won, and then I saw us celebrating, so I knew we had won the series," Mutombo explained in *Sport.*

Mutombo was a force inside the rest of the series, blocking shots and intimidating the Sonics. "Their game was from the paint, from the inside," he stated in *Sports Illustrated.* "To me, going for blocks was the only way we could win. I kept telling them [the Seattle players], 'Don't come!'" In one of the greatest comebacks of all-time, Denver became the first eighth-seeded team to defeat a number one seed since the NBA adopted its current playoff system by sweeping the last three games against Seattle. Mutombo blocked more shots against the Supersonics than any player ever had in a five game series—31. When the game ended, Mutombo laid on his back, kicking his feet in the air.

In the second round the Nuggets again found themselves on the brink of elimination, falling behind 3-0 to the Utah Jazz in their best-of-seven series. Denver made another remarkable comeback, but this time they fell one game short, losing the seventh and deciding game. Mutombo blocked 38 shots against the Jazz—the most ever by a player in a seven-game series.

DEFENSIVE PLAYER OF THE YEAR. Mutombo reached several important milestones during the 1994—95 season. Western Conference coaches named him to the all-star game roster after an injury forced Cedric Ceballos of the Los Angles Lakers to miss the game. Mutombo led the league in blocked shots for the second straight season and also had the most total rebounds of any NBA player (1029). The most intimidating player in the league, he finally earned recognition when he won the 1994—95 NBA Defensive Player of the Year Award.

"Dikembe doesn't get the credit he deserves," Minnesota Timberwolves forward Stacey King told *Sports Illustrated*. "A lot of people don't consider shot blocking and defense, they consider it a last resort. But if you've got an intimidator back there [under the basket], so that anybody going to the hole has a 90 percent chance his shot's going to get thrown out . . . it's big."

SIGNS WITH HAWKS. Mutombo repeated as an NBA all-star in 1996, playing for the Western Conference in San Antonio, Texas. He remained a defensive force, leading the NBA in blocked shots for the fourth straight season (4.49 per game). Mutombo, however, became increasingly frustrated because he felt the Nuggets did not include him in their offense. He scored a career-low 11 points per game, and his scoring average had dropped every year of his career. "I was not allowed to participate in the offense, to touch the ball, to even set a pick," Mutombo stated in *Sports Illustrated*. "I was told to run down the floor and then go stand over there. What good is that?" The

WORLD TRAVELER

During the summer of 1994 Mutombo joined his fellow Georgetown alumni Patrick Ewing of the New York Knicks and Mourning on a trip to South Africa. "The trip is of great importance to me," Mutombo stated in the *Sporting News*. "I feel I have to give something back to the people where I'm from." Mutombo got a big thrill when he met South African president Nelson Mandela, a man who spent 27 years in prison because he opposed the South African policy of apartheid (the official policy of legal and economic discrimination against nonwhites).

Mutombo is a hero on his native continent. "I've tried to educate people about my continent and visited it often, and I've kept my citizenship, so people haven't seen me as a sell-out," he explained in *Sport*. "I'm one person who has [left Africa] but tried to maintain his culture, and I think people realize and respect that."

Mutombo is active with the international relief agency CARE. He receives no pay for his trips to Africa, where he puts on basketball clinics for children in some of the poorest areas in the world. "Although I am from Zaire, I consider all of Africa my home and all Africans my people," he told *Sports Illustrated*.

Nuggets won only 35 games in 1995—96 and missed the playoffs.

Mutombo became one of the most sought-after free agents in the summer of 1996. He could sign with any other NBA team. The Detroit Pistons, Boston Celtics, and Milwaukee Bucks were interested, but Mutombo told those teams he did not want to play in a cold-weather city. He eventually signed a five-year, $56 million contract to play with the Atlanta Hawks. "Sometimes you have to leave home and start over," Mutombo explained in *Sports Illustrated*. "I hope to do that here."

TEAM SPONSOR. Mutombo made headlines in the summer of 1996 when he sponsored the Olympic women's basketball team from Zaire that participated at the Summer Olympics in Atlanta, Georgia. Zaire won the African tournament, becoming the first team from his country to qualify for the Olympics. Mutombo paid the team's expenses, including airplane tickets, uniforms, and basketballs. "There are a couple of girls on the team that I grew up with, we went to school together," Mutombo explained.

The team from Zaire was not a medal contender, and they did not win a game at the Olympics. They lost to the gold-medal winning U.S. team, 107-47. Mutombo tried to encourage the players and make them feel good about themselves. "I told them, 'Don't be upset if you don't win the Gold or because you didn't win the game, but be happy that you made it here,'" Mutombo revealed. "Because this is the biggest thing and it doesn't happen to everyone."

Mutombo was proud to see a team from his home country play in the Olympics. "That means a lot," he admitted. "Just to see them play in front of 31,000 people and see my flag be waved—that means a lot. It means a lot to the players where I came from, where I grew up as a child."

WHY SO GOOD? Mutombo's strength is his ability to change the offensive game of other teams with his shot-blocking ability. "I always think that when I block a shot, I'm protecting my house," he explained in *Sport*. "It means I didn't let anybody come in and steal [anything], take the furniture, you know? It makes me feel good."

Mutombo is still awkward and his movements seem difficult. He does not run smoothly and seems to struggle with offensive moves. His scoring average has declined in each of his seasons in the NBA and he needs to develop a good shooting touch. Despite his lack of offense, Mutombo is still a dominating player. "Whatever he gives us offensively is gravy," Nuggets coach Bernie Bickerstaff confessed in the *Sporting News*. "We want him thinking only of blocking shots, rebounding and playing defense. That's where he earns all his money."

OFF THE COURT. Mutombo lives with his wife in Potomoc, Maryland. He adopted a son and daughter of his brother, Kamba, after his sibling died of brain cancer; he also adopted the daughter of another late brother and the son of his sister. "These kids have changed my life," Mutombo admitted in the *Sporting News*. "I feel like I have to grow up to set a good example for them. I want them to see only positive things when they see me on TV, or when the read about me."

Mutombo purchased a new house in Zaire for his parents and bought cars for each of his two surviving brothers. He also provides his family members with clothes and gifts and pays for them to visit the United States. The big center is currently active in building Polyclinique-55, a hospital in Kinshasa named after his number. The hospital will serve those who cannot afford health care. Mutombo enjoys being generous with his wealth. "It is an African thing to share your money with your family," he explained in the *Sporting News*. "Besides, I don't want to just make money and be happy by myself."

Mutombo works out in the off-season with his two famous ex-Georgetown centers, Mourning and Patrick Ewing of the New York Knicks. "I always see Patrick as a brother," Mutombo told *Sport*. "He still inspires me a lot. I can't even describe it as a friendship; it's more like we come from the same family. And Alonzo, too. He lives just a few blocks away, and we all spend a lot of time together."

Mutombo speaks French, Spanish, Portuguese, English, and five African dialects. After his basketball career is over, he is considering a career in diplomacy. "I told my dad I wanted to work for the United Nations or the International Monetary Fund," Mutombo told *Sport*. "I want to be the first 7-footer to sit in the U.N., the first former basketball player."

Mutombo owns a German shepherd. He likes Chinese food and enjoys reading. He enjoys what he does best—blocking shots—most of all. "It means a lot to me to block shots," he explained in the *Sporting News*. "When I block a lot of shots, I feel like I'm in charge. I'm The Man. Don't come in here. This is my place."

Sources

Sport, March 1995.
Sporting News, November 7, 1994; March 25, 1996.
Sports Illustrated, December 9, 1991; October 11, 1993; November 7, 1994;
    April 24, 1995.
Additional information provided by the National Basketball Association.

WHERE TO WRITE:

C/O ATLANTA HAWKS,
1 CNN CENTER, SUITE 405, SOUTH TOWER,
ATLANTA, GA 30303.

Gary Payton

1968—

Gary Payton of the Seattle Supersonics has two nick-names. Other players call him "The Glove" because of his ability to guard opponents as tightly as a glove fits on a hand. Payton's defensive ability earned him the 1995—96 National Basketball Association (NBA) Defensive Player of the Year award. Stopping high-scoring opponents— along with a sweet shooting touch—made the Sonics point guard an all-star and a member of the 1996 gold-medal-win-ning U.S. Olympic men's basketball "Dream Team III." Pay-ton earned his other nickname—"The Mouth"—through his trash-talking (excessive bragging and celebrating) on the court. His high-octane play has made the Supersonics one of the best teams in the NBA.

"The thing is, he's a great winner." —Seattle Supersonics coach George Karl.

Growing Up

LEARNS FROM DAD. Gary Payton was born July 23, 1968. His father, Alfred (also called Al), owns a restaurant in Fremont, California, and his mother's name is Annie. Payton grew up in the projects of Oakland, California, until his father won $30,000 through a gambling bet. Al Payton used the money to move his family to a nicer neighborhood while Gary was still a young child.

His father worked to keep Payton and his four siblings out of trouble. "I had him on a very tight schedule," Al Payton recalled in *Sport*. "I made him take vitamins, eat his vegetables, and kept him off the streets."

Payton learned how to intimidate opponents from his father. "I am mean," Al Payton admitted in *Sports Illustrated*. "I taught the kid the look, the intimidations, yeah, the meanness." Payton also says that his older sister, Sharon, was tough. "On the softball field, I'm tellin' you, Sharon would punch out boys," he told *Sports Illustrated*.

TRASH-TALKING TEENS. Payton learned how to trash-talk on the inner-city playgrounds of Oakland. He was a star basketball player at Skyline High School in the Oakland Athletic League (OAL). The OAL was a tough league, both on the court and in the stands. Armed guards were necessary to protect both the players and the fans. "You talk about rowdy," Payton recalled in *Sports Illustrated*. "In Oakland the players were on you. The refs were on you. The stands were on you. You had to talk back or you were a sissy; you'd get run out of the league. Afterward? Yeah, it was kind of a, uh, struggle to get out of the gym. Cops had to be everywhere. Which was lucky."

Payton had to learn that his schoolwork was as important as his basketball ability. Halfway through his sophomore high school season, the basketball coach suspended him for bad grades and for getting in trouble. "I messed up—fighting, trashing teachers and coaches, everybody," Payton admitted in *Sports Illustrated*. Al Payton helped his son get back on track. He went to school and sometimes told Gary off in front

Payton (left) makes a breakaway layup.

of other students. "I started growing up," Payton told the same magazine.

OREGON STATE BOUND. Although he had the ability to be a successful college player, Payton's off-court problems worried many college coaches. "He had an air, like a guy who might cause trouble," former UCLA coach Jim Harrick explained in *Sports Illustrated*. Because of Payton's troublesome behavior, St. John's University offered him a scholarship, but then withdrew the offer.

Payton finally accepted a scholarship to play for Oregon State University (OSU) of the Pacific-10 (Pac-10) conference. Oregon State coach Ralph Miller was tough, and he let his young player know where he stood right away. Miller told Payton that he had to play defense if he wanted to start for the Beavers. "In high school, I was offensive-minded," Payton explained in the *Detroit Free Press*. "I liked George Gervin [a high-scoring forward for the San Antonio Spurs] a lot, and you know he didn't play no D [defense]. He didn't play no D at all."

Payton responded to the his coach's challenge, earning Pac-10 Freshman of the Year and Defensive Player of the Year honors. He averaged 12.5 points per game his first season and dished out 229 assists, the sixth most ever for a first-year college player.

PLAYER OF THE YEAR. Payton started every game in his four-year career at Oregon State. He left OSU as the school's all-time leading scorer (2172 points), assists man (938), and thief (321 steals). Payton had a great season as a senior, averaging 25.7 points per game, compiling 235 assists, and stealing the ball 100 times. He earned first-team All-American honors and *Sports Illustrated* selected him as the college Player of the Year. "My first year in college I was OK," Payton explained in *Sport*. "My second year I got better. My third year I was on the verge of being an All-American, and then my senior year—pow!—I'm Mr. Everything."

"I've loved my days at Oregon State," Payton told *Sports Illustrated* during his senior year. "If I had gone to New York, maybe I'd have made All-American two years ago, but who knows what trouble I might have gotten into in the big city? Here, I settled down, slept a lot, started to take care of my body. The trash-talking and stuff—I've calmed down. At this level it's all business."

Payton calmed down his sharp tongue, but he did not become quiet on the court. "[The trash-talking has] been a touchy thing for me," Miller admitted in *Sports Illustrated*. "But you cannot take away this kid's style. His cockiness is what makes him tick." Other players did not take Payton's words personally. "Payton doesn't mean any harm with his trash," University of Washington player Eldridge Recasner told the same magazine. "It's just his competitiveness. He doesn't get in fights, because he backs up everything he says."

SONIC BUST? The Seattle Supersonics chose Payton with the second overall pick in the 1990 NBA Draft. (The New Jersey Nets chose Derrick Coleman of Syracuse University with the first pick.) Payton led NBA rookies in steals (165) and assists (528) and averaged 7.2 points per game. The NBA named him to the 1991—92 All-Rookie second team, but many basketball experts thought Seattle made a big mistake by taking Payton with such a high draft pick.

Payton had a hard time adjusting to the NBA, and he did not get along with the Sonics coach, K.C. Jones. "When I came out of college, I thought I was just going to keep rolling," he told *Sport*. "But I was forced to play a style of basketball that I couldn't play—a slowdown game—and Jones didn't have confidence in me. The mental part was my fault because I let the coach get to me. I questioned myself. I came home to Oakland that summer after my rookie year and I didn't work out. I thought I was through; one year in the league and that's that. I thought I would be bouncing around from team to team."

NEW COACH. Payton and the Sonics continued to struggle at the beginning of the 1991—92 season. In January 1992, George Karl replaced Jones as Seattle's coach. Payton credits new assistant coach Tim Grgurich with making him an all-star. "Coach Grg was really the one who turned me around," he explained in *Sport*. "We let the rest of that ['92] season go by and I picked it up a little bit, but my head was still messed up and I still didn't think I could play in this league."

Grgurich invited Payton to his home in Utah to work out, walk, and talk. "We actually walked for hours, and all we talked about was what I did at Oregon State," Payton recalled in *Sport*. Most importantly, Grgurich showed Payton videotapes of games he played at Oregon State. Seeing how well he could play when things were clicking for him, Payton started to get his confidence back.

"[Grgurich] didn't change my shot," Payton explained in *Sport*. "All he did was bring my confidence back. Before, I was thinking every time I shot the ball it was never going in, and now, each time I shoot I think the ball is going in. I don't care if I miss seven or eight shots in a row, I know eventually one is going to fall."

ALL-STAR. Payton's game continued to improve, and he became an all-star during the 1993—94 season. He averaged 16.5 points and 6 assists per game. Payton also stole the ball 188 times and earned his nickname—"The Glove"—because he covered his opponents as tightly as a glove fits on a hand. The NBA named him to the All-Defensive first team.

The Supersonics also earned the best record in the NBA during the 1993—94 season, winning 63 games to become a playoff contender. Payton and forward Shawn Kemp became one of the most dangerous combinations in the league, with the flashy point guard's feeding the flying forward for a slam dunk on the fastbreak becoming a regular feature on the highlight reel."Gary and I are a good combination, and his game has really improved the last couple years," Kemp explained in *Sport*. "I love playing with Gary and I wouldn't want him to be on any other team."

Unfortunately, Seattle lost a tough five-game first-round playoff series to the Denver Nuggets. The Nuggets had barely qualified for the playoffs, and the loss disappointed Payton. "I didn't come home [to Oakland] for about a month after the Denver loss," he confessed to *Sport*. "I stayed in Seattle and thought about what happened."

THE POINT MAN. Payton made the Western Conference all-star team for the second consecutive year in 1995. He finished second in the voting for the NBA All-Star Game's Most Valuable Player to **Mitch Richmond** of the Sacramento Kings. Payton had 15 assists in the game. For the season, he averaged a career-best 20.6 points per game and dished out 7.1 assists per contest. Experts now considered him one of the best point guards in the game. "I think Gary Payton is certainly one of the best point guards in the West and in the NBA," Phoenix Suns point guard Kevin Johnson admitted in *Sport*.

Payton's teammates also noticed his improvement. "A lot of times, he is toying with opposing point guards," teammate Nate McMillan told the *Oregonian*. "Gary has grown tremendously the last couple of years. The confidence level has gone up a great deal. He is making things look easy this season." The Sonics won 57 games during the regular season, but for the third straight season lost in the first round of the NBA playoffs, this time falling to the Los Angeles Lakers.

Superstar

DAD'S ADVICE. The Sonics' early exits from the NBA playoffs bothered Payton, especially since point guards Robert Pack of the Nuggets and Nick Van Exel of the Lakers outplayed him in the last two playoff upsets. He talked to his father about his problems. "My father sat me down and put a lot of things in my mind," Payton explained in the *Oregonian*. "He reminded me when he had yelled at me, I'd responded by going out and working harder. He said the only reason Coach Karl is on you is because he cares about you and wants to help you. He reminded me that's the way it was with Coach Miller at Oregon State. In both situations, they're trying to get our team to another level."

DEFENSIVE PLAYER OF THE YEAR. Payton had his best all-around season in 1995—96. He led the NBA in steals with 231 (2.85 per game), and was a force on offense, averaging 19.3 points per game clip and setting up his teammates at a career-best 7.5 assists per game rate. In recognition of his skill at stopping high-scoring opponents, the NBA named him the 1996 Defensive Player of the Year. Payton became the first guard to win the award since Michael Jordan in 1988. "I am the best point guard in the league—at playing defense," Payton told *Sport*.

Payton was now the Sonics' team leader. "The biggest difference now is that [I'm directing] this team a little bit bet-

SILENCE IS GOLDEN?

Payton is the undisputed king of NBA trash-talking. "When you're done, you just want to go find a library or something, someplace totally silent," former teammate Michael Cage told *Sports Illustrated* about playing against Payton. The Sonics' star feels that his constant jabbering gives him an advantage over his opponent. "I can't let that go," Payton explained in the *Oregonian*. "That's Gary. I can try to change a lot of things, but I can't change that [trash-talking]. That's what keeps the fire in me. That's what energizes me. Like my father says, 'That's your game. That's you. You can control it, but don't lose it.'"

Even though he will always talk on the court, Payton has calmed down in the last few years. "I think I've grown up a lot," he admitted in *Sports Illustrated.* "I mean, I'm always going to talk, but I know how to control it better now, when to tone it down. I don't worry that much about what people think of me, but nobody wants to be known as a loudmouth his whole career."

ter than I have in the last two or three years," he explained in the *Sporting News.* "I'm more serious now. I'm more productive. I'm showing myself on the court not by talking but by doing the other things."

THE FINALS AT LAST. Seattle set a team-record with 64 wins during the 1995—96 season. The Sonics also ended their playoff frustration. They defeated the Sacramento Kings, 3-1, in the first round, then swept Hakeem Olajuwon and the Houston Rockets in their second playoff series. "[Payton's] the key to everything they do, that's all," Houston coach Rudy Tomjanovich told *Sports Illustrated.* "He's the engine behind their offense with the way he penetrates and pushes the ball on the break, and he sets the tone for the way they attack you on defense."

In the Western Conference Finals, the Supersonics faced the Utah Jazz, with its future Hall of Fame duo of Karl Malone and John Stockton. The series featured a showdown between the two best point guards in the NBA—Payton and NBA career assist and steals leader Stockton. Seattle took a 3-1 lead, but then lost two straight to the stubborn Jazz. Seattle ultimately won Game Seven, 90-85, and earned a trip to the NBA Finals. Payton outplayed Stockton throughout the series and scored 22 points in the Supersonics Game Seven victory.

BULLED OVER. The Sonics faced a difficult challenge in the NBA Finals. Their opponent, the Chicago Bulls, set an NBA record with 72 wins in the 1995—96 season and featured two of the best players in the league—Michael Jordan and Scottie Pippen. The Bulls entered the finals with a 12-1 playoff record and continued to roll through the first three games of the finals, threatening to sweep the Sonics. Payton struggled against the tough defense of Bulls' guard Ron Harper, failing to score 20 points in any of the first three games.

Seattle did not quit, however, and came back strong to win Games Four and Five on their home court. Team captain Nate McMillan provided a spark by playing with an injured back, and Karl assigned Payton the full-time job of guarding Jordan for the first time in the series. The change also ignited Payton's offensive game, as he scored 21 and 23 points respectively in the two Sonics' victories. "If we can play like we did in the last two games, we have a chance of beating them," he said.

The series then returned to Chicago, and the Bulls proved they deserved the championship, winning Game Six, 87-75. Payton scored 19 points and dished out 7 assists in Game Six, but the 19 rebounds by Chicago's Dennis Rodman broke Seattle's back. "We take our hats off to the Bulls," Payton stated in the *Chicago Sun-Times*. "They did a great job and I congratulate them on winning a championship."

DREAM TEAMER. Payton received another great honor following the 1995—96 season when USA Basketball named him to the men's basketball team—called "Dream Team III"—that would represent the United States at the 1996 Summer Olympics in Atlanta, Georgia. A spot on the team became available when Glenn "Big Dog" Robinson of the Milwaukee Bucks withdrew because of an Achilles tendon injury. The "Dream Team" swept through the best competition in the world, easily winning the gold medal.

Payton became a free agent after the 1995—96 season, meaning that he could sign with any other NBA team. The Miami Heat and New York Knicks expressed interest in signing him, but he decided to stay in Seattle. Payton remained because he felt the Supersonics had the best chance to win an NBA championship.

OFF THE COURT. Payton lives in the Oakland, California, area, with his wife, Monique, and their two children, Gary II

WHY SO GOOD?

Payton has become one of the best point guards in the NBA because of his unique combination of offensive and defensive abilities. He is also durable, missing only two games in his career. "Gary doesn't like to come out [of the game]," teammate Earvin Johnson told the *Detroit Free Press*. "He likes to play and he likes to win."

Payton and Karl—who are both very competitive—have had a stormy relationship. Despite their differences, Karl appreciates the talent of his superstar. "He's not a great shoot, he's not really quick, he's not a great jumper, he's not a great ballhandler," Karl explained in the *Oregonian*. "The thing is, he's a great winner. Stockton is a better playmaker, there are better shooters and so on. But the total package, what he brings defensively and all the other assets, he's the best. Gary has an attitude of no non-sense, get it done, get after people."

and Raquel. "Gary is a really good father in regards to spending time with his kids every chance he gets, and he is very disciplined with them," Monique Payton told *Sport*. "That's why they're so good."

Fatherhood has had a positive effect on Payton. "Once you become a father, you have to grow up, just like they're growing up," he admitted in the *Oregonian*. "Being a father with a lot of responsibility at home has made me grow up in basketball, too. Don't want my kids' friends talking about how their father is acting like a crazy clown on the court."

In August 1995, Oregon State named Payton to its Hall of Fame. "A young guy like me, in a Hall of Fame?" Payton asked in the *Oregonian*. "I don't know. But, it's a great thing. I think I made a great choice going to Oregon State."

Payton is active with charities that help children and the homeless, and he contributes to the March of Dimes. When his career is over, he would like to own or manage a sports bar or restaurant. Before he retires, however, Payton plans to lead the Sonics to an NBA title. "I can't imagine a better point guard for our style," Karl admitted in *Sports Illustrated*. "There are some great point guards in this league, but there's not one I'd rather have playing for me than Gary."

Sources

Chicago Sun-Times, June 17, 1996.
Detroit Free Press, April 20, 1995; May 7, 1996; May 15, 1996; May 30, 1996; June 3, 1996; June 6, 1996; June 8, 1996; June 10, 1996; June 11, 1996; June 14, 1996; June 15, 1996; June 17, 1996.
Esquire, April 1994.
Jet, June 3, 1996; July 15, 1996.

Oregonian, April 16, 1995.

Philadelphia Inquirer, June 16, 1996.

Sport, January 1995.

Sporting News, May 27, 1996.

Sports Illustrated, March 5, 1990; January 16, 1995; May 13, 1996.

Sports Illustrated for Kids, November 1996.

Additional information provided by the National Basketball Association and Oregon State University.

WHERE TO WRITE:

C/O SEATTLE SUPERSONICS,
190 QUEEN ANNE AVENUE, N., SUITE 200,
SEATTLE, WA 98109.

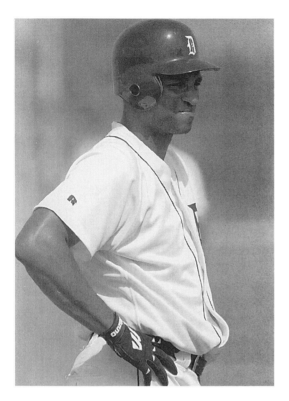

Curtis Pride

1968—

Imagine being a professional baseball player and not being able to hear the crowd cheer, the crack of the bat, or even the umpire calling balls and strikes right behind you. If you can imagine that, you will begin to understand what life is like on the field for Curtis Pride, outfielder for the Detroit Tigers. Born 95 percent deaf, he played 95 games for the Tigers in 1996 and batted an even .300. The young outfielder is living proof that it is possible to overcome obstacles, even when other people tell you it's not.

Growing Up

GROWING UP DEAF. Curtis John Pride was born December 12, 1968, in Washington, DC. He grew up in Silver Spring, Maryland, with his mother, Sallie, a registered nurse, and his father, John, a consulting firm executive. When Pride was five months old, his parents began to worry that their son was not responding to the sounds around him. "I had a hard time reacting to them [his parents] around the house," Pride explained in the *Sporting News*. By the time he was 17 months old doctors discovered that Pride was 95 percent deaf. Experts believe the disease rubella—which Sallie Pride suffered from during her pregnancy—caused the deafness.

Pride attended special classes designed to help him read lips. Unlike many deaf children, he did not learn how to use sign language. Pride was determined to learn to speak, and his parents feared that learning sign language would slow his speech development. (Often deaf children give up trying to speak because it is difficult to make themselves understood.) With a hearing aid, Pride can hear noises but cannot tell one sound from another.

By fourth grade Pride began to take some classes with hearing students. Unfortunately, other kids made fun of the way he talked. Pride came home crying one day and said he did not want to go back. "You know, Curt sees all the world as good," Sally Pride explained in the *Sporting News*. "He likes people and wants them to like him. I remember as a boy he came to me and said he didn't understand why kids made fun of the way he talked. He really meant, he didn't understand."

"I'M GOING TO BE A BASEBALL PLAYER." In order to learn to be comfortable with hearing children, Pride got involved in sports. At the age of six, he began to play Tee-ball, a form of baseball for young children, after his father threatened legal action against the league that would not let him play because of his disability. In his first game, Pride hit a ball over head of the center fielder. "I'm going to be a baseball player!" he said repeatedly the night after that first game, according to *Reader's Digest*.

Pride's parents encouraged their son to get involved with hearing children. "My parents were a constant support to me,"

SCOREBOARD

ONLY THE FIFTH DEAF MAJOR-LEAGUE PLAYER.

MADE MAJOR LEAGUE DEBUT WITH MONTREAL EXPOS ON SEPTEMBER 14, 1993.

HIT .300 IN 1996 WITH THE DETROIT TIGERS DURING HIS FIRST FULL MAJOR-LEAGUE SEASON.

PRIDE HAS OVERCOME THE OBSTACLES PRESENTED BY DEAFNESS TO EARN A CHANCE TO BE A MAJOR LEAGUE BALLPLAYER.

A diving Pride (left) makes the catch.

Pride explained in the *Sporting News*. "They kept feeding me information. They treated me just like my sisters [Jackie and Christine], except they spent more time with me. They encouraged me to play sports and realize I had a variety of choices in life. Still, I was very shy around other kids. They made fun of me. They thought I was retarded. It's hard for people to feel comfortable around me, so I make a great effort to put them at ease."

BIG DECISION. When it was time to enter seventh grade, Pride made a decision. He insisted on taking all of his classes at the neighborhood school, not the school with special programs for the hearing impaired that his teachers wanted him to attend. "I told my parents it was my chance to be independent," Pride explained in the *Sporting News*. "To function in the normal world."

Pride ran into unique problems at his new school. The teachers tried to remember that he read lips, but sometimes they forgot and spoke facing the blackboard. Pride also had trouble carrying on conversations with other kids on the playground.

Pride made friends with a boy named Steve Grupe, who offered to help him. In return, Pride offered to give Grupe help with his baseball. The two boys became best friends. Grupe helped Pride take notes and the two young athletes played soccer and baseball.

HIGH SCHOOL STAR. Athletics helped Pride fit in. He was a three-sport star at John F. Kennedy High School. Pride earned Parade Magazine All-American honors for soccer and played for the American national under-eighteen team at the 1985 world championships in China.

A point guard on the basketball team, he earned a scholarship to play at the College of William & Mary.

Pride's best sport, however, was baseball. The New York Mets drafted him in the tenth-round of the 1986 major league free-agent amateur draft. An all-star in the classroom, Pride graduated from high school with a 3.6 grade-point-average.

COLLEGE BOUND. After high school Pride accepted the basketball scholarship to the College of William & Mary. He started as the team's point guard and graduated with a degree in finance. "I think the most we won in any one season while I was there [William & Mary] was 11 games," Pride recalled in the *Detroit Free Press*. "But we had to play some tough teams—Virginia, Duke, [and] Navy when David Robinson was there."

LIFE ON THE ROAD. Each summer Pride played baseball in the Mets farm system. (A farm team is a minor-league team where young players are trained to be professional players. These teams are usually affiliated with a major-league team.) When he went to join his first minor league team in Kingsport, Tennessee, it was the first time he had been away from home. "I remember leaving him on the steps of the motel," John Pride recalled in the *Sporting News*. "He looked so sad, like he was about to cry. My wife and I thought maybe we should take him home with us. But we left him."

The adjustment to living on the road was hard on Pride, and his deafness caused special difficulties. "I was lonely that first year," he told the *Sporting News*. "But it helped me mature. To handle responsibility. I got confident in the world. But still, a deaf person's biggest fear is to be alone when something bad happens to them. You can't even call someone on the phone. I just had to learn not to be afraid. I can't speak for other deaf people, but I don't think deaf persons should isolate themselves from the hearing world."

FULL-TIME BALLPLAYER. Attending college hurt Pride's baseball career, because he had to wait until the end of the school year to join his minor league team. After graduating from William & Mary in 1990, Pride could devote himself full-time to baseball. In 1991, he played his first full minor league season, hitting .260 for the Mets St. Lucie team in the Single A Florida State League. He earned league all-star honors and the Mets promoted Pride to the Double A team at Binghampton, New York, for the 1992 season.

Pride slumped badly in 1992, finally finding himself benched. After one game, he noticed that his teammates were making fun of him. This made Pride angry, because he expected his teammates to be his friends. He walked over to the group of players and began to speak. "I can't hear you, but I can think and I can feel, just like you," Pride told them, according to *Reader's Digest*. "My handicap is deafness. Yours is intolerance. I'd rather have mine." His teammates turned away, embarrassed by what they had done.

CLOSE TO QUITTING. Pride's poor performance in 1992—he hit only .227—and his teammate's actions tested the young ballplayer's confidence. He called his parents and told them he was thinking about giving up on baseball. Mr. and Mrs. Pride drove to Binghampton to meet with their son. Pride's father convinced him not to quit. "Honor your commitment to finish the season," John Pride advised his son, according to *Reader's Digest.* "Then, if you choose not to play baseball that's fine. Just make sure it's your decision."

The Mets gave up on Pride after the 1992 season. "They told me I'd be better off signing with someone else," he recalled in the *Sporting News.* During the off-season Pride worked as a tutor for students with learning and physical disabilities. The determination and courage of his students inspired him, and he decided he could not give up on baseball. "I'd be letting them, and myself, down if I quit now," Pride explained to his mother, according to *Reader's Digest.*

NEW START. Fortunately, the Montreal Expos offered Pride a contract and a chance to play every day. Montreal general manager Dan Duquette told *Sports Illustrated* that he had a "chance to play every day in the big leagues." The Expos sent Pride to their Double A Harrisburg, Pennsylvania, farm club. His manager in Harrisburg convinced him to stop trying to hit for power and instead concentrate on using his speed to get on base. Pride batted .356, hit 15 home runs, had 39 runs batted in (RBI), and stole 21 bases in 50 games for Harrisburg.

Pride then moved up to the Triple A Ottawa Lynx, where he batted lead-off (first). "With Curtis as our centerfielder, it might sound kind of scary that we have a guy directing traffic out there who can't hear," Ottawa manager Mike Quade admitted in *Sports Illustrated.* "It hasn't been a factor." Pride continued to produce, hitting .302, with 6 home runs, 22 RBI, and 29 steals for Ottawa.

Superstar

STANDING OVATION. On September 11, 1993, the Expos called Pride up to the major leagues after the Ottawa season

WILLIAM ELLSWORTH HOY

The first deaf person to play in the major leagues was William Ellsworth Hoy. He played 14 seasons (1888—1902) with 6 different teams. He hit .287 in his career, with 40 home runs and 594 stolen bases. Because Hoy could not hear their calls, umpires began to use hand signals for balls and strikes.

ended. He became only the fifth deaf player in major league baseball. (The last was Dick Sipek, who batted .244 in 82 games with the Cincinnati Reds in 1945.) Pride made his big-league debut as a defensive replacement on September 14.

Pride's first major-league hit was a big one. On September 17, he pinch-hit (batted as a substitute) with two runners on base and the Philadelphia Phillies leading the Expos 7-4 in the seventh inning. Phillies relief pitcher Bobby Thigpen threw Pride a slider, and the young hitter drove it into the gap between the outfielders all the way to the wall. He slid into second base with a double, driving in two runs.

Standing on second base, Pride did not realize that the 45,000 fans in the crowd were giving him a standing ovation. His third base coach, Jerry Manuel, called him over and told him to tip his hat because the fans were cheering. Pride took his cap off and waved to the crowd. Even though he could not hear the ovation, he could feel the noise vibrate throughout the stadium. "It brought tears to my eyes," Pride recalled in the *Detroit Free Press.* "It still does when I watch it on a tape I have." The Expos went on to win the game in extra innings.

Pride finished his first major-league stint with 4 hits in 9 at-bats—a .444 average—and 5 RBI. Expos manager Felipe Alou liked what he saw of his young outfielder. "He's a terrific fastball hitter," Alou stated in the *Sporting News.* "He has power, speed, and confidence. You know, when he first got here last September, we worried about him. How to treat him. But after three days we forgot he couldn't hear. Curt's just a normal player."

TIGER BY THE TAIL. Hampered by a strained stomach muscle and a sore left thumb, Pride hit only .111 in the spring training of 1994. Montreal sent him back to the Ottawa farm team. Despite returning to the minors, Pride thought he had made an impression. "Playing in the majors showed me that I've come a long way," he explained in *Sports Illustrated for Kids*. "It showed others they can be successful in whatever they put their minds to."

Pride spent the entire 1994 season in the minors, hitting .257 at Ottawa. He then bounced back and forth between Ottawa, where he led the Lynx to the International League Championship, and the Expos in 1995. Pride could only manage a .175 average in Montreal, however, and the Expos released him after the 1995 season.

The Detroit Tigers—a rebuilding team looking for young talent—invited Pride to tryout in spring training. "He's an interesting player," Detroit general manager Randy Smith stated in the *Detroit Free Press*. "He's obviously a good athlete—a guy who can run well and has some pop in his bat."

Pride hit .265 during the Tigers' spring training camp in 1996, but he did not know if that would be good enough to make the team. "There were a lot of sleepless nights for me," he admitted in the *Detroit Free Press*. "I would just toss and turn and wonder if I was going to make it. I've worked really hard, and I've shown what I can do. I've put up good numbers, but I knew it would be close." When the final cuts came and went, Pride was still on the team. He would start a season in the major leagues for the first time in his career.

The 1996 Detroit Tigers were a terrible club. They lost 109 games—a franchise record—and finished with the worst record in major league baseball. One bright spot for the Tigers was Pride, who batted .300, hit 10 home runs, and stole 11 bases. "It has been a good season for me but a tough season because we've been losing a lot," he admitted in the *Detroit Free Press*. "My goal now is to be an everyday player in the majors."

Pride's play impressed manager Buddy Bell. "I think Curtis has had a good year," Bell told the *Detroit Free Press*. "He's been an important guy for us coming off the bench. But I've told him that he's got to improve his defense to get more playing time."

JUST A BALLPLAYER

Pride does not want people to treat him any differently than they would anyone else. "I'm successful because my handicap made me work harder," he stated in the *Sporting News*. "I'm not trying to prove myself to others. But for my own self-esteem. A lot of handicapped people worry about what people think of them. I used to, too. Now I don't because I can't control that. I just focus on what I have to do. My handicap forces me to focus better. It frees me from unpleasantness around me. I can't let my mind wander. All my life, I worked hard to be normal. To prove I wasn't stupid. I never thought there was anything I couldn't do. I'm not afraid of anything. My handicap taught me not to quit. Not to need sympathy from people or have them treat me differently. I think I've been fortunate. I had talent, a good family, people to support me. I get a lot of affection from people pulling for me. I'm lucky."

SPECIAL PLAYER. As a deaf player, Pride has to work harder to be successful. Since he cannot hear the crack of the bat, he has to rely on his vision to get a good jump on fly balls hit to the outfield. "I can tell how hard a ball is hit by the angle it comes off the bat," Pride explained to *Sports Illustrated*. "If I misjudge the ball, I have my foot speed to make up for it."

When batting Pride has to look back at the umpire to find out if each pitch is a ball or strike. Some umpires have gotten mad at him, thinking he is questioning their calls. To prevent problems, Pride's manager reminds the umpire before each game about his deafness.

Pride has great speed, but he has to run with his head up at all times, watching his coaches to know when to take an extra base. Most importantly, he must concentrate very hard and learn about the game. "I have to put 100 percent concentration into every second," Pride admitted in the *Sporting News*.

OFF THE FIELD. Pride is single and lives in West Palm Beach, Florida. He receives a lot of fan mail, much of it from deaf and handicapped children. Pride is a spokesperson for the Better Hearing Institute and spends much of his time speaking to groups that support the hearing impaired. In the off-season, he tutors handicapped and learning disabled students. The television show "48 Hours" did a report on Pride during the 1996 season. He likes to fish and play on his computer. When his career is over, Pride wants to be a financial counselor or investment banker.

Being the only deaf person playing professional baseball, Pride wants to be a role model for hearing impaired children. "My message for people with disabilities—or to any person who has been told he can't do something—is simple," he explained in *Reader's Digest*. "Ignore it. The answers are inside your own heart."

Sources

Detroit Free Press, February 24, 1996; March 30, 1996; August 6, 1996; August 8, 1996; September 26, 1996.
Reader's Digest, May 1994.
Sporting News, May 2, 1994.
Sports Illustrated, July 12, 1993.
Sports Illustrated for Kids, September 1994.
Additional information provided by the Detroit Tigers.

WHERE TO WRITE:
C/O DETROIT TIGERS,
2121 TRUMBULL AVENUE,
DETROIT, MI 48216.

Dot Richardson

1961—

"When you watch me play, I hope you see an expression of pure joy."—Dot Richardson.

Dot Richardson is a surgeon, on the softball field and off. As an orthopedic surgeon, her scalpel helps patients recover from their muscle and bone injuries. As a member of the U.S. national team, Richardson uses her bat and glove to operate on the best female softball players in the world. Richardson's career is a perfect example of how hard work and not giving up can make a dream come true.

Growing Up

SUPPORTIVE FAMILY. Dorothy Gay Richardson was born September 22, 1961, in Orlando, Florida. Her father, Ken, is a retired Air Force mechanic. Richardson—who spent much of her childhood living on military bases—credits her family with encouraging her. "There's a drive within my family to see how high you can go and what you can reach," she explained in *Southern Living*. Richardson's mother and father had high hopes for their daughter. "The whole family always knew that Dorothy was going to turn out to be something," her mother, Joyce, told *People Weekly*. "We just didn't know what."

Richardson's parents excelled in athletics. "My dad was a football, baseball, track-and-field, and basketball player," Richardson explained in *People Weekly*. "My mom was a cheerleader who ran faster than my dad, so he says."

"BOB." Richardson began playing baseball at an early age. Although she showed excellent skills, at the time the local Little League team would not take girls. "I'd understand if I didn't have a strong arm," Richardson admitted in the *New York Times Magazine*. "But I was just as good as the boys, if not better." Her parents told her not to pitch to boys, because their parents got mad when she struck them out.

A coach of a boy's team wanted to sneak Richardson onto his squad. "Honey, we'd love to have you on our team," the coach told her, according to *Sports Illustrated*. "If you don't mind, we'll just cut your hair and call you Bob." The incident hurt Richardson's feelings. "I was crushed, because I had this dream and all of a sudden the loss was right in front of me because I would have to change who I am," she recalled in the *San Jose Mercury News*.

GETS HER CHANCE. Luckily, one day the coach of the Union Park Jets women's softball team saw Richardson playing. The coach invited her for a tryout. "I didn't even know there was women's softball," Richardson admitted in the *New York Times Magazine*. "I said, 'not another rejection.'"

Richardson should not have worried because the coach invited her to join the team. She was 10 years old and the average age of the team was 26. Not only did Richardson play, she made the league's all-star team. "I was so happy that

DOT IN A BOX

Richardson is a very energetic person. Her parents say she has always been that way. "Dorothy never walked as a baby," Joyce Richardson recalled in *People Weekly*. "She ran." Once her parents put Richardson in a box during a cross-country trip because she was crawling all over the car. "We put her in a box in the backseat," Ken Richardson told *Sports Illustrated*. "That's how she got across the country—in a box."

when I said my prayers at night, I'd say, 'If I should die before I wake, please God, let there be a softball field in Heaven,'" she recalled in *People Weekly*.

At age 13, Richardson became the youngest player ever in the national Women's Major Fast Pitch league, starring for the Orlando Rebels. She played for two years before needing to make a decision. Richardson could turn professional—and make money for playing—or remain an amateur, or unpaid, player. In the end she decided to remain an amateur, because she hoped that one day woman's softball would be added as an Olympic sport. What Richardson did not know is that she would have to wait 20 years for her dream to come true.

HIGH SCHOOL STAR. Richardson starred in five sports during her junior high days—softball, basketball, tennis, volleyball, and track and field. "Dorothy could have excelled in any sport," Joyce Richardson stated in *People Weekly*. Richardson played softball during junior high, despite the fact that other kids teased her. Other girls quit playing because of the pressure. "They didn't want to be stereotyped," Richardson explained in the *New York Times*. "They had trouble getting dates. Guys would say to them, 'Why do you want to be like a man?' They would get pressure from their parents. I was lucky. Through all the years I've played, my mom never said, 'Dot, you should think about quitting, about getting married.'"

PLAYER OF THE DECADE. Richardson earned all-conference honors in tennis, softball, and track and field while attending Colonial High School. When it came time to choose a college, Richardson picked Western Illinois University. She played there for one year, leading the nation with a .480 average in softball while also playing basketball and field hockey.

Richardson then transferred to the University of California at Los Angeles (UCLA), where she led the Bruins to the first-

Tagging out the competition, Richardson (right) helped the United States to win a gold medal during the 1996 Summer Olympics.

ever National Collegiate Athletic Association (NCAA) women's softball championship. She led UCLA in hitting for three straight seasons, earning All-American honors each year. The NCAA named Richardson the woman's softball Player of the Decade for the 1980s. She also played junior varsity basketball for the Bruins.

DR. DOT. Richardson also had another dream: she began studying medicine at UCLA. "Those are my passions, medicine and softball," she stated in *Sports Illustrated*. Richardson completed the pre-med curriculum at UCLA, then attended medical school at the University of Louisville. She studied to become an orthopedic surgeon, a doctor who treats people with bone and muscle problems. "I would frequently be playing a doubleheader, and then sprinting to the opposite end of the campus for my chem lab," Richardson recalled in *People Weekly*. "I'd still be in my uniform, dirty from sliding."

After graduating from medical school, Richardson continued her medical training at the University of Southern California (USC). The young surgeon installed a pitching machine and net in the bedroom of her apartment so that she could practice her swing at night after coming home from the hospital. Richardson practiced late into the night, driving her neighbors crazy. But the hard work paid off: she signed a bat endorsement contract, the first woman to be so honored.

FREQUENT FLYER. Keeping both of her dreams alive has often been difficult for Richardson. "I've had to juggle my sport and medicine for a couple of years," she admitted in *Southern Living*. "I was prepared at one point to give up softball. When I was accepted to medical school, I felt that was what God wanted me to do." To protect her hands for her future as a surgeon, Richardson decided to slide feet-first only.

In order to continue playing softball while studying at Louisville, Richardson had to fly each weekend during the season to Stratford, Connecticut. There she would play for the Raybestos Brakettes, a national championship softball team. "I'd fly cross-country, be picked up at the airport by a fan and driven to the field, changing clothes in the car because I didn't want to wear my uniform on the plane," Richardson recalled in *Southern Living*. "My teammates would see me running onto the field in the second inning of a doubleheader game to jump in at shortstop." Her coach on the Brakettes, Ralph Raymond, gave her the nickname "Tiger."

Besides playing on the Brakettes, Richardson also became a fixture on the U.S. national team. She played shortstop and batted lead-off (first) on almost every national team for two decades. Richardson played for three Pan American

Game champions and three International Softball Federation world champions. Three times she won most valuable player honors at the Amateur Softball Association (ASA) national championship, 14 times the ASA named Richardson to its All-American team, and six times she won the Erv Lind Award, given to the outstanding defensive player at the ASA national championship.

KEEPING THE DREAM ALIVE. Still, Richardson's dream of playing in the Olympics did not come true. "When we didn't make it into the games in '92, I felt like I'd missed my last shot at the Olympics," she admitted in *Esquire*. Richardson—now 30—did not give up, even though some experts said she was over the hill.

The drive to include women's softball in the Olympics began in 1965. At the time, only five national teams existed to compete in the first-ever world championship, far short of the forty teams required for recognition as an Olympic sport. The International Softball Federation established clinics and held exhibition games throughout the world. Soon, women in many countries were playing softball.

The Olympic dream of Richardson and thousands of other women came true when the International Olympic Committee announced they would include women's softball in the 1996 Summer Olympics in Atlanta, Georgia. U.S.A. Softball announced the women's team in September 1995, and Richardson made the squad.

"I can only imagine the Olympics," Richardson confessed in *Southern Living*. "When I'm jogging or running around, I think about how it will feel to enter that Olympic stadium for the first game, going for the gold medal—and winning. You cry for the people who didn't make it who are deserving and for those who played before you who weren't in any Olympic Games. I hope and pray that anyone who has ever seen me, played against me, or played with me knows I'm there to represent her."

The American Medical Association gave Richardson a one-year leave of absence from her surgical training to play in the Olympics. The leave ended the day after the Olympic soft-ball competition's championship game. "Two days after the gold medal game, I have to go back to work," Richardson explained in *Sports Illustrated for Kids*.

Superstar

DREAM TEAM. Woman's softball experts rated the U.S. team as the overwhelming favorite to win the gold medal at the Olympics. The team had a 110-1 record over the last decade and outscored their last 61 opponents leading up to the Olympics by a cumulative score of 441-3. The one loss suffered by the Americans came at the hands of the People's Republic of China in the fall of 1995, a defeat that ended a 106-game winning streak. The U.S. team came back, however, and defeated China, 8-0, in the championship game of the same tournament.

Richardson enjoyed the fact that other teams were closing the gap with the Americans. "Not winning by as large a margin anymore makes it exciting," she admitted in *Southern Living*. "In 1982, we beat China 38 to 0 in 4 1/2 innings. Four years later, we beat China 2-1 for the world championship. That shows how other countries have developed in such a short time."

GOING FOR GOLD. In the first-ever women's Olympic softball game—a 10-0 U.S. victory over Puerto Rico—Richardson got the first hit, scored the first run, and hit the first home run. "I had a lot of dreams about hitting that first homer," she said after the game. "I was looking for my parents in the stands as I came around the bases, because they knew what I had dreamed. I'm feeling things I've never felt before."

The U.S. team suffered their first loss in Olympic competition when Australia defeated them, 2-0, in 10 innings. Despite the loss, the Americans easily reached the semifinals, where they faced their old nemesis, the Chinese. In another 10-inning struggle, the United States prevailed, 1-0, earning a place in the gold-medal game.

SHOT HEARD 'ROUND THE WORLD. In the gold-medal game the United States once again faced the Chinese, who earned their place in the title game with a 4-2 win against the Australians. The game was a classic between the two best teams in the world. In the top of the third inning, Richardson threw a runner out at the plate on a controversial play to keep the game scoreless.

In the bottom of the third, Laura Berg led off for the United States with a single up the middle. The next batter was Richardson. She faced Liu Yaju of China, a pitcher with an 0.40 earned run average (ERA) in 15 previous Olympic tournament innings. The first pitch to Richardson was a strike, but on the second offering she swung, blasting a curving drive down the right field line.

As the ball disappeared over the fence, the U.S. team held its breath. That is until the umpire signaled that the ball was fair, curving around the foul pole, even though it landed in foul territory in the seats. The Chinese argued that the ball went foul, but replays showed it was fair. "I have felt that swing over and over again, and the feeling will never leave me," Richardson stated in *People Weekly*.

The United States scored one more run in the third inning, then tried to hold on to their 3-0 lead. The Chinese scored one run in the sixth off starting pitcher Michele Granger, but **Lisa Fernandez** came on in relief to get out of the jam. She struck out the first three Chinese batters she faced in the seventh to clinch the gold medal with a 3-1 victory. "I think we'll never be the same," Richardson admitted in *People Weekly*. "My cleats never touched the ground."

After the victory, Richardson acted as host for an interview with the team on NBC. When she returned to USC, the school's marching band played for her. Richardson let sick children try on her medal when she visited the pediatric ward. "Everybody shared in it," she explained to *People Weekly*. "I never stopped smiling." Richardson was also thrilled to learn that she came in second place in voting for the U.S. Olympic

LIVE YOUR DREAM

Richardson did not have many softball role models growing up. She hopes the exposure women's softball received during the Olympics gets more girls involved in sports. "As an Olympian, I think it's important to give back," Richardson stated in the *San Jose Mercury News.* "I hope to give back in competition, if I can, and also do more clinics and camps and appearances and speaking because I didn't have those role models when I was young. I hope that I can develop into a role model for young girls, if they feel that I'm worth enough."

Richardson likes to tell kids to work hard to make their dreams come true. "When you have a passion for something, you can overcome all obstacles," she explained in *Women's Sports and Fitness.* "Having that drive in sports has given me the drive in medicine. I'm the luckiest woman alive. I'm living the two dreams of my life."

Committee's Sportswoman of the Year award. (American swimmer **Amy Van Dyken** was the winner.)

OFF THE FIELD. Richardson is single and is finishing her training at USC. She has two brothers and two sisters. As a result of her Olympic success, Richardson now endorses gloves for Rawlings. The Colorado Silver Bullets—a women's professional baseball team—offered to sign Richardson, but she turned them down. "I admire them, but I think softball is the way for women to go," she explained in the *New York Times.*

Richardson says that softball has aided her preparation for a career in medicine, helping her to develop her concentration, deal with stress, and set priorities. She hopes to keep playing as long as she can. "After the Games, I'll compete as long as it doesn't hinder my career," Richardson told *Southern Living.* "I just love orthopedic surgery. Whether it's a child with a birth defect whom I'm able to help walk better or an athlete working to get back on the field in a safe way, it's very rewarding."

Softball is one of the loves of Richardson's life, and she hopes it shows on the field, as she told the *Oregonian:* "When you watch me play, I hope you see an expression of pure joy."

Sources

Columbus Ledger-Enquirer, August 4, 1995; September 4, 1995.
Daily Oklahoman, September 5, 1996.
Dallas Morning News, September 5, 1995.
Esquire, July 1996.
Hartford Courant, July 23, 1995.
New York Times Magazine, June 23, 1996.
Oregonian, July 24, 1995.

People Weekly, June 24, 1996; August 19, 1996.
Sacramento Bee, April 28, 1996.
San Jose Mercury News, July 27, 1995.
Southern Living, February 1996.
Sports Illustrated, July 18, 1994.
Sports Illustrated for Kids, July 1996.
Women's Sports and Fitness, July/August 1996.
Additional information provided by the Amateur Softball Association of America and UCLA.

 WHERE TO WRITE:
C/O AMATEUR SOFTBALL ASSOCIATION,
2801 NE 50TH STREET,
OKLAHOMA CITY, OK 73111-7203.

Mitch Richmond

1965—

Mitch Richmond is the best-kept secret in the National Basketball Association (NBA). The shooting guard of the Sacramento Kings has averaged over 21 points per game in each of his first eight seasons, only the seventh NBA player to accomplish this feat. Despite his consistent excellence, Richmond has not gained the national exposure that other NBA stars receive. In 1996, however, the NBA recognized the Kings' star by naming him to the men's basketball "Dream Team III" that represented the United States at the Summer Olympics in Atlanta, Georgia.

Growing Up

MITCH AND MOM. Mitchell James Richmond was born June 30, 1965, in Fort Lauderdale, Florida. His mother—Ernell O'Neal—has always been his best friend. "We were always close," O'Neal recalled in *Sports Illustrated.* "I wouldn't let him sleep over at his friends' houses. I wanted to know where he was at night." Richmond sang in a church choir when he was a child and dreamed of becoming a singer someday. His favorite singer was Marvin Gaye.

GROWTH SPURT. Richmond's favorite sport as a child was football. His boyhood friend was Michael Irvin, now a wide receiver with the Dallas Cowboys. Richmond also hung out with future National Football League (NFL) players Brett Perriman and Benny and Brian Blades. "I played football until the tenth grade," he recalled in the *Sacramento Observer.* "I enjoyed basketball though, especially after I started getting taller."

Richmond took up basketball after experiencing a growth spurt as a teenager. Soon the game became his first love. "Ever since he hit that basketball, he's known where he was going," Ernell O'Neal explained in *Sports Illustrated.* "Everything has gone so well." His basketball idol as a child was Julius "Dr. J" Erving, the legendary star of the Philadelphia 76ers.

Richmond began playing organized basketball in tenth grade. He started on the varsity team and scored thirteen points in his first game, despite suffering from a bad case of nerves. "That definitely was big for me," Richmond recalled to the Associated Press. "Just being nervous, jittery like I am now before games. I was really shaky before that one. I wasn't used to playing in front of a crowd. That was my first time playing basketball in front of people."

MOM'S SUPPORT. Richmond struggled in high school to keep his grades high enough to play basketball. He attended three high schools in the Fort Lauderdale area. Richmond credits his mother with helping him make it through. "She's definitely been behind me every step of the way," he admitted in the *San Antonio Express-News.* "She always told me she did it for my own good. I remember she pulled me off the teams a cou-

Richmond is fouled while going for two.

ple of times. At the time, I didn't understand it. But she always told me I had to get the grades to make it."

At the end of his senior year, Richmond was one-half credit short of the total he needed to graduate. He thought about quitting school—and giving up a basketball scholarship—when he discovered he would not graduate with his classmates. O'Neal would not let her son quit, telling him, according to *Sports Illustrated:* "You need three weeks of summer school to go to college, to get a $100,000 scholarship, and you don't want to do it? I've got news for you, Mitchell, you're going to summer school. You're going to prove to that teacher that you can do something with your life."

HOMESICK. Richmond attended Moberly Area Junior College in Moberly, Missouri, after earning his high school diploma in summer school. Being so far away from home made the young player homesick. Several times Richmond went to his coach, Dana Altman, saying he wanted to quit. "He really struggled with homesickness," Altman told *Sports Illustrated*. Altman spent time with Richmond, and O'Neal encouraged her son to stick it out.

HIGHER LEARNING. Richmond averaged 13.1 points at Moberly and led the team to a 69-9 record in his two seasons there. He earned Junior College All-America honors his senior season. Richmond credits Altman with transforming his game. In high school he could play forward and overpower smaller opponents. To succeed in college, however, Richmond had to play guard. Altman worked to improve his player's outside shot. Richmond also learned another important lesson at Moberly. "I learned to study," he explained in *Sports Illustrated.*

WILDCAT WONDER. Before the 1986—87 season Kansas State University offered Altman a position as an assistant coach. He accepted and brought his best player along with him. Richmond became a national star during his senior season (1987—88) with the Wildcats. He averaged 22.6 points, 6.3 rebounds, and 3.7 assists per game, and shot .469 from beyond the 3-point arc. Richmond set the Kansas State single-season record for most points in a season (768), scored more points at the school than any other 2-year player (1327), and earned second team All-American honors.

Richmond played his best in the National Collegiate Athletic Association (NCAA) tournament. He averaged 26.7 points and 9.2 rebounds in 8 tournament games during his career. In his senior year, Richmond led Kansas State to the Elite Eight of the tournament. The Wildcats lost in the Midwest Regional Finals to arch-rival Kansas, led by Danny Manning, now with the Phoenix Suns. "However far we went, Mitch got us there," Altman confessed in *Sports Illustrated*.

In his senior season, Richmond learned to be a leader at Kansas State. "The biggest compliment you can pay Mitch is to say how his teammates feel about him from Moberly to Kansas State," Altman explained in *Sports Illustrated*. "Everyone wants him to be successful." Richmond was also a success in the classroom. He earned his degree in social studies. O'Neal traveled to Kansas and proudly attended the graduation ceremonies.

OLYMPICS I. Richmond got his first taste of international competition in 1987, participating on the silver-medal-winning U.S. World University Games team in Zagreb, Yugoslavia. He led the team in scoring with 16.7 points a game.

In 1988, Richmond tried out for and made the men's basketball team that represented the United States at the Summer Olympics in Seoul, South Korea. The Americans lost to the Soviet Union in the semifinals, 82-76. "I can't even remember what happened during the loss to the Soviets," Richmond recalled in *Newsday*. "I can remember going back to the hotel after the game. It was the longest bus ride I ever took."

The United States defeated Australia to win the bronze medal, but the team's performance disappointed Richmond. "It [the loss to the Soviet Union] was devastating, probably the most devastating thing that's ever happened to me in sports," he explained to *Newsday*. Richmond averaged 8.9 points, 3.4 rebounds, and 2.1 assists in 8 games. He did not think he would ever have another chance to win an Olympic gold medal.

RUN TMC. The Golden State Warriors chose Richmond with the fifth overall pick in the 1988 NBA Draft. With the Warriors he teamed was with forward Chris Mullin and point guard Tim Hardaway to form the "Run TMC" high-scoring trio that helped the Warriors lead the NBA in offense for two out of three seasons from 1989-1990. (TMC stood for Tim, Mitch, and Chris.) His new teammates gave Richmond the nicknames Rock and Hammer. "I like to call him Rock, as in rock solid," Mullin declared in *Sports Illustrated*. "He's a hard body."

ROOKIE OF THE YEAR. Richmond made an instant impression on the NBA. He averaged 22 points (sixteenth in NBA), 5.9 rebounds, and 4.2 assists per game his first season. Those numbers were good enough to earn Richmond the 1988—89 NBA Rookie of the Year award. "What I love most about Mitch is that he's raw," Golden State coach Don Nelson stated in *Sports Illustrated*. "He's just starting to blossom as a player and as a human being. It's a wonderful time for him. Mitch is doing just about everything I've asked of him. I need him to be dominant, but in the flow of the team, and he's doing that."

TOUGH TRADE. While the Warriors were the top offensive team in the NBA, they suffered defensively because they did not have a quality big man. In order to fill this need Golden State traded Richmond and Les Jespen to the Sacramento Kings in exchange for forward Billy Owens. Parting with Richmond was a difficult decision since he had averaged 22.7 points per game in his 3 seasons with the Warriors.

The trade hurt Richmond, who liked his teammates on the Warriors. He also did not want to go to Sacramento, a team that had never made the playoffs since moving to that city. Richmond walked out of the locker room before his first game with the Kings and was very unhappy. "Those were tough times," he explained in the *San Antonio Express-Times.* "I liked the team I was on [the Warriors]. I felt it needed just a couple of pieces to get to the next level. It was heart-breaking to leave them."

ALL-STAR. Richmond began to earn recognition during the 1992—93 season. For the first time Western Conference coaches named him to the NBA All-Star Game, in his fifth NBA season. Richmond was the first Kings player to make the team since the franchise moved to Sacramento. It was the first of four straight elections to the big game for the high-scoring guard. "I've been disappointed that I never made it before," Richmond told the *Sporting News.* "I think I was good enough. That's been a goal of mine since I came into the league. And you're not totally happy until you reach your goals." A broken right thumb forced Richmond to miss his first all-star game and the rest of the 1992—93 season.

In 1994 and 1995, Richmond earned second team All-NBA honors, the first Kings player to make the list since guard Otis Birdsong in 1981. Unfortunately, Sacramento could not earn its way into the playoffs. "It's so frustrating," Richmond admitted in *USA Today.* "I've been on a losing team three years. You don't want to be considered a loser. You've got to play through it."

Superstar

MVP. In 1995, Richmond earned the NBA All-Star Game Most Valuable Player Award in the game played in Phoenix, Arizona. He scored a game-high 23 points, grabbed 4 rebounds, and dished out 2 assists in only 22 minutes of action. Richmond made 10 of 13 shots, including 3 for 3 from 3-point range. "It hasn't been great playing in Sacramento the last few years because of our record, but this year, I could come to the all-star game with my head up high and say with pride that I am a Sacramento King," he told *Jet.*

Richmond's mother was at the game sharing in her son's extraordinary achievement. "She was at the game, and that made it special," Richmond confessed in the *San Antonio Express-News*. "To see her face and to see her smile like that, it was nice." Sacramento declared March 1, 1995 as "Mitch Richmond Day." Sacramento won 39 games in the 1994—95 season, barely missing the playoffs.

FINALLY. During the 1995—96 season, Richmond led the Kings to their first-ever playoff appearance since the franchise moved to Sacramento during the 1995—96 season. The last time the team made the NBA playoffs was ten years before, in 1986. Despite a 3-1 first-round loss to the Seattle Supersonics, Richmond felt that the future looked bright. "We have a good team," he explained in the *San Antonio Express-News*. "We have a lot of guys who can play. The sky is the limit for this team."

Richmond led the Kings with a 23.1 per game scoring average, becoming only the seventh player to average over 21 or more points in each of his first eight seasons. He had the ninth-highest 3-point shot percentage in the league (.437) and made the second most 3-point shots, hitting 225 of 515. When Richmond entered the NBA his outside shot was his major weakness, but his hard work made this part of his game a strength. "He's a great player and a hard worker," teammate Tyus Edney told the *San Antonio Express-News*. "He brings it every night. You know he's going to play as well as he can to help you win the game."

DREAM TEAM III. Richmond finally took his place among the best players in the world when the NBA named him to the "Dream Team III" squad that represented the United States at the 1996 Summer Olympics in Atlanta, Georgia. Playing in the Olympics again gave him a second chance to earn an Olympic gold medal. "I never knew if I would get this opportunity to go back to the Olympics again, so I'm happy to be

MR. CONSISTENCY

When Richmond averaged 23.1 points per game in the 1995—96 season, he joined an elite group of players who have averaged more than 21 points per game in their first 8 seasons. The following chart lists these players and the years during which they accomplished this feat.

Player	Years
Wilt Chamberlain	1960—66
Oscar Robertson	1961—67
Rick Barry	1966—73
Kareem Abdul-Jabbar	1970—76
Larry Bird	1980—86
Michael Jordan	1985—91
Mitch Richmond	1989—96

WHY "DREAM TEAMS"?

The loss by the U.S. men's basketball team at the 1988 Summer Olympics in Seoul, South Korea, set off shock waves throughout international basketball. Improved competition in the rest of the world made it impossible for American college players to win. Before the 1992 Olympics, the International Basketball Federation voted to allow professional players to participate. "I think it's good the pros are here because the college players are no longer guaranteed to win," Richmond, who played on the last U.S. Olympic men's basketball team to feature college players, admitted in *Newsday.*

here," Richmond explained in *Newsday.* "I'm trying to reverse what happened to me eight years ago."

American Olympic men's basketball coach Lenny Wilkens—who leads the Atlanta Hawks in the NBA—gained new respect for Richmond when he saw him play in practice. "Now that I've had a chance to spend some time with him, I've come to realize how hard he works," Wilkens told the Gannett News Service. "He can defend and play on both ends of the court. For years he's had to carry the offensive load with the Kings but he's a [great] all-around player. People don't appreciate all the things he can do."

Richmond looked at his "Dream Team" selection as a chance to show the world that he was one of the best players in the world. "Basically I just want to show people what I can do," Richmond stated in the Gannett News Service. "I want to play well, play hard and help us win. We have a lot of great players on this team, but I have a role, maybe a big role. Maybe this experience will open some doors for me, show people what I'm about. That would be nice." The "Dream Team" easily won the Olympic gold medal. Richmond played every game, averaging 9.6 points, 1.6 rebounds, and 1.3 assists in 8 U.S. victories.

UNKNOWN KING? Playing in Sacramento has made Richmond one of the NBA's best-kept secrets. The Kings play in the smallest media market in the league and have been in the playoffs only once since Richmond joined the team. Even though he has put up great numbers, Richmond has not been voted a starter on an all-star team and was passed over for the first two "Dream Team" squads.

Richmond does not call attention to himself by making flashy plays or trash-talking, and his steady play does not create many plays for highlight films. "I'm not the high-flying dunker or anything fancy," he admitted in *Sports Illustrated.* "Maybe my game isn't what they want for the commercials and the TV appearances. It bothered me a little when I was younger, but I don't worry about it anymore. If the recognition comes, it comes. If not, I'll just keep doing what I've been doing."

The high-scoring guard is also proud of his consistently excellent play. "I'm proud of the fact that I've been consistent in this league, consistent almost every night," Richmond told *Newsday.* "What you see is what you get. I'm very happy where I'm at. I think my numbers stack up with anyone's. Maybe it's good that I don't play in a place like New York. Maybe I wouldn't handle myself as well if I was a big-market guy. Maybe playing in Sacramento is a blessing."

Richmond can make the three-point shot, hit jumpers when defended, and drive to the goal. He is also a physical defender and good rebounder for a guard. "Mitch can post you up, shoot the jump shot, put the ball on the floor and drive past you—and he plays defense," former NBA guard Doc Rivers told *Sports Illustrated.* "If you trap him, he finds the open man. If you don't trap him, he scores. Pick your poison. He's a great, unselfish player, and that's the worst kind."

In his career, Richmond has never averaged less than 21 points per game, a remarkable record of consistency. His career scoring average at the end of the 1995—96 season was 22.8, a mark that ranks him in the top-ten among active players. "From the day he walked in as a rookie with Golden State, he was a guy you could count on to give you two things: about 20 points a night and every ounce of effort he had," Sacramento coach Gary St. Jean explained in *Sports Illustrated.* "And he could do it without ever once calling attention to himself."

OFF THE COURT. Richmond lives in Granite Bay, California, with his wife Julianna and their children, Phillip and Jerin. He likes to listen to music, go to plays, play video games, and bowl. Beside basketball, Richmond also follows boxing, football, and track and field. His favorite athletes are Jackie Joyner-Kersee, Mike Tyson, Evander Holyfield, and Hakeem Olajuwon; his favorite singers are Marvin Gaye, Luther Vandross, and Babyface.

Richmond likes to make his teammates laugh by imitating other NBA players, including Hakeem Olajuwon and Alonzo Mourning. "I'm telling you, there's nobody in the league I can't do," Richmond bragged in *Sports Illustrated.* "I watch a lot of tape and pick things up like that."

Richmond is involved with "Smart Clothes," a fashion design business. He sponsors the Solid As a Rock foundation that grants scholarships to high school-student athletes from his hometown of Fort Lauderdale, Florida. The National Committee to Prevent Child Abuse gave Richmond the Special Friend Award for the commercials he did that highlighted this problem.

Richmond is now happy to play for Sacramento. "There were a lot of things here I didn't like at first," he confessed in the *Sporting News.* "But we've got a new owner, a new coach and a new attitude. I know we're headed up." The Kings are glad to have him as the foundation around whom they can build a winning tradition. "Talk about the Kings, and you start with Mitch Richmond," St. Jean told the *San Antonio Express-News.* "He's one of the finest two guards in the league."

The Kings hope that Richmond can continue to star for many years to come. "Things have been happening to me all my life," he told *Sports Illustrated.* They pop up, and I see if I can handle them. So far, I've been doing pretty well."

Sources

Jet, February 27, 1995.
Newsday, February 11, 1996; July 20, 1996.
Sacramento Observer, February 22, 1995; April 19, 1995.
Sporting News, January 18, 1993; January 15, 1996.
Sports Illustrated, February 6, 1989; December 4, 1995; April 15, 1996.
Sports Illustrated for Kids, August 1996.
Time, April 29, 1996.
USA Today, January 4, 1994.

Additional information provided by the Gannett News Service, the Sacramento
Kings and USA Basketball.

 WHERE TO WRITE:

C/O SACRAMENTO KINGS,
1 SPORTS PARKWAY,
SACRAMENTO, CA 95834.

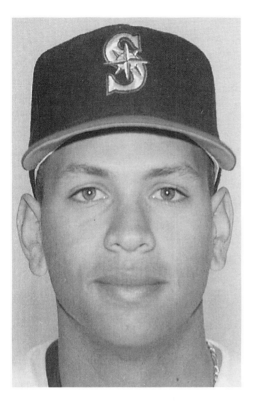

Alex Rodriguez

1975—

When he was a child, Alex Rodriguez of the Seattle Mariners idolized Cal Ripken Jr., the legendary shortstop of the Baltimore Orioles. In 1996, Rodriguez produced what many experts believe is one of the greatest seasons a shortstop has ever had. He led the American League in hitting (.358), doubles (54), and runs (141). As Ripken's career comes to an end, Rodriguez is the greatest bet to replace his hero as the best all-around shortstop in baseball.

Growing Up

BEST FRIEND. Alexander Emmanual Rodriguez was born July 27, 1975, in New York City. His parents moved to the Dominican Republic when he was four years old. Rodriguez's father, Victor, played catcher in professional baseball in the Dominican Republic during the 1970s.

Rodriguez and his family moved to Miami, Florida, when he was in fifth grade, and soon after the move, his parents divorced. The breakup was hard on Rodriguez. "I kept thinking my father would come back, but he never did," he admitted in *Sports Illustrated*. "But it was O.K. All the love I had for him I just gave to my mother. She deserved it. Sometimes people ask why I still live at home, and I say, 'Why shouldn't I? I like living with my mother. She's one of my best friends.'"

His mother, Lourdes Navarro, raised Rodriguez, his brother, Joe, and his sister, Susy, on her own. "I always wanted to be like my dad," Rodriguez explained in *Sports Illustrated*. "But my mom is my role model." Navarro worked as a secretary and waitress so that her son could attend private school.

STARTS PLAYING. Rodriguez got his start playing baseball while his family was still living in the Dominican Republic. "In the [Dominican Republic], playing ball was tougher," he explained in *Sports Illustrated*. "No one had anything. In the United States there were $200 gloves, and the fields were like paradise."

Rodriguez grew up idolizing Baltimore Orioles shortstop Cal Ripken Jr. and former Atlanta Braves star Dale Murphy. He chose number 3 because that was Murphy's number. "My mom always said, 'I don't care if you turn out to be a terrible ballplayer, I just want you to be a good person,'" Rodriguez recalled in *Sports Illustrated*. "That's the most important thing to me. Like Cal or Dale Murphy, I want people to look at me and say, 'He's a good person.'"

HIGH SCHOOL STAR. Rodriguez attended Westminster Christian High School in Miami. He helped make Westminster one of the most highly rated high school teams in the country. Rodriguez posted a .419 batting average in 3 seasons at the school, with 17 home runs, 70 runs batted in (RBI), and 100

SCOREBOARD

WON THE 1996 AMERICAN LEAGUE BATTING TITLE (.358), THE FIRST SHORTSTOP TO ACCOMPLISH THIS FEAT SINCE 1944.

IN 1996, SET SINGLE-SEASON RECORDS FOR MAJOR LEAGUE SHORTSTOPS IN THE FOLLOWING CATEGORIES: RUNS SCORED (141), HITS (215), DOUBLES (54), EXTRA BASE HITS (91), AND SLUGGING PERCENTAGE (.631).

VOTED 1996 *SPORTING NEWS* MAJOR LEAGUE PLAYER OF THE YEAR BY FELLOW PLAYERS.

RODRIGUEZ STANDS READY TO REPLACE HIS IDOL, CAL RIPKEN JR., AS THE BEST ALL-AROUND SHORTSTOP IN BASEBALL.

Shortstop Rodriguez making a spectacular throw.

stolen bases in 100 games. Westminster earned an 86-13-1 record during those three seasons.

During his senior season Rodriguez hit .505 with 9 home runs and 35 stolen bases in 35 attempts. Those numbers earned him several awards, including USA Baseball Junior Player of the Year and Gatorade's National Student Athlete of the Year in baseball. Rodriguez was the only high school player invited to try out for Team USA in 1993 and he played for the U.S. Junior National Team. "Coaching Alex is a once-in-a-lifetime experience," his high school coach Rich Hofman recalled in *Sports Illustrated*.

Rodriguez also excelled in football at Westminster, playing quarterback his junior year and leading the team to a 9-1 record. He considered playing both sports in college, but gave up football before his senior year in high school. In addition to his success on the athletic field, Rodriguez was an honor roll student.

TOP PICK. After graduating from high school, Rodriguez accepted a scholarship to play baseball at the University of Miami. Major league scouts, however, crowded around to see him play and practice in high school. Many experts said he would be the number-one pick in the 1993 major league baseball free-agent amateur draft.

"My mom told me that all the scouts are here because they see something they like," Rodriguez explained in *Sports Illustrated*. "She said, 'Don't change, just be yourself.'" The Seattle Mariners held the draft's first pick. The Mariners used their pick to choose the young shortstop. At first Rodriguez worried that Seattle would be too far away from home, but after lengthy negotiations he signed a three-year, $1.3 million contract.

CALLED UP. The Mariners sent Rodriguez to their Class A Appleton, Wisconsin, farm team in the spring of 1994. (A farm team is a minor-league team where young players learn to play as professionals.) He hit .319 in 65 games and earned a promotion to the Class AA Jacksonville, Florida, team.

Rodriguez batted .288 there in 17 games before Seattle manager Lou Pinella called him up to the majors. He was 18 years old at the time, only the third shortstop in history to make his major league debut at such a young age.

Center fielder Ken Griffey Jr.—who came to the majors at the age of 19—helped the rookie adjust to the big leagues. He insisted that Rodriguez take a locker next to his. "It's funny," Rodriguez explained in *Sports Illustrated*. "Last year I would have paid anything to go watch a major league game. This year I'm playing in one."

MAJOR LEAGUER. In July 1994, Rodriguez started his first game for the Mariners, playing in Fenway Park in Boston, Massachusetts. He went hitless in his first contest, but picked up his first two major-league hits in his second game, in addition to stealing a base. "I know I'm ready," Rodriguez told *Sports Illustrated*.

Rodriguez struggled in his first stint in the majors. He batted only .204 in 17 games and the Mariners sent him down to their Triple A Calgary team. Rodriguez returned to the Dominican Republic to play in the winter of 1994—95. "It was the toughest experience of my life," he admitted in *Sports Illustrated*. "I learned how hard this game can be. It was brutal, but I recommend it to every young player." Rodriguez batted only .179 during the winter, but the experience prepared him to return to the major leagues the next year.

COMEBACK. Rodriguez spent the early part of the 1995 season bouncing back and forth between Seattle and the minors. On August 31, he returned to the big-league Mariners permanently. Rodriguez—who batted only .232 in the majors for the season—served as a backup for starting shortstop Luis Sojo. From the Seattle dugout Rodriguez witnessed one of the most remarkable comebacks in major league history.

The Mariners trailed the California Angels in the American League West Division by 11 games on August 9. Going on an incredible hot streak, Seattle not only caught up to California, but took the division lead late in the season. The two teams finished the season tied, and Seattle won the deciding game, 9-1, behind their ace pitcher, Randy Johnson. The Mariners were in the playoffs for the first time in their history.

PLAYOFF BOUND. The Mariners lost the first two games of their best-of-five division series to the New York Yankees. Facing elimination in each game, Seattle came back to sweep three straight games at their homefield in the Kingdome. Rodriguez waited on deck as Griffey scored from first base on a double to win the fifth and deciding game against the Yankees in the eleventh inning, 6-5. Seattle's Cinderella season came to an end in the American League Championship Series, as the Cleveland Indians eliminated the Mariners, 4 games to 2.

Rodriguez enjoyed Seattle's playoff run, although he did not see much action. "It was an awesome experience," he explained in *Sports Illustrated.* "I was 20 years old. It would have been [silly] for me to think I should have been in there. I understood my role—I was there to pinch run or fill in if someone got hurt—and it didn't bother me at all." Rodriguez played in just two games in the postseason—one against New York and the other against Cleveland—and was hitless in two at bats.

STARTING SHORTSTOP. Sojo left Seattle to join the Yankees before the 1996 season, and Rodriguez took over as the Mariners' starting shortstop. He joined a lineup that already included Griffey, slugger Jay Buhner, and defending American League batting champion Edgar Martinez. Rodriguez began the season batting ninth and Pinella hoped he could hit .270 for his team. "The first thing I've got to understand is my role on this team," Rodriguez explained to the *Everett Washington Daily Herald* before the season. "If my role is to play good defense or to be a contact hitter or to hit home runs or to bunt, whatever I have to do, then that's my role."

Rodriguez got off to a solid start, hitting .279 on May 7. On that day, Pinella decided to move him up in the lineup to second, just ahead of Griffey. The move turned Rodriguez's season around. Teams had to pitch to him, or face his hardhitting teammate. "The most obvious thing Junior [Griffey] does

RIPKEN AND RODRIGUEZ

Many experts compare Rodriguez to his longtime hero, Cal Ripken Jr. Both are tall men—Rodriguez is 6 feet, 3 inches—and good hitters. "He's a big, physical shortstop like Ripken, but he's a better athlete," Indians general manager John Hart explained in *Sports Illustrated*. "He probably has more power than Cal, and he might be a better all-around hitter." Ripken had this to say about his admirer in the *Sporting News:* "All that Alex seems to need is experience to become the shortstop everyone else will be watching in our league. I'm still having a good time out there, just playing. But the future belongs to Alex Rodriguez."

for me is get me better pitches," Rodriguez told the *Sporting News*.

ALL-STAR. Rodriguez steadily improved, hitting .393 in May, .324 in June, .383 in July, and .435 in August. He made his first all-star game appearance, serving as backup for his childhood idol, Ripken. "I'm excited, but I'm not really surprised [by being an all-star]," Rodriguez admitted in the *Sporting News*. "I have a lot of confidence in my ability."

RECORD BREAKER. The Mariners suffered two devastating injuries during the 1996 season. Johnson sat out most of the season with a bad back, and Griffey missed several weeks with a broken hand. With the two superstars out, Rodriguez stepped up and had a fantastic season. He led the major leagues with a .358 average, hit 36 home runs, drove in 123 runs (eighth in the American League), and scored 141 more (first in the American League). Rodriguez finished second in the American League with 215 hits and his 54 doubles led the league.

Rodriguez also broke several records in 1996. He set single season marks for major league shortstops in five categories—runs scored, hits, doubles, extra base hits (91), and slugging percentage (.631)—and his 379 total bases tied the major league record for a shortstop set by Ernie Banks of the Chicago Cubs in 1958. Rodriguez became the third youngest batting champion in history and the youngest since 20-year-old Al Kaline of the Detroit Tigers hit .340 in 1955. He was also the first shortstop to lead the American League in batting since Lou Boudreau of the Cleveland Indians in 1944.

PLAYER OF THE YEAR. In addition to his offensive production, Rodriguez committed only 15 errors in the field and finished second in the American League voting for the Gold Glove, awarded for fielding excellence. Following the season, fellow major league players voted Rodriguez the *Sporting News* Major League Player of the Year. In voting for the American League Most Valuable Player Award, Rodriguez finished second, only three votes behind Juan Gonzalez of the Texas Rangers. "Let's be honest, the year he had could be the best year a shortstop had ever had," Detroit Tigers shortstop Alan Tramell told the *Sporting News.*

OFF THE FIELD. Rodriguez lives with his mother in Miami during the off-season and calls her five times a week while playing with the Mariners. He has a German shepherd named Ripper. When not playing baseball, Rodriguez enjoys playing golf and Nintendo.

Rodriguez has not let success go to his head, and other players recognize him as one of the nicest players in baseball. "Alex has a lot of respect for the game, for the players who have gone before him," Paul Molitor of the Minnesota Twins stated in the *Sporting News.* "Compared to many young players, I look at him as a breath of fresh air. He doesn't take for granted his accomplishments of this season." Rodriguez loves to sign autographs and answer his fan mail.

Although Rodriguez hesitated to play for Seattle because it was so far from home. Now he is happy to be a Mariner. "At first, I didn't want to play in Seattle," Rodriguez admitted in *Sports Illustrated.* "Now I can't imagine playing anywhere else. This is the perfect place for me. It's got great fans, and it's an easy city to play in."

Rodriguez has the ability to be a great player for many years to come. "I really feel like I've been given this gift, that I've been blessed," he admitted in the *Sporting News.* "I thank

GRIFFEY AND RODRIGUEZ

The Mariners are blessed with two of the best young players in baseball, Rodriguez and Griffey. Rodriguez understands, however, that Griffey is the team's leader. "Whatever attention I get is going to be secondary to Junior because Junior's gotten the ultimate," he stated in the *Everett Washington Daily Herald.* "He's the Michael Jordan of our game and the Michael Jordan of our era. To me, it's just a blessing to be next to him."

Griffey hopes that fans do not have unrealistic expectations for his young teammate. "I just hope people don't expect him to put up those same numbers every year," he explained in the *Sporting News.* "I hope that they're not going to say he's had a bad year if he hits .330 with 25 homers and 90 RBI. I don't want him feeling he has to do this every year or he's come up short."

the Lord for that, but I have to remember that it can be taken away, too."

Sources

Daily Herald (Everett, Washington), March 21, 1996; July 28, 1996.
Dallas Morning News, July 30, 1995.
Oregonian, May 16, 1995.
Seattle Times, December 16, 1994; October 18, 1995.
Sporting News, August 12, 1996; September 23, 1996; October 14, 1996.
Sports Illustrated, March 22, 1993; June 14, 1993; July 18, 1994; October 7, 1996.
Additional information provided by the Seattle Mariners.

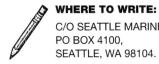

WHERE TO WRITE:

C/O SEATTLE MARINERS,
PO BOX 4100,
SEATTLE, WA 98104.

Chanda Rubin

1976—

Chanda Rubin was practically born with a tennis racket in her hand. She came from a tennis-playing family and grew up on the court her father built in the backyard. Rubin has now gone from her backyard to the most important arenas in the sport, earning the number seven ranking in the world. The top-ranked American-born female player, she has been a success on the court and off through hard work and a desire to be the best.

"Chanda is definitely at the top of the new group of stars."
—Monica Seles.

Growing Up

JUDGE'S DAUGHTER. Chanda Renee Rubin was born February 18, 1976, in Lafayette, Louisiana. Her father, Edward, is a judge, and her mother, Bernadette, is a retired elementary school teacher. The Rubins met at Louisiana State University when both were students. Edward Rubin became the first African American elected a district judge in Lafayette Parish.

Rubin told *Tennis* that her parents make a good team.

"My parents make decisions together, but they take different roles," she explained. "Dad sees the ideal; he has a feeling for the long-term goals and ambitions. If mom agrees with him, she makes it happen. She takes care of the details. I take after Dad in that I can be very stubborn, but I'm also more patient than he is. My mom is very organized, and I guess I inherited that from her."

Rubin always liked things just so. "I was always picky about things," she admitted in *Tennis*. "Things just had to be in their right places in my room. If you went in my room and messed it up, I got really upset. I guess I went a bit too far sometimes, because even my mom would get annoyed with me."

INHERITS LOVE OF GAME. Bernadette Rubin was a high-school basketball player and track and field participant. She also competed in tennis and passed on her love of the game to her children. Rubin's sister, LaShon, played four years on the tennis team at Southern University. Her brother, Ed Jr., plays tennis at Louisiana State University.

Rubin's parents played tennis on a court her father built in their backyard. One day, Chanda woke up from a nap and found the house was empty. Looking outside, she saw her parents on the tennis court "laughing, playing and just having a good time," Rubin recalled in *Essence*. "I still remember thinking, 'This is a good place to be, a safe place.' I wanted to be out there with them."

Rubin took a racket from the closet and asked to play, still in her red nightgown. "They sat me on a fence and made me watch, because I was such a pain," she told *Sports Illustrated*. Rubin's parents let her hit balls against the fence so she would stop interrupting their game. "It's not like it was fun, but I was determined to play," she revealed in *Cosmopolitan*.

SOMETHING SPECIAL. Rubin began playing tennis seriously at

the age of five. "My mom was really surprised at how easily I returned her shots," she recalled in *Sports Illustrated for Kids*. Bernadette Rubin believed her daughter had potential. "I knew she had something special right then," Bernadette Rubin confessed in *Tennis*. "When I told Ed later that day, he didn't believe me. I made him come out to the court to see for himself."

When she turned seven, Rubin began taking tennis lessons at a tennis club near her home. "My parents had let me hit the balls on the second bounce to make it easier," she stated in

Tennis. "So when the pro told me the ball could only bounce once, I was shocked." Rubin practiced almost every day and rapidly improved.

BIG WINS. When she was 11, Rubin won the national championship at the 12-year-old-and-under tournament. She won the 14-and-under national title the next year. In 1992, Rubin won the Girls' Singles Championship at Wimbledon, the most prestigious tournament in the world. Rubin played well in the senior tournament as well, despite losing to Jennifer Capriati of the United States, 6-1, 7-5.

Also in 1992, Rubin and her doubles partner, Lindsay Davenport, finished second in the French Open junior competition. Playing as a single at the senior level of the U.S. Open, she reached the fourth round, beating fifteenth-seeded Katerina Meleeva along the way. Rubin was now able to play with the best players in the world.

TURNS PRO. Rubin had to make a tough decision in 1991. She could turn professional—and join the tour full-time—or complete her high school education. Her parents wanted her to stay in school, but Rubin wanted to play on the tour. Rather than pick one or the other, she decided to do both. During the week Rubin attended school, but she also played 12 tournaments a year on the Women's Tennis Association (WTA) tour.

Rubin did homework during free-time at tournaments and graduated from the Episcopal School of Acadiana with an A-average. "I was never number one in my class," she admitted in *USA Today.* "It was impossible. I was always behind. Every summer, I was turning in work from the previous year. When I finally graduated, the slates were clean."

Unlike many other young players, Rubin's parents never pushed her to become a star and refused to send her to a high-pressure tennis academy. "It's funny, but we never thought about all this 'tennis parent' stuff," Ed Rubin told *Tennis.* "Our actions were always guided by our instincts as parents. We never thought of sending our kids off to an academy. Our philosophy always was to keep them within striking distance, so that if any of them did decide that they wanted to play tennis badly enough, they could turn on the afterburners for themselves and make it happen. She could have quit any time she wanted to. We had realized a while back that if tennis is going to be primary, just let it happen. Don't force it in any way, because there's enough pressure there in the situation already."

TOURS FULL-TIME. With her high school diploma in hand, Rubin could concentrate on tennis full time in the summer of 1993. She rapidly moved up in the rankings, but had a hard time defeating top-ten players. Several times Rubin stood on the verge of upsets, but then let them slip away. "Everyone had always said Chanda Rubin is going to be the next great American female tennis player, or the next great black tennis player," her coach, Marcel Freeman, stated in *Tennis*. "She just felt too much pressure to succeed." Freeman told Rubin to not worry about winning and just play the same way no matter what the score.

Rubin also had to learn to be more patient and realize that she had to raise the level of her game to defeat the best players in the world. "I need to hit a few more balls to win a point," she admitted in *Sports Illustrated*. "Usually when I hit a certain shot, I expect it to be a winner, and if it comes back, I get a little impatient."

MOVING UP. In the spring of 1995, Rubin reached the quarter-finals of the Family Circle Cup, losing to top-ranked Steffi Graf. It was clear she needed more experience to beat a player like the legendary champion. "She went for too many shots," Graf told *Sports Illustrated*. "I showed her I could stand up to it. She needs to wait a little bit longer."

Superstar

CLASSIC COMEBACK. At the 1995 French Open, Rubin faced fifth-ranked Jana Novatna in the third round. Rubin got off to a fast start, pulling ahead, when the bottom fell out. She soon found herself behind 0-5 in the third set, one point away from being eliminated. "At that point I got upset with myself because it was like the same old story," Rubin recalled in *Tennis*. "When I was down triple-match point, I started saying, 'I just want this one point, just this point.' Then I had to win the second point, then the third point."

One point at a time, Rubin began one of the most remarkable comebacks in tennis history. She worked hard to keep her shots in the court and make Novatna beat her. Rubin saved nine match points and captured the third set, 8-6. It was her first win against a top-ten player and meant that Rubin reached the quarterfinals of a Grand Slam event for the first time. (The Grand Slam tennis tournaments are the Australian, French, and U.S. Opens, and Wimbledon.)

"That was probably the biggest win yet for me," Rubin confessed in *Tennis*. "It isn't the comeback, although that's what people remember and always ask about, as much as it was the fact that I beat a top player at a Grand Slam event. It gave me confidence and motivation, and I was able to follow up with more wins. That's what made it so good." By the end of 1995 Rubin had climbed from number 23 to number 13 in the world rankings. *Tennis* named Rubin the magazine's female Most Improved Pro.

The victory over Novatna showed that Rubin had arrived as a top player. "I never really lacked confidence," she acknowledged in *Tennis*. "It was just a matter of the level of confidence. Before, in big matches, I sometimes had opportunities on which I didn't follow through. When it got a little sticky against a top player, and she challenged me to take the match, I would maybe pull back a little, not be as willing as I am now to be aggressive, get to the net, close out the points. A lot of it has to do with coaching, and a lot has to do with my own maturity."

THUNDER DOWN UNDER. Rubin had the best performance of her career in a Grand Slam tournament at the 1996 Australian Open. In the quarterfinals she met third-seeded Arantxa Sanchez Vicario, who only recently had held the world number-one ranking. The two players—who slugged it out for an Australian record for females of three-and-a-half hours—split the first two sets, Rubin winning the first, 6-4, and Sanchez Vicario the second, 6-2.

The final set was remarkable. It went to a tiebreaker and to claim victory one player had to win two more points than her opponent. Amazingly, the two players were still tied with the score at 14-14. "I just wanted to stay in there and keep fighting," Rubin admitted to the Reuters News Service. "I wanted to keep fighting no matter how long it took."

Finally, the young American prevailed, 16-14, when she hit a powerful forehand on match point that Sanchez Vicario could not reach. It was the biggest win ever for Rubin and put her in her first Grand Slam singles semifinals. "It's great to be in the semifinals of a Grand Slam," she said after the match. "It's huge."

In the semifinals Rubin faced Monica Seles, the co-number-one ranked player in the world. The young challenger took the first set in a tiebreaker, 7-6, hitting hard, deep shots that kept Seles on her heels. Seles came charging out in set two to win 6-1. When Rubin took a 5-2 lead in the third and final set, it seemed like she would add Seles to the list of her victims. Unfortunately, at this point Rubin's serve, so tough all day, failed her. Seles won the next five games, the third set, and the match.

Seles might have won the match, but Rubin made her work for the victory. "I was lucky to win in three long sets," Seles told *Sports Illustrated for Kids.* "Chanda runs down balls most people would not go after." Rubin was happy with her performance. "I tried to stay aggressive and get in [to the net] a little bit, and I think I did that pretty well," she explained to the Reuters News Service. "I gave myself chances but I didn't close it out." Rubin won the doubles title with Sanchez Vicario, who forgave her partner for knocking her out of the singles competition.

Rubin's ranking soared—from number fifty-three in May 1995 to number seven. She was now the number-one ranked

HERO WORSHIP

Rubin did not have many role models as child, because there were only a few black female tennis players. One of those players was Zina Garrison-Jackson, a top-ten star who once reached the finals of the legendary Wimbledon tournament. "I always like watching her play," Rubin explained in *Sports Illustrated for Kids.* "She's one of the very few black female players at the top of the game." Rubin put a poster of Garrison-Jackson up on the door to her room when she was ten and left it there for nine years.

Garrison-Jackson is impressed by her biggest fan. "[Rubin's] not intimidated by anything at all, and nothing seems new to her," Garrison-Jackson told *Tennis.* "She's also very competitive, and I like that. She's more like a 'typical' tennis player than I was, in that she grew up with a court in her own backyard, and she comes from a real tennis family. She knew a lot coming in, where I had to learn it all on the job. Chanda's at home in her own little world, with Chanda and nobody else. And in tennis, that's O.K."

As one of the few African American players on the tour, Rubin realizes that she may be a role model for young players like Garrison-Jackson was for her. "I'm not comfortable being a role model, but I'm doing my best," she admitted in *Essence.*

American-born woman player in the world. "I guess I just got tired of losing really close matches," Rubin explained in *Cosmopolitan.* "I had chances, and instead of letting them go by, I took advantage of them."

YEAR ENDS EARLY. Returning to the United States, Rubin reached the final of the Lipton Championships, where she once again faced Graf. Despite the fact that she had lost all six times when she had previously faced the German champion, Rubin was confident. "I can play with anybody," she declared in *Sports Illustrated.* "Including her." Unfortunately, Graf was still too tough, winning 6-1, 6-3.

The rest of the 1996 tennis season was frustrating for Rubin. She suffered a stress fracture in her right wrist that kept her out of action for the remainder of the year. Her biggest disappointment came in July when she had to miss the Summer Olympics in Atlanta, Georgia. "I'm disappointed that I can't play," Rubin told *Jet.* "But my health comes first."

ONE OF THE BEST. Rubin works hard to improve her game. She practices tennis six times a week, three to four hours per day. In order to improve her strength, Rubin lifts weights five days a week and runs every other day. She has a powerful serve and huge forehand. Rubin's speed enables her to reach shots others let go by, and she is able to move effortlessly around the court.

Rubin's hard work has paid off. "Chanda is definitely at the top of the new group of stars," Seles stated in *Sports Illustrated for Kids.* "Nothing seems to bother

her. She's always smiling and really looks like she enjoys the competition."

OFF THE COURT. Rubin's home is still in Lafayette, but she spends most of her time on the professional tour. "I've always gained a lot of strength from Lafayette," she acknowledged in *USA Today.* "I feel grounded here, truly centered. I can relax and be myself. It's home." Lafayette held a Chanda Rubin Day in 1995. The local post office honored her with a special postmark, and local businessmen put up a billboard with her picture on it that said "Tennis, Anyone? Chanda is making a racket."

Rubin likes to read. "I've always loved to read and learn about new things," she explained in *Sports Illustrated for Kids.* She likes to watch figure skating and ride horses. Rubin has a black toy poodle named Cocoa. She gives free tennis clinics for kids and donates equipment to auctions. Her favorite subjects in high school were math and science.

Edward Rubin is an elected official and has to run for re-election. His children, including his famous tennis-playing daughter, campaign for him. "It was hard work," Rubin told *Sports Illustrated for Kids* after the last election. "But it paid off. He won."

Rubin has a simple goal for the rest of her career, as she declared in *Sports Illustrated for Kids:* "To be the best player I can be, work as hard as I can, for as long as I can."

Sources

Cosmopolitan, June 1996.
Essence, August 1996.
Jet, August 12, 1996.
Newsday, August 31, 1995; September 4, 1995.
New York Amsterdam News, November 11, 1995.
Sports Illustrated, April 19, 1993; April 8, 1996.
Sports Illustrated for Kids, August 1996.
Tennis, January 1996; August 1996.
USA Today, April 8, 1996.
Additional information provided by the Reuters News Service.

WHERE TO WRITE:
C/O U.S. TENNIS ASSOCIATION,
70 W. RED OAK LANE,
WHITE PLAINS, NY 10604-3602.

John Smoltz

1967—

"I'm thinking about nothing but pitching out there on the mound now. It's fun."
—John Smoltz.

Atlanta Braves righthander John Smoltz has struggled throughout his career to live up to other people's expectations. Despite compiling an above-average record in his first seven seasons, he never could become one of the best pitchers in baseball. That all changed in 1996 when Smoltz quieted all his critics with a spectacular season. He won a major-league high 24 games and earned the National League Cy Young Award as that league's best pitcher. Now that he has arrived as one of the top hurlers in the major leagues, Smoltz can enjoy playing baseball once again.

Growing Up

TIGER TODDLER. John Andrew Smoltz Jr. was born May 15, 1967, in Warren, Michigan but grew up in Lansing, Michigan, the state capital. He is the oldest of John and Mary Smoltz's three children. His father owned an electronics shop and his mother was a homemaker.

Smoltz grew up as a Detroit Tiger fan. His father worked as an usher at Tiger Stadium. After the Tigers won the 1984 World Series, the family took home a piece of sod from the stadium and planted it in the backyard. Smoltz skipped his high school homecoming dance to go see Detroit play the San Diego Padres in the 1984 World Series. "That was the place I wanted to be," he explained in *People Weekly.* Smoltz is also related to Tiger royalty. Charlie Gehringer, Detroit's Hall-of-Fame second baseman, is his second cousin.

CHILD PRODIGY. Smoltz's parents both play accordion. John Sr. played the instrument at the Tigers' 1968 World Series victory party. Smoltz began to play the accordion when he was four and soon became an expert. He won contests in places as far away as Chicago.

Even though Smoltz was good at playing the accordion, he hated the pressure of the competitions. "What I remember is being on stages and getting trophies," he recalled in *Sports Illustrated.* "And I remember all the people. I remember a hundred people watching me. I used to throw up before I played. By the time I was seven, I'd had it. I hated to practice. I told my parents, 'That's it. I don't want to play this thing any more.'"

NEW CAREER. Smoltz parents said he could quit playing the accordion. He then concentrated on what he really wanted to do: play baseball. "From seven years old I said I was going to be a major leaguer," he revealed in *People Weekly.* "My mom said, 'That's great, but you need something to fall back on.' I told her, 'A gas station attendant looks pretty fun.' She said, 'Well, don't tell your dad.'"

Baseball became Smoltz's life. "I never had any other interests," he stated in *People Weekly.* After giving up 3 home runs in one inning to lose a tournament game when he was 16, Smoltz taped a strike zone against the back of the house, with

Smoltz prepares to throw one of his amazing pitches.

small squares in each corner. He spent his spare time throwing against the house, working to develop control of his pitches. "That is when I knew that he would be something special," John Smoltz Sr. recalled in *Sports Illustrated*.

DREAM COME TRUE. Smoltz attended Waverly High School in Lansing. He earned all-state honors in both baseball and basketball. Smoltz wanted to play baseball and his dream was to be drafted by the Tigers. His dream came true when Detroit picked him in the twenty-second round of the 1985 baseball free-agent draft. Smoltz moved up through the Detroit system, earning a promotion to the Glen Falls (New York) Double A team in 1987.

TRADED. The major league Tigers were in the middle of a tough pennant race in 1987. They were battling the Toronto

Blue Jays for the American League East Division lead, but they realized they needed an experienced starter to help put them over the top. The Atlanta Braves offered Doyle Alexander, a 36-year old-veteran righthander. In return, the Braves wanted Smoltz. Detroit agreed to the deal and Alexander went 9-0 the rest of the season for the Eastern Division champion Tigers.

At first the trade disappointed Smoltz because he wanted to play with the Tigers. The Braves, however, offered him the opportunity to move up more quickly to the major leagues. On July 23, 1988, Atlanta brought Smoltz up to the big club. He started and defeated the New York Mets that same day, 6-1, pitching 8 innings. Smoltz and the Braves struggled the rest of the season, however. He finished with a 2-7 record with a 5.48 earned run average (ERA), and Atlanta finished the season with 106 losses.

UPS AND DOWNS. In 1989, Smoltz started strong. He was 11-6 and became the youngest pitcher in Braves history to earn a spot in the all-star game. "People started talking about 20 wins," Smoltz explained in *People Weekly.* "But the second half [of the season] was a total flop." He finished the season with a 12-11 record, but his 2.94 ERA was one of the best in the league.

Smoltz reached a low point in 1991 after starting the season 2-11. "I felt like I was letting my father down," he admitted in *Sports Illustrated.* The fans at Fulton-County Stadium began to boo Smoltz, the first time in his career this had happened. To get help he turned to sports psychologist Jack Llewellyn. "We tried to teach him how to recover faster from adversity," Llewellyn explained in *People Weekly,* "and how to tell when he was losing his focus and how to get it back."

Smoltz worked to control his temper and focus on pitching. "I had a very difficult three years when I didn't handle things off the field very well," he confessed in the *Sporting News.* "I took in a lot of problems." The work with Llewellyn seemed to help, as Smoltz turned his season around. He went on to post a 12-2 record in the second half of the 1991 season and was 8-0 after August 15.

WORST TO FIRST. Smoltz's late-season heroics helped the Braves pull off one of the most remarkable turnarounds in baseball history. A last place team in 1990, Atlanta won the National League West Division title in 1991. Smoltz joined with Cy Young Award winner Tom Glavine and Steve Avery to form one of the best starting rotations in baseball. He finished the year 14-13 with a 3.80 ERA and a National League-leading 215 strikeouts.

The Braves faced the Pittsburgh Pirates in the 1991 National League Championship Series. Smoltz won Game Three, 10-3, giving Atlanta a 2-1 edge in the best-of-seven series. Pittsburgh won Games Four and Five, pushing the Braves to the brink of elimination. Avery, however, shut the Pirates out 1-0 in Game Six setting up a deciding Game Seven. Smoltz came through in a pressure-packed situation, throwing a complete-game shutout 4-0 win, giving Atlanta its first-ever National League Pennant.

WORLD SERIES I. The Braves faced the American League champion Minnesota Twins in the 1991 World Series. The Twins matched Atlanta with their own "worst-to-first" improvement during the 1991 season. Neither team would ever quit, and the series was one of the best ever. The Braves and Twins battled for seven games, with five of the contests being decided in the last at-bats.

Smoltz pitched Game Four and gave up two runs in seven-and-two-thirds innings in a game the Braves finally won 3-2 in the bottom of the ninth. With the Series tied at 3-3, he again took the mound with Atlanta's season in the balance. Smoltz came through, holding Minnesota scoreless for seven innings before leaving the game. Unfortunately, Jack Morris of the Twins did the same to the Braves. Minnesota finally scored a run in the bottom of the tenth to capture a 1-0 victory and their second World Series championship. Morris, who won the game for the Twins, had been Smoltz's idol when he played with the Tigers.

Even though Atlanta lost, Smoltz still remembers 1991 as his greatest sports moment. "Pitching the three most important games for Atlanta—the clinching game versus Houston [for the National League West title], the clinching seventh game versus Pittsburgh, and the seventh game of the World Series—all three in one year," Smoltz declared. "And that was after going 2-11 in the first half and after people were wishing I had went to AAA or out of the rotation. It was a pretty gratifying year."

BEST SEASON YET. Smoltz continued to improve in 1992, putting together the best numbers of his career so far. He went 15-12 with a 2.85 ERA and led the National League with 215 strikeouts. The Braves repeated as National League champions, but lost for the second straight year in the World Series, this time to the Toronto Blue Jays in six games.

Smoltz continued to be a big-money pitcher, remaining undefeated in postseason play. His two wins in the National League Championship Series against the Pittsburgh Pirates earned him most valuable player honors. Smoltz also had one victory against the Blue Jays in the World Series, staving off elimination for the Braves in Game Five.

PITCHING THROUGH PAIN. Smoltz won 15 games again in 1993 (15-11), but his ERA jumped to 3.62. He also lost his first playoff game, dropping a 2-1 decision to the Philadelphia Phillies in the National League Championship Series. When Smoltz finished the strike-shortened 1994 season with a 6-10 record, it was obvious something was bothering the big righthander.

The problem was a bone spur in his right elbow. The injury had begun to cause him pain in 1991, and had grown steadily worse. By the end of the 1994 season he could not move his arm because of the pain. "I was out there on the mound thinking about so many things except the hitter and how to pitch," Smoltz told *Sports Illustrated*. "I worried about whether throwing the next pitch would hurt."

Despite the misery caused by the bone spur, Smoltz missed only one start in his career. In September 1994, he finally had surgery to remove the bone spur. "The one way the injury really hurt was in preventing me from working on things to become better—working on the side, working on my control," Smoltz stated in *Sport*. "The thing I couldn't do was master my control, improve my pitches, and the quality wasn't as good at times."

Smoltz pitched well in the shortened 1995 season, earning a 12-7 record, with a 3.18 ERA, and 193 strikeouts. He tired as the season went on, however, and it showed in the postseason. In his worst playoff performance ever, Smoltz gave up 11 runs in 15 innings in the playoffs and did not get a victory or a loss. The Cleveland Indians knocked him out of Game Three of the World Series in the third inning. Despite Smoltz's poor performance, the Braves won their first World Series since the team moved to Atlanta from Milwaukee.

Superstar

GOOD STUFF? Entering the 1996 season, many baseball experts considered Smoltz a disappointment, feeling he had not lived up to his potential. Despite having the best stuff—or pitches—in the majors, he had only compiled a 90-82 record with a high of 15 wins in one season. Smoltz was hurt by the criticism he received. "I let all the criticism and the expectations rule my life," he admitted in *Sports Illustrated*. "I wasn't happy. There were times when the last place I wanted to be was at the ballpark."

Smoltz claimed that his mediocre record was the result of bad luck. "I still maintain that there were a ton of games I could've won with any breaks, with one or two runs," he explained in the *Sporting News*. " But I was never going to complain. I was just going to try to find a better way to win. I'll compare my numbers with anybody except Greg Maddux or Randy Johnson—career ERAs with anybody. But yet there seems to be guys with 30 more wins than me."

FINDS PEACE. Smoltz needed to find a way to deal with the anger he felt about people who criticized him. He and his wife, Dyan, began to attend Bible-study groups. Strengthening his faith helped Smoltz deal with adversity. "Brett Butler [the Los Angeles Dodgers outfielder] once told me, 'If you were in a room with 100 people and 98 said nothing but positive things about you, you'd worry about the other two,'" he told *Sports Illustrated*. "He was right. I know I'm going to lose some games and have some rough spots. The difference now is, I won't be concerned about what people say."

HOLY SMOLTZ. Smoltz was confident before the 1996 season began. "This is my year," Smoltz told his teammates, according to *Sports Illustrated,* in spring training. "This time it's my turn for the Cy Young." After losing his first start, Smoltz ran off a streak of 14 straight victories, a new Braves record. He reached double-digits in wins faster than any National League pitcher since Joe McGinnity of the New York Giants in 1904. "I think I've kind of been in a time lapse," Smoltz explained in *Sport*. "I've kind of been stuck for two or three years, and now I feel like I'm going to emerge as one of the better pitchers in the game."

Smoltz earned the starting pitching spot in the 1996 All-Star Game and got the win as the National League defeated their American League rivals. He became the ace of the Braves' staff and pitched the National League Eastern Division championship-clinching game against the Montreal Expos on September 22. Smoltz led the majors in wins (24) and strikeouts per 9 innings (9.8) and led the National League in strikeouts (276) and innings pitched (253). He finished second in the National League with six complete games and finished fourth in the league with a 2.94 ERA. "I got every break this year," he declared in the *Sporting News*. "The bullpen never blew a lead for me, and the hitters came through incredibly almost every game."

The big difference for Smoltz on the mound was his control. He learned how to throw his overpowering pitches where he wanted to and cut down on his walks. "When you do that [throw strikes], with the stuff he has, generally nobody is going to get any runs," Atlanta manager Bobby Cox stated in the *Sporting News*. Pitching without pain also helped with Smoltz's control.

MR. OCTOBER

Throughout his career, Smoltz has earned his reputation as a big-game pitcher. His regular season record was 114-90 with a 3.45 ERA at the end of the 1996 season, but his post-season statistics were much better. When the games really count, Smoltz has a 9-2 record in the playoffs with a 2.20 ERA. In the 1996 playoffs, he was 4-1 with a 0.95 ERA.

Smoltz says that pitching in the playoffs is what baseball is all about. "I don't know how everybody else feels about these situations, but as a kid this is all I dreamed of doing," he told the *Sporting News*.

Smoltz also learned how to control his temper. "Everybody has a boiling point," he explained in the *Sporting News*. "But my faith allows me to stay even-keeled and not get carried away with what people think." Teammate Greg Maddux, the best pitcher in the National League over the previous four seasons, helped keep Smoltz focused. "He helped me out a lot," Smoltz declared to the Associated Press. "He kept telling me, 'This is a special year. Make every game count.' Coming from him, it meant a lot."

TOUGH LOSS. Smoltz continued his great pitching in the playoffs. He beat the Dodgers in Game One of the Division Series, which the Braves won three games to one. Smoltz then beat the Cardinals in Game One and Game Five of the National League Championship Series, which Atlanta also won. The Braves were now in the World Series for the fourth time in six years, and this time they faced the New York Yankees.

In Game One against the Yankees, Smoltz had a no-hitter for four-and-two-thirds innings. He pitched six innings and gave up two hits in a game the Braves won 12-1. "John is about as locked in now as you're ever going to see anybody," Glavine told the *Sporting News*. The Braves won the first two games of the Series in New York and hoped to be able to win the championship with the next three games set to be played in Atlanta.

The Yankees, however, had different ideas. They won the next two games to tie the series and Smoltz took the mound in Game Five trying to salvage one victory for the Braves at home. The ace of the staff pitched an outstanding game, giving up only 4 hits and striking out two New Yorkers. The only run the Yankees could score came on an error by Atlanta center fielder Marquis Grissom. Unfortunately for Smoltz, that one run was enough to ensure New York a 1-0 victory.

"You're going to have some bad hops," Smoltz told the Associated Press after his Game Five loss. "You're going to have some bad luck. There's not a guy here [in the Braves locker room] who doesn't feel like we can still win it. We're still the defending champs." Unfortunately for Smoltz and the Braves, the Yankees won Game Six and the series.

CY YOUNG. Smoltz received recognition for his great season when he won the 1996 National League Cy Young Award, given to the league's best pitcher. "Everybody felt I needed this to be on par with Greg [Maddux] and Tommy [Glavine]," Smoltz declared to the Associated Press. "At least winning the award takes the pressure off of that. I know down the road I'll be honored to have played with those two guys. Everybody felt I needed to win it more than I did. For years things did not go my way and I was pitching hurt. Aside from us winning the World Series, this is the greatest thing that's ever happened to me."

OFF THE FIELD. Smoltz lives with his wife Dyan, their two children, Andrew and Rachel, and their dog, Ginger, in Duluth, Georgia. After the 1996 season, he signed a four-year, $31 million contract with the Braves that made him the highest-paid pitcher in baseball. Smoltz loves to play golf. He competes with his teammates throughout the season and hosts his own tournament for charity. Smoltz's nicknames are Marmaduke and Duke.

Smoltz enjoys baseball now. "I'm thinking about nothing but pitching out there on the mound now," he explained in *Sports Illustrated*. "It's fun."

CY GUYS

When Smoltz won the 1996 National League Cy Young Award, it marked the fourth year in a row that an Atlanta pitcher had won the award. (Greg Maddux first won the award in 1992 when is was still playing for the Chicago Cubs.) This was the first time a team had accomplished this feat, and the Braves had the only staff in baseball history with three Cy Young Award winners in the same starting rotation. The following chart lists these pitchers and when they won this prestigious honor.

Pitcher	Year
Tom Glavine	1991
Greg Maddux	1993—95
John Smoltz	1996

Sources

People Weekly, July 15, 1996.

Sport, November 1996.

Sporting News, June 17, 1996; October 28, 1996.

Sports Illustrated, July 8, 1991; November 4, 1991; June 10, 1996.

Additional information provided by the Atlanta Braves, the Associated Press, and the Gannett and Reuters news services.

 WHERE TO WRITE:

C/O ATLANTA BRAVES,
PO BOX 464,
ATLANTA, GA 30302.

Kordell Stewart

1972—

Kordell Stewart is one of the most dangerous players in the National Football League (NFL). Blessed with extraordinary athletic ability and an exceptional knowledge of the game, he burst on the scene in 1995 as "Slash," the multi-dimensional threat of the Pittsburgh Steelers offense. Playing quarterback, running back, and wide receiver, Stewart confused defenses and helped his team reach the Super Bowl. Despite his success, he still has not reached his number-one objective: to quarterback the Steelers to a Super Bowl victory.

> *"I want to be the man here and get us to the Super Bowl as many times as I can."*
> —Kordell Stewart.

Growing Up

SLASH SR.? Kordell Stewart was born October 16, 1972, in New Orleans, Louisiana. He was raised in Marrero, Louisiana, just across the Mississippi River from New Orleans. Stewart's father, Robert, worked at many different jobs to support his family. "I'm Slash junior," Stewart declared in *Sports Illustrat-*

ed for Kids, referring to his versatile father. "Slash senior is a barber slash house painter slash carpenter. He does more things than I do, believe me!" Stewart helped his father cut hair and helped around the house, cooking dinner and doing laundry. When he later attended the University of Colorado, Stewart cut the hair of his teammates.

GROWS UP FAST. Stewart's mother Florence died from liver cancer when he was just 11. "My mom passed away when I was eleven and my dad's been there for me ever since," Stewart explained to the Reuters News Service. "It's been a rough one for me, but when things like that happen to you, you can either be a person who goes astray or understand that things happen for a reason and that's the approach that I have taken."

His mother's death forced the young man to grow up fast. Even though he lived in a poor neighborhood, and many of his friends turned to drugs and crime, Stewart stayed out of trouble. "From the time my mother passed on, my father treated me like a man," he recalled in *Sports Illustrated.* "As I look back, I think I needed that discipline. Things got pretty rough down where I live, and I have to thank Daddy for keeping me in line."

ONE MAN TEAM. Stewart did not get a chance to start in football at John Ehret High School until his junior year. He made the most of his opportunity. That season Stewart threw for 1645 yards and 19 touchdowns and ran for 522 yards and another 10 scores, leading Ehret to a 6-4 record.

As a senior, Stewart was almost a one-man offense. Running an option-attack, he passed the football for 942 yards and 17 touchdowns, and carried the pigskin for 923 yards and 23 touchdowns. Altogether, Stewart had a hand in 40 touchdowns for his team. Ehret went 8-3 and won the district championship. Stewart earned Louisiana Most Valuable Player and

Stewart dashes toward the end zone.

New Orleans Player of the Year awards. *Prep Football Report* named him to its All-American team.

BECOMES BUFFALO. Stewart was one of the top-rated high school option-quarterback prospects in the United States, and he accepted a scholarship to the University of Colorado. He saw only limited action in his freshman season, but became the team's starting quarterback in his second year (1992). Stewart threw for a Colorado season-record 2109 yards and tied the school record with 12 touchdown passes, despite missing time with a sprained foot. He broke his own single-season passing record as a junior, throwing for 2299 yards, and he started every game of the season even though he had a broken bone in his left hand.

GOOD COACHING. Before his senior season at Colorado, Stewart worked hard with assistant coach Rick Neuheisel. He gives Neuheisel credit for his improvement as a quarterback. "If I'd had [Neuheisel as a coach] since my freshman year, I would have gone in the first round [of the NFL Draft]," Stewart told *Sports Illustrated.* "He taught me about coverages and gave me confidence." Neuheisel had previously worked at the University of California—Los Angeles (UCLA), where he had helped develop the talents of Troy Aikman, the Super-Bowl-winning quarterback of the Dallas Cowboys.

BUFFALO STAMPEDE. The offense of the 1994 Colorado team was almost unstoppable. In addition to Stewart, the team featured Heisman-Trophy-winning running back Rashan Salaam, who rushed for 2055 yards and 24 touchdowns in 1994. "With this offense, if everyone's doing what he's supposed to do, I don't think anybody can stop this team," Stewart declared in *Sports Illustrated* after Colorado defeated Wisconsin 55-17.

"HAIL MARY." Stewart became a legend by throwing one pass. Colorado trailed the University of Michigan, 26-21, in Ann Arbor, Michigan, with six seconds left to play in the game. "Coach [Bill McCartney] was saying just stick with it and pray and hope to get it done," Stewart recalled in the *Sporting News.* The ball was on the Colorado 36 yard line, 64 yards from the end zone.

Colorado lined up to try the "Hail Mary" play. (A "Hail Mary" pass occurs when the offensive team sends several receivers to one spot in the end zone. The quarterback throws the football high in the air and hopes that one of his wide receivers can catch the ball, or that a defensive player is called for pass interference.) "We work on that play every Thursday in practice," Colorado receiver Michael Westbrook told the *Sporting News.* Stewart took the snap from center, rolled to his right, and then rolled back to his left. He heaved the ball as far as he could, into a jumble of players.

Michigan's cornerback Ty Law had a chance to knock the ball away, but missed it, and Colorado receiver Blake Anderson tapped it. As the ball fell to the ground, it came down in Westbrook's arms in the end zone. The touchdown won the game for Colorado, 27-26. Stewart ran into the end zone and mobbed his teammates. "I kissed the end zone, I licked the grass, I kissed my teammates on the lips," he recalled in *Sports Illustrated for Kids.*

Colorado finished Stewart's senior season with an 11-1 record. In his final game as a Buffalo, Stewart and the team defeated Notre Dame 41-24 in the Fiesta Bowl. Stewart earned game Most Valuable Player honors by throwing for 226 yards and rushing for 143 more. Colorado finished second in the final polls, behind Nebraska, the only team to beat them all season.

RECORD BREAKER. During his four years at Colorado, Stewart set school records for yards passing (6481), touchdown throws (33), and total offense (7770 yards). He ran for 1289 yards in his career, averaging 4.3 yards per carry, and 15 touchdowns. Colorado was 26-5-1 with Stewart as the starting quarterback.

Superstar

QB OR BUST. Stewart announced after his final season at Colorado that he wanted to play quarterback in the NFL. Professional scouts told him that he could be drafted higher if he agreed to play other positions, but Stewart stood firm. Many scouts doubted that he had the ability to be an NFL signal-caller.

The Pittsburgh Steelers selected Stewart with their second-round draft choice in the 1994 NFL Draft. "The Steelers were obviously a team that wanted me and figured I was good enough to be on the team and to be a quarterback," Stewart stated in the *New Pittsburgh Courier.* He came to training camp hoping to get a shot at playing quarterback, but the Steelers already had an established starter at the position, Neil O'Donnell. After the exhibition season, Stewart was listed as the team's fourth-string quarterback, behind O'Donnell, veteran Mike Tomczak, and second-year-man Jim Miller.

To show what position he wanted to play, Stewart chose a quarterback's number: 10. (Quarterbacks wear numbers 1 through 19.) "I'm convinced I can play quarterback in this league, but I also know it's not my time," he explained to *Sports Illustrated.* "It's a very tough thing to come into this league and play quarterback right away."

SLASH IS BORN. Stewart spent the first game of the season, a 23-20 Pittsburgh victory over the Detroit Lions, watching from the sideline in street clothes. When O'Donnell missed the next four games with an injury, he suited up but still did not play. Sitting out was hard on a player like Stewart, who was so used to being in the middle of the action. "It's a transition for me because in high school I was the man pretty much," he explained to the *New Pittsburgh Courier.* "I was running the show. Then ever since my sophomore year up until my senior year [in college] I was the starter. I never had to sit on the bench again and now it's different. I just have to sit back and learn and understand everything and wait my turn."

The Steelers got off to a 3-4 start and the offense was struggling. Coach Bill Cowher realized he needed a spark, and watching Stewart in practice gave him an idea. "This kid has so much talent," Cowher told his staff, according to *Sports Illustrated for Kids.* "Can't we find a way to use him?"

The coaching staff devised a plan to use all of Stewart's skills. They decided to use him at three different positions on offense: quarterback, running back, and wide receiver. Cowher came up with his nickname, "Slash," because Stewart was now a quarterback (slash) running back (slash) wide receiver.

Used this way, Stewart presented a difficult problem for defenses. As a former quarterback, his strong arm made him a threat to throw the ball, and his speed made him a dangerous runner and pass receiver. Stewart was happy to be able to contribute to the team. "I'm just having a lot of fun right now," he stated in *Sports Illustrated*. "I'll play whatever position they want me to play, and I'll take the ball whenever they want to give it to me."

SECRET WEAPON. In the Steelers' eighth game, against the Jacksonville Jaguars, Stewart ran for 16 yards on a quarterback sneak. "Now that was fun!" he admitted in *Sports Illustrated for Kids*. The next week he ran the ball twice, made two catches, and threw his first pass, a touchdown throw he made after scrambling from one side of the field to the other. The next week, Stewart caught a 71-yard touchdown pass against the Cincinnati Bengals.

Most importantly, the Steelers began to win after unleashing their new secret weapon, reeling off eight straight wins. Pittsburgh finished the season with an 11-5 record, an American Football Conference (AFC) Central Division title, and home field advantage throughout the NFL playoffs. "I'm not bragging or trying to be cocky or say anything wrong," Stewart stated in *Sports Illustrated*, "but I just feel if a guy is in front of me, just me and him, I'm going to get open."

The plan to use all of Stewart's abilities worked very well. "Slash" ran or caught the ball 49 times, with 30 of those plays resulting in first downs or touchdowns. Stewart ran the ball 15 times for 86 yards, a 5.7 average, and 1 touchdown, a 22-yard scamper against the New England Patriots. He also caught 14 passes for 235 yards—an average of 16.8 yards—and another score. As a quarterback, Stewart completed 5 of 7 passes for 60 yards and 1 touchdown. Just his presence on the field made Pittsburgh's offense more dangerous, because defenses had to worry about him even if he never touched the ball.

SUPER SLASH. Stewart continued to excel in the playoffs. In a 40-21 victory over the Buffalo Bills, he added a new position to his resume when he punted. "Coach never gave me a play, so I'm like, 'What's going on?'" Stewart recalled in *Newsday*.

"'What play am I running?' Finally, one of the lineman told me I had to punt."

After their victory over the Bills, Pittsburgh faced the Indianapolis Colts in the AFC Championship Game. Stewart scored a big touchdown on a 5-yard reception that gave the Steelers a 10-6 lead at halftime. Pittsburgh eventually won the game 20-16, and "Slash" was a big reason for their victory. He ran the ball 4 times for 12 yards and caught 2 passes for 18 more.

The Steelers now faced the Dallas Cowboys in the Super Bowl. "It's always been a dream of mine to be a quarterback in the Super Bowl," Stewart revealed in *Newsday*. "To be a rookie and playing in the Super Bowl; it's a great feeling." Stewart ran the ball twice as a quarterback and twice as a running back, picking up 3 first downs. He also caught a pass for a touchdown. Despite Stewart's great playing, the Cowboys won the game, 27-17, taking advantage of two O'Donnell interceptions to sneak past the Steelers.

QB CONTROVERSY. Despite his success the season before, Stewart still wanted to play quarterback. "Right now, I'm Slash," Stewart told the Reuters News Service. "Hopefully next year [1996] I'll get all the attention at quarterback because that is something I really love to do. Playing receiver is something that I feel I won't be doing for a very long time. I just have to wait my turn and be patient."

When O'Donnell left the team as a free-agent and signed with the New York Jets, Stewart thought he might have a chance in 1996. He came into training camp competing with Tomczak and Miller for the starting job. Eventually, Tomczak's experience won out, and Stewart returned to his multi-position role. "It puts everything at ease for me," he confessed to the Gannett News Service. "It's gotten to the point where I'm just ready to move on. As far as just being a receiver, that will never be the case. To be just a receiver, I won't settle for just that. I'm a quarterback with the capabilities of being a receiver."

PLATOON PASSER. Stewart again proved to be a vital part of the Steelers' offense. He ran for 171 yards and 5 touchdowns and caught 17 passes for 293 yards and 3 scores. Less effective as a quarterback, Stewart completed only 36.7 percent of his passes (11 of 20), for 100 yards, no touchdowns, and 2 interceptions.

Pittsburgh finished the season at 10-6 and repeated as AFC Central Division champions. They struggled down the stretch, however, losing three of their last four games behind a slumping Tomczak. In an effort to get the sagging offense back on track, Cowher decided to use both of his quarterbacks in the final game of the season against the Carolina Panthers. Stewart took advantage of his opportunity, setting an NFL record for quarterbacks with an 80-yard run, in an 18-14 Pittsburgh victory.

Cowher announced that the platoon system would continue in the playoffs. "We're going to continue to use him [Stewart]," Cowher told the Associated Press. "It's more of a 'feel' thing, based on where you're at and how things are going. They're both going to play in the upcoming weeks, but how much, I can't say."

PLAYOFF UPS AND DOWNS. The Steelers played the Colts in a rematch of their classic playoff game the year before. This time the game was not close, with Pittsburgh capturing a 42-14 victory. Both Tomczak and Stewart played, and "Slash" tore through the Indianapolis defense for 2 touchdowns and 48 yards. "There were a few plays I knew I was going to have the opportunity to run," Stewart explained to the Associated Press. "But to sit here and say I'd have as many plays as I did, no, I didn't know at all."

DREAM COME TRUE

Stewart always dreamed of playing in the NFL. When he was in middle school, his seventh-grade history teacher tried to explain the realities of making a professional team to his student. "When I was in middle school I had a teacher who said, 'Kordell, there's probably only one out of every so many thousand players who have the opportunity to make it to the NFL,'" Stewart recalled in the Reuters News Service. "I'd like to meet him and say, 'Hey, I made it.'"

The Steelers' drive to return to the Super Bowl ended against the New England Patriots in the second round of the playoffs. The Patriots dominated the game, winning 28-3, on a foggy day that made it difficult for the quarterbacks to see their receivers. Tomczak started the game for Pittsburgh, but Stewart saw action. Unfortunately, New England's defense was too tough forcing Stewart to throw 10 incomplete passes.

OFF THE FIELD. Stewart owns an Akita dog, Dice. He likes to play drums and listen to rap, reggae, rhythm and blues, and jazz music. Stewart majored in communication at Colorado and was a member of the team's "Academic Starters" squad because he had the highest grade point average among quarterbacks.

Stewart still considers himself the Steelers' quarterback of the future. "Quarterback is my specialty," he told the Associated Press. "I know there will come a time when I'll be the starter. I'm very capable of leading this team." Stewart has one goal, as he revealed to *Sports Illustrated for Kids:* "I want to be the man here [in Pittsburgh] and get us to the Super Bowl as many times as I can."

Sources

Dallas Morning News, January 29, 1996.
New Pittsburgh Courier, August 26, 1995.
Newsday, January 10, 1996; January 15, 1996.
Sporting News, October 3, 1994.
Sports Illustrated, September 26, 1994; November 27, 1995; December 11, 1995; December 25, 1995.
Sports Illustrated for Kids, September 1996.
Additional information provided by the Associated Press, the Gannett and Reuters news services, and the University of Colorado.

WHERE TO WRITE:
C/O PITTSBURGH STEELERS,
300 STADIUM CIRCLE,
PITTSBURGH, PA 15212.

Kerri Strug

1977—

Before the 1996 Summer Olympics in Atlanta, Georgia, Kerri Strug was not a household name. Although a solid performer, her more famous teammates always overshadowed her. "She has always been the bridesmaid, never the bride," legendary gymnastic champion Mary Lou Retton stated in *People Weekly*. Experts questioned Strug's toughness and wondered if she would ever succeed in a big competition. That all changed in one magical moment in the Georgia Dome. Strug—mustering courage that few have shown in Olympic history—vaulted the U.S. women's gymnastics team to their first ever Olympic gold medal.

"Anything in life, to be successful, you've got to work really hard."
—Kerri Strug.

Growing Up

TUMBLING TODDLER. Kerri Strug was born November 19, 1977, in Tucson, Arizona. Her father, Burt, is a heart surgeon and her mother, Melanie, is a homemaker. The youngest of three children, Strug admits her parents spoiled her.

Strug began gymnastics when she was four. Her older sister Lisa and older brother, Kevin also competed in the sport. Lisa Strug trained with the famous gymnastics coach Bela Karolyi, whose prize student at the time was the great Mary Lou Retton, the 1984 Olympic women's all-around gold medal winner. Strug wanted to follow in her sister's footsteps. "[Kerri's] quiet, driven, an overachiever," Burt Strug recalled in *Sports Illustrated*. "She's totally self-motivated and wants to be perfect all the time."

LEAVES HOME. Strug began training with Jim Gault, the gymnastics coach at the University of Arizona. The college gymnasts helped the youngster learn new skills. "I saw how in college everything was team oriented, and everyone had a lot of fun," Strug explained in *Sports Illustrated*. "That was my goal before I ever dreamed of competing in the Olympics."

When she turned 12, Strug told her parents that she wanted to go to Houston, Texas, and train with Karolyi. He coached Retton as well as former Olympic great Nadia Comeneci of Romania and world champion Kim Zmeskal and is considered the top gymnastics coach in the world. "I knew if I was going to make the '92 [Olympic] team, I had to make a change," Strug stated in *Sports Illustrated*.

Strug moved to Houston and lived with a family near Karolyi's gym. Her parents visited her every couple of weeks to keep her from becoming too lonely. "I didn't want her to leave," Melanie Strug admitted in the *Atlanta Journal-Constitution*. "She was my baby." Training at a high level was expensive, costing the Strugs tens of thousands of dollars. The expense was worth the cost. "You don't put a price tag on seeing your child succeed," Burt Strug told the same newspaper.

MOVING ON UP. Strug first made the U.S. Senior National Team in 1991, becoming the team's youngest member at 13

years of age. She won the vault at the 1991 U.S. Gymnastics Championships and finished third in both the all-around competition and uneven bars. In her first ever World Gymnastics Championships, Strug won a silver medal as the United States finished second in the team competition.

OLYMPICS I. Strug established herself as one of the best gymnasts in the United States with a solid performance at the 1992 U.S. Gymnastics Championships. She won both the vault and balance beam, finished second in the all-around competition and floor exercise, and took third in the uneven bars.

Then, at the U.S. Olympic Trials, Strug finished third in the all-around competition to earn a spot on the U.S. team for the 1992 Summer Olympics in Barcelona, Spain. She was the

Strug performing her unforgettable vault during the 1996 Summer Olympics.

youngest member of the American team. Strug won a bronze medal as part of the third place U.S. team, but was disappointed when she failed to qualify for the all-around competition finals. She was determined not to fall short at the 1996 Summer Olympics in Atlanta, Georgia.

STRUG'S STRUGGLES. Karolyi announced his retirement from coaching after the 1992 Olympics. Strug repeatedly changed coaches, training at five different gyms in five years. During this time she lived at home for only one year, and that was because she was recovering from a torn stomach muscle. Strug's travels took her to Orlando, Florida, and then to Oklahoma City, Oklahoma, where she worked with Steve Nunno, the coach of world champion Shannon Miller.

Despite her solid performances, experts questioned whether Strug had the toughness to be a champion. She showed great speed and power in her routines, but she also earned the nickname "Scary Kerri," because she often seemed nervous and let minor injuries keep her out of competition. "She is just a little girl who was never the roughest, toughest girl, always a little shy, always standing behind someone else," Karolyi explained in *Sports Illustrated*. "I always had to handle her as a baby. That's what we called her, the Baby, because she was always the youngest."

In 1994, Strug earned a silver medal at the World Gymnastics Championships as part of the U.S. team. She then had her best-ever individual finish in international competition with a seventh-place result in the all-around competition at the 1995 World Gymnastics Championships in Sabae, Japan. Strug also earned a bronze medal at that competition as part of the U.S. team.

BRIDE'S MAID. Despite being a solid member of the U.S. team for five years, Strug had not become a star. Nagging injuries slowed her down and she remained in the background to her more famous teammates, Shannon Miller and Dominique Dawes. Miller had won two world all-around championships and Dawes won every event at the 1994 U.S. Gymnastics Championships.

To prepare for the 1996 Summer Olympics, Strug decided to return to Karolyi's gym after the famous coach and his wife, Martha, came out of retirement. "Everybody has their niche, and I think I've been in enough places to know mine," Strug told the *New York Times*. "There is no questioning Bela's and Martha's record for producing medalists."

Even at Karolyi's gym Strug took a backseat to Dominique Moceanu, the newest U.S. gymnastics star. Moceanu burst on the scene by winning the all-around competition at the 1995 U.S. Gymnastics Championships. Strug finished fifth. "You'll never see Kerri on a Wheaties box," Karolyi admitted in *People Weekly*.

Superstar

MAGNIFICENT SEVEN. Strug earned a place on the 1996 U.S. Olympic team by finishing second in the all-around competition at the U.S. Olympic Trials. Even though the U.S. had never won a team gold medal at the Olympics, the American women were confident. The team included Miller, Dawes, and Moceanu, and every member of the U.S. squad had international experience.

The U.S. women's team trained for a week in North Carolina before the Olympics and then moved into their headquarters outside Atlanta. The team stayed at a fraternity house at Emory University, but their whereabouts were a closely held secret. Staying together, the team grew close and became good friends. They also gave themselves a nickname: The Magnificent Seven. The togetherness the team developed would help them when the going got rough.

OLYMPICS II. Entering Olympic competition, experts made the U.S. one of the favorites, along with the world championship team from Romania and the always powerful squad from Russia. The compulsory, or required events, took place on the first day of competition at the Georgia Dome. Strug and the rest of her U.S. teammates finished second the first day, only .127 points behind the Russians and ahead of the world champion Romanians. The Romanians struggled after losing three members of their team to injuries before the competition began.

OLYMPIC CHAMPION. The finals of the 1996 Olympic women's team gymnastics championship occurred July 23 at the Georgia Dome. The Americans took the lead in the competition on their first event, the uneven bars. Strug's routine earned a score of 9.787. The U.S. then held onto their lead during the balance beam and the floor routine. By the time of the final event—the vault—the U.S. team had a .897 lead over the Russians. Knowing that only a miracle could save them, a few members of the Russian team broke out in tears.

Then disaster struck. Miller took a short hop on her landing, earning a low score on what is usually a strong event for the great gymnast. Then, Moceanu, competing next to last for the Americans, fell on both of her vaults. "I saw Dom fall the first time, and I thought I can't believe it," Strug recalled in *Sports Illustrated*. "Then she fell a second time, and it was like time stopped. The Russians, I knew, were on the floor [exercise], which can be a high-scoring event, and my heart was beating like crazy. I thought, 'This is it, Kerri. You've done this vault a thousand times.'"

Strug was the last U.S. gymnast to compete. She needed at least a score of 9.6 to bring the United States to victory, and was confident because she had not missed her vault—a 1 1/2 twisting Yurchenko—for nearly three months. Strug stood at the end of the runway and began running toward the vault. She flew through the air, landed on her heels, and fell backward.

"My first thought was, 'How could you do that?'" Strug told *Sports Illustrated*. "Maybe I lost my concentration worrying about things I shouldn't have been worrying about. I heard a crack in my ankle, but you hear a lot of cracks in gymnastics. Then I tried to stand up, and I realized something was really wrong. I couldn't feel my leg. I kept thinking with each step it would go away, but it didn't." Strug had rolled over on her left ankle and torn two ligaments. Her score—9.162—was not good enough to assure the United States of victory.

LEAP OF FAITH. Strug looked to Karolyi and her teammates for help in deciding what to do. "I don't think they understood there was something wrong," she explained in *Newsweek*. "I felt the gold medal was slipping away." Strug asked Karolyi if she needed to jump again, but she knew she had to.

In the stands Melanie Strug worried about her daughter. "I could see she was hurt, and as a parent, I'd have said, 'Don't do the vault'" Melanie Strug told *Sports Illustrated*. "But knowing Kerri, you couldn't have stopped her unless you'd dragged her off." Strug tried to concentrate on what she had to do. "I knew if I didn't make it, we wouldn't win the gold," she explained in *People Weekly*. "So I said a quick prayer and asked God to help me out."

Obviously in great pain, Strug took off for her second vault. "I was thinking about the vault and nothing else," she recalled in *Sports Illustrated*. "I felt pretty good in the air, but I'd felt good the time before, too. Then when I landed, I heard another crack."

As Strug landed, a grimace covered her face. She hopped twice, but raised her hands over her head to complete the vault and then fell to the mat. When the score came up—9.712—Strug and the Americans knew they had the gold medal, the first ever by an American Olympic gymnastics team. "I don't know how I did the vault, but I knew I had to do it," Strug admitted in *People Weekly*.

Karolyi carried Strug to a waiting stretcher after her vault. Medics put her in a cast and were taking her away to the hospital. Strug called out to Karolyi, who came and picked her up off the stretcher and carried her to the medal ceremony. "Not even the New York City police can stop me taking you up," Karolyi told her, according to *Sports Illustrated*. "Kerri, you're an Olympic champion now. Enjoy it." Her teammates had waited for Strug, refusing to get their medals until their valiant teammate joined them.

GOOD REASON

Many people wondered why Strug did her historic vault despite being injured. She said the decision was easy. "I didn't want to be remembered for falling on my butt in my best event," Strug admitted in *Sports Illustrated*.

ACT OF COURAGE. Afterwards the American team discovered that they would have won without Strug's second vault because the last two Russian performers turned in poor performances. But Strug and her teammates did not know that at the time. "When she nailed that second vault, I had tears of overwhelming joy because it was such a courageous thing to do," Retton told *People Weekly.* "It was one of the most heroic acts in the Olympics I've ever seen." In honor of her heroic jump, Strug earned the Olympic Spirit Award, along with track and field legend Carl Lewis.

VICTORY AND DISAPPOINTMENT. With her historic vault Strug injured herself to the point where her Olympics were over. "I've had a lot of mixed emotions," she stated in the *New York Times.* "It's great that the U.S.A. won the gold medal and made history. I'm ecstatic about that. But I'm upset because of my injury."

The fact that she would miss the individual all-around competition—a goal of hers since barely missing out on qualifying for the same competition at the 1992 Summer Olympics—disappointed Strug greatly. "She had the best day of her life and the worst day of her life in five seconds," Burt Strug explained in *Sports Illustrated.* Moceanu replaced Strug in the all-around competition.

STARDOM. Strug had turned down all financial opportunities connected with gymnastics during her career. She wanted to remain an amateur and be able to compete in college, accepting a scholarship to the University of California at Los Angeles (UCLA). Strug graduated from high school with a 4.0 grade point average. "Look, gymnastics are fine, and I love this sport, but I also want to have a college experience," she told the *New York Times* before the Olympics.

Her Olympic performance and the attention it brought her made Strug change her mind. "Things have changed a bit," she admitted in *People Weekly.* "It's exciting and at the same time scary for me because I don't have complete control. For the first time in my life, I don't know where I'm going. It's weird." Rather than go on tour with the rest of the victorious U.S.

team, Strug decided to go on a tour of her own. After the tour is over, she plans on attending UCLA, even though she will not be able to compete in gymnastics.

OUT OF THE GYM. Strug lives in Houston, Texas. She likes to read, shop, and spend time with her family and friends. Strug and her teammates appeared on a Wheaties box and Strug guest-starred on *Beverly Hills 90210* and *Saturday Night Live.* Her favorite events in gymnastics are the floor exercise and the uneven bars.

Strug knows what it takes to be a champion: "Anything in life, to be successful, you've got to work really hard."

Sources

Atlanta Journal and Constitution, July 27, 1996.
Cincinnati Enquirer, August 24, 1996.
Dallas Morning News, August 14, 1995.
Entertainment Weekly, October 18, 1996.
Gazette Telegraph, September 19, 1995.
Newsweek, August 5, 1996.
New York Times, July 24, 1996; July 25, 1996; July 26, 1996.
People Weekly, August 5, 1996; August 19, 1996.
Sports Illustrated, August 5, 1996; August 12, 1996; September 9, 1996;
    October 7, 1996.
Time, August 5, 1996.
Washington Post, October 9, 1995; July 30, 1996.
Additional information provided by USA Gymnastics.

WHERE TO WRITE:

C/O USA GYMNASTICS,
PAN AMERICAN PLAZA,
201 S. CAPITOL AVENUE, SUITE. 300,
INDIANAPOLIS, IN 46225.

DREAM DATE

Now that her competitive gymnastics career has probably ended, Strug might have more time to date. At 4 feet, 9 inches and 87 pounds, she has strict standards for a boyfriend. "I don't want a party animal guy, but I don't want a nerd," Strug told *Sports Illustrated.* "I don't want some macho hunk jock guy, but I don't want him to be a wimp. And he can't be tall, either."

Amy Van Dyken

1973—

When Amy Van Dyken was in high school, her swimming teammates teased her. They said she swam so slowly that they did not want her on their team anymore. Other students made fun of Van Dyken because she was so tall and acted like a "nerd." In addition to the teasing, she also suffered from asthma, a disease that made it so hard for her to breathe that she could not even climb stairs. Despite all these obstacles, Van Dyken kept swimming. Soon she was so good that she became the star of her team. In July 1996—at the Summer Olympics in Atlanta, Georgia—Van Dyken swam into the record books by becoming the first American woman to win four gold medals in one Olympic Games.

Growing Up

ASTHMA ATTACKS. Amy Deloris Van Dyken was born February 15, 1973, in Denver, Colorado. She grew up in Englewood, Colorado, with her father, Don, a software-company president, her mother, Becky, and her brother and sister.

Van Dyken has suffered from asthma since she was a child. Her parents often took Van Dyken to the hospital emergency room because she could not breathe. Van Dyken's mother slept on the floor near her daughter to make sure she continued to breathe.

"When I was a kid, I couldn't go on field trips because I was so highly allergic that a little dust could trigger an attack," Van Dyken recalled in *Women's Sports and Fitness*. "I couldn't stay at friends' houses. I couldn't even walk up the steps."

DOCTORS PRESCRIBE SWIMMING. To help with her asthma, doctors recommended that Van Dyken take up swimming at the age of six. Humid—or wet—air helps people with asthma to breathe better, and swimmers have to learn to control their breathing. Van Dyken could not swim even one length of the pool before she was 12, but she enjoyed her new sport. "I fell in love with it," she admitted in *Women's Sports and Fitness*.

TOO SLOW? Van Dyken grew to 6-feet-tall by the time she entered Cherry Creek High School. Her asthma and her height made her awkward and she describes herself as a "nerd." Van Dyken continued to swim, but other swimmers on the high school team teased her. They felt that she swam too slowly to be on their team. Her teammates went to the coach, according to Van Dyken, and said, "I refuse to be on the relay with Amy because she's so terrible." Her teammates threw Van Dyken's clothes in the pool and even spit at her.

The teasing just made Van Dyken more determined to succeed. "I'm really stubborn," she explained in the *Sporting News*. "If someone tells me I stink, I'm going to try to prove them wrong."

> ## SCOREBOARD
>
> VOTED SPORTSWOMAN OF THE YEAR IN 1996 BY THE U.S. OLYMPIC COMMITTEE.
>
> WON FOUR GOLD MEDALS AT 1996 SUMMER OLYMPICS IN ATLANTA, GEORGIA (50-METER FREESTYLE, 100-METER BUTTERFLY, 400-METER FREESTYLE RELAY, AND 400-METER MEDLEY RELAY).
>
> FIRST AMERICAN WOMAN TO WIN FOUR GOLD MEDALS IN ONE OLYMPIC GAMES, SUMMER OR WINTER.
>
> NINETEEN-TIME COLLEGE ALL-AMERICAN.
>
> VAN DYKEN OVERCAME ASTHMA AND THE TEASING OF HER HIGH SCHOOL CLASSMATES TO MAKE HISTORY.

Van Dyken continued to work hard, and soon she was the team's star. Six times she earned high school All-American honors, set three state records, and broke five school marks. Van Dyken earned Colorado Sportswoman of the Year honors in both 1990 and 1991 and was named Colorado Swimmer of the Year in 1991.

COLLEGE STAR. After graduating from high school in 1991, Van Dyken spent two years at the University of Arizona. While a freshman at Arizona, she finished fourth in the 50-

meter freestyle at the 1992 U.S. Olympic Trials, just missing a place on the Olympic team. Van Dyken also earned silver medals at the 1992 U.S. Swimming Championships in the 50-meter and 50-yard freestyle races.

Van Dyken finished second in the 50-meter freestyle and third in the 100-meter butterfly at the 1993 National Collegiate Athletic Association (NCAA) Swimming Championships. After earning All-American honors 14 times at Arizona, Van Dyken decided to move closer to home, transferring to Colorado State University.

Van Dyken set seven school and Western Athletic Conference (WAC) records as a junior. Colorado State named Van Dyken the school's 1994 Female Athlete of the Year and the WAC gave her the Joe Kearney Award, recognizing the conference's best female athlete of the year. "Amy Van Dyken is the type of athlete most coaches only dream about having in their program," Colorado State coach John Mattos said. "She possesses that rare instinct that thrives on competition at the highest levels."

RECORD BREAKER. At the 1994 NCAA Swimming Championships, Van Dyken set a new American record in winning the women's 50-meter freestyle at 21.77 seconds. She became only the second woman in the world to break the 22-second barrier in the event. Van Dyken also earned All-American honors in the 100-meter freestyle, 200-meter freestyle relay, and 200-meter medley relay.

Van Dyken was the first swimming national champion from Colorado State, and the Collegiate Swimming Coaches Athletic Association named her National Swimmer of the Year. She also earned places in the Colorado Sports Hall of Fame and the Sportswomen of Colorado Hall of Fame.

TAKES ON WORLD. In 1994, Van Dyken won three medals at the World Swimming Championships in Rome, Italy, the most by an American woman at the competition. She earned a bronze medal in the 50-meter freestyle and won silver medals in both the 400-meter freestyle and 400-meter medley relays. A

BATTLE TO BREATHE

Van Dyken takes in only 35 percent as much oxygen into her lungs as a person without asthma. Swimming authorities have banned steroids—medications used by asthmatics to help their breathing—because some athletes use them to illegally improve their performance. There are drugs she can take that are not banned, but they do not work very well. "It's kind of difficult, because there are medicines out there that would basically almost cure my asthma, but I'm not allowed to take them," Van Dyken explained in the *Sporting News.*

During her time at Colorado State, Van Dyken caught mononucleosis. The illness—combined with her asthma—made her think about giving up swimming. "I thought, 'This is too hard. I want to be normal,'" Van Dyken admitted in the *New York Times.* "Then I realized how much I missed the sport...."

"I'm not supposed to be here at all," she admitted in *Women's Sports and Fitness.* "Swimming, just swimming, is a victory for me." Van Dyken cannot swim races longer than 100-meters because of her asthma, but the effort is worth it. "Oh yeah, it's worth it," she told the *Sporting News.*

year later, Van Dyken won three gold medals and one silver at the Pan American Games.

Van Dyken's efforts earned her an invitation to join the U.S. Resident National Team, a program designed to help American swimmers train for the Olympics. By accepting the invitation, she had to give up her last season at Colorado State. "It was the toughest decision I've ever made," Van Dyken said. "I really love the school and the team, but this is something I felt I had to do. I only have one chance to go for the gold."

Superstar

WHAT HAVE YOU BEEN UP TO? Van Dyken achieved one of her goals by qualifying for the 1996 U.S. Olympic team. She won the 50-meter and 100-meter freestyle races and finished second in the 100-meter butterfly at the U.S. Olympic Trials. The victories were satisfying for Van Dyken, and she told *Time* a story about seeing some girls at the mall who gave her a hard time in high school. "[It] felt good to walk into the mall and see these girls who wouldn't swim a relay with me because I swam so bad," Van Dyken said. "I said, 'Hi, how're you doing? By the way, I'm swimming in five events in the Olympics. What have you been up to?'"

ROUGH START. The 1996 Summer Olympics in Atlanta, Georgia, got off to a horrible start for Van Dyken. In the finals of the 100-meter freestyle, she suffered from leg and neck cramps. After finishing a disappointing fourth, Van Dyken crawled out of the pool and laid down at the side, trying to relax her muscles. "For the 100 freestyle,

I was really nervous," she admitted in the *New York Times*. "I didn't know what to expect. It was like the Super Bowl with the crowd. I didn't know how to handle it. I was overanxious."

GOOD AS GOLD. Van Dyken came back strong from her early disappointment to win her first gold medal of the Olympics as part of the victorious U.S. 400-meter freestyle relay. She swam her leg of the relay in a time of 53.91, the second fastest relay leg ever. Even after winning a gold medal, Van Dyken entered the 100-meter butterfly as a longshot. She admitted later that she had not even practiced swimming this race leading up to the Olympics.

Van Dyken trailed world champion Liu Limin of China for most of the race. Then, in the last 25 meters, the American came on strong, cheered on by the home crowd. Van Dyken touched the wall, but did not think she had won. When she looked at the scoreboard and saw her lane number in first place, she mouthed the words, "Oh, my God," with an astonished look on her face.

Van Dyken defeated Limin by one one-hundredth of a second, with a time of 59.13. "I had no idea what was happening," she explained in the *Detroit Free Press*. "I just tried to swim between the lines. At the turns I could hear the crowd, so I had an idea something was going on. But there were two Americans, and I didn't know where anyone was." Angel Martino of the U.S. won the bronze medal.

Van Dyken won her third gold medal as part of the victorious U.S. 400-meter medley relay team. A medley relay includes four teammates each swimming 100-meters of their specialty— either the backstroke, breaststroke, butterfly, or freestyle. Van Dyken swam the last 100-meters, bringing the U.S. team the victory by almost two seconds over the silver-medal-winning Australian team.

DASH FOR THE RECORD. Van Dyken now had the chance to make history in the 50-meter freestyle. She held the American record in the race, but her main rival, Le Jingyi of China, held the world record. Van Dyken got off to a slow start in the 50-

STARDOM

After her record shattering Olympic performance, Van Dyken became a big star. So many people called her at her hotel that she began to use a false name. "It still has not sunk in yet," Van Dyken told the *Detroit Free Press*. "We were driving in here, and people were running up beside the car, trying to take pictures. I had to tell them, 'Don't worry. I'm still Amy. You can take my picture.'" Van Dyken tried not to let her new fame go to her head. "I hope my life won't change all that much, because I like me and I like my life," she explained to the same newspaper. "I know, though, I'm going to be on some TV shows, so probably I'll have to learn how to do my hair and put my makeup on."

meters final, but rapidly made up ground with strong, swift strokes. She reached the wall first in a time of 24.87, a new American record. Jingyi finished second, three one-hundredths of a second behind. "I knew the girl from China [Jingyi] was going to be really tough, and 25 seconds is a big barrier for anyone," Van Dyken said after the race. "To do it in this pool in front of my home crowd is really great."

The victory in swimming's shortest race earned Van Dyken the title of world's fastest female swimmer. "This is a victory for all the nerds out there," she announced in the *New York Times*. "Here I am. Those girls who gave me such a hard time, I want to thank you." The victory also gave Van Dyken four gold medals in one Olympic games, the first time an American woman had ever accomplished this feat. The Women's Sports Foundation named Van Dyken the Sports Woman of the Year and USA Swimming voted her Swimmer of the Year.

Van Dyken was the biggest star for a dominant American swimming team. The U.S. men and women won 26 medals—13 of them gold. The Americans also swept the relays. "I think for underdogs, we have quite a big bite," Van Dyken told the *New York Times*. "People weren't expecting a lot out of us. We were expecting a lot out of ourselves. We have a lot of heart and we're having fun."

OUT OF THE POOL. Van Dyken lives in Denver with her husband, Alan. She knows sign language and hopes to teach deaf high school students after her swimming career is over. Van Dyken has a poodle, named Buttons, who drinks coffee with sugar and cream. Buttons sent her a congratulatory telegram at the Olympics. "She's [Buttons is] brilliant, but we could only read every third word because of the paw prints," Van Dyken joked in the *New York Times*.

Van Dyken is a spokesperson for Speedo and appeared on a Wheaties box because of her Olympic success. "They called me after my last race," she explained in the *Detroit Free Press*. "My jaw dropped." Van Dyken also made appearances on the David Letterman and Rosie O'Donnell shows. She received another honor in December 1996 when the U.S. Olympic Committee voted her Sportswoman of the Year. Van Dyken stated that the honor was even more special since "there were a lot of women out there who deserved the award because these were the Olympics of women."

In addition to swimming, Van Dyken likes shopping and volleyball along with other sports. She also majored in human development at Colorado State. Van Dyken hopes to compete through the 2000 Summer Olympics in Sydney, Australia. Even though she seems nice out of the pool, she is a fierce competitor. "When I get ready to swim, I might bite your head off if you joke with me," Van Dyken admitted in *People Weekly.*

Van Dyken hopes her Olympic performance can be an inspiration to young people. "I was 6-feet-tall in high school," she told the *New York Times*. "I was easy to pick out of a crowd and easy to pick on. So for all the kids who are struggling, their peers saying they're terrible, I hope I'm an inspiration to them, that if they love it, keep plugging away at it, something good will come out of it."

Sources

Detroit Free Press, February 2, 1995; June 7, 1995; July 18, 1996; July 20, 1996; July 24, 1996; July 27, 1996; July 30, 1996; August 5, 1996.
Newsweek, August 5, 1996.
New York Times, July 24, 1996; July 27, 1996.
People Weekly, August 19, 1996.
Sporting News, March 20, 1995.
Time, August 5, 1996.
Women's Sports and Fitness, September 1995.
Additional information provided by Colorado State University and USA Swimming.

WHERE TO WRITE:

USA SWIMMING,
ONE OLYMPIC PLAZA,
COLORADO SPRINGS, CO 80909-5770.

Ricky Watters

1969—

"He thirsts for the football and there's nothing wrong with that. —Philadelphia Eagles defensive end William Fuller.

Running back Ricky Watters of the Philadelphia Eagles has always wanted to be his team's main man. He led the San Francisco 49ers in rushing for three straight seasons (1992—94) and helped them win Super Bowl XXIX by scoring 3 touchdowns in the big game. Despite his success, Watters's more famous teammates—Steve Young and Jerry Rice—overshadowed him. In 1995, he joined the Philadelphia Eagles, and no one now doubts that he has arrived as one of the best running backs in the National Football League (NFL), especially after leading the league in total yards during the 1996 season.

Growing Up

SPECIAL DELIVERY. Richard James Watters was born April 7, 1969, in Harrisburg, Pennsylvania. He was the adopted child of Jim and Marie Watters. The couple had tried for several years to have a child of their own but had been unsuccessful.

Watters's biological mother was the daughter of Marie Watters's friend. The couple had already adopted a daughter—Rhonda—and Jim Watters wanted a son. Marie Watters arranged for the adoption as a surprise for her husband, and the couple picked up their son in a Trailways bus depot. "I was lucky," Watters admitted in *Sport*.

Watters grew up in the tough uptown section of Harrisburg, Pennsylvania, the state capital. Jim Watters worked as a postal worker until a disability forced him to retire. He had grown up in poverty in rural Alabama and won four Bronze Stars and two Purple Hearts as a demolition expert during the Korean War.

Marie Watters worked as a licensed practical nurse and admits she spoiled her children. "I had waited so long for children, and I wanted them to have all the things I didn't have," she explained in *Sports Illustrated*. "We always had a good income. Our house at Christmas was like a department store. Our sofa was filled with nothing but toys. Ricky always had the best basketball, the best football."

Jim Watters was tougher on the children and kept his son out of trouble. "I wanted him concentrating on school work," Jim Watters stated in *Sports Illustrated*. "And sports." The proud father rarely missed one of his son's football or basketball games. "My dad would push me and get on my case," Watters told *Sport*. "If there was something I couldn't do right, he'd have me working. To this day, if I ever have a problem with blocking or something, I'm out there working on it, and that's from him."

"SKINNY RICK." Watters played football whenever he could as a child. He usually played with older and bigger kids. Many times Watters came home with bloody and torn clothes. "They always made me cry," he recalled in *Sports Illustrated*. "I'd want to stop or go home, but they wouldn't let me. Afterward

I'd be all skinned up and my dad would say, 'I told you so.' My mom would say, 'Don't play with those big boys anymore.' But I wouldn't give up." The other players called Watters "Skinny Rick."

The older boys played tricks on Watters and would not throw him the ball. These games taught him he would have to work hard to succeed. "I couldn't have beaten anybody if I had only hoped to do it," Watters declared in *Sports Illustrated*. "I had to hear myself say, 'I can do it!' to feel invincible. The older boys liked my cockiness. The rougher the games got, and the tougher they were on me, the tougher I got."

ATTRACTS ATTENTION. Watters earned all-state honors in football his junior and senior seasons at Bishop McDevitt High School. He also lettered in basketball and track. College scouts began to attend games his senior year, during which he ran for 1598 yards and 17 touchdowns. Coach Lou Holtz of Notre Dame worked hard to get Watters to attend his university. "Now, Rick, we think you're the finest tailback in the nation," Holtz told Watters, according to *Sports Illustrated*. "If you want to win the Heisman [Trophy], where else would you go but Notre Dame." That was all the young player needed to hear to decide to play for the Fighting Irish.

NOTRE DAME DAYS. Watters contributed immediately to Notre Dame's success as a freshman (1987). He played every game for the Fighting Irish and finished second on the team in rushing with 370 yards. The third time Watters touched the ball, he scored on a 18-yard touchdown run against the University of Michigan.

Heisman Trophy-winning flanker (a halfback stationed to the side of the linemen, chiefly used as a pass receiver) Tim Brown graduated in 1987, and Holtz needed someone to try to fill his shoes. He picked Watters, moving the young player to flanker during his sophomore year. The change paid dividends

Dancing into the end zone, Watters makes another touchdown.

for Notre Dame, as Watters led the team in receiving with 15 catches for 286 yards and 2 touchdowns. He also returned 2 punts for scores, helping the Fighting Irish win the national championship with a perfect 12-0 record.

Despite the team's success, Watters was unhappy playing flanker. He felt that Holtz had gone back on his promise to make him the featured tailback. "He [Holtz] was moving a lot of people around, and they all moved," Watters explained in *Sports Illustrated.* "I was the only one who said, 'Wait a minute. You said I'd be a running back for four years.' He didn't like that. He said I had an attitude."

Watters had his best season as a junior (1989). Moving back to tailback, he rushed for 791 yards and 10 touchdowns.

He also set a Notre Dame record by returning a punt 97 yards for a touchdown against Southern Methodist University. Watters closed out his career in South Bend by rushing for 623 yards and 9 touchdowns in 1990. In his last two seasons he gained 1652 yards combined as a receiver and running back and scored 18 touchdowns.

WATTERS VERSUS HOLTZ. During his career at Notre Dame, Watters constantly argued with Holtz over how much playing time he received. Because the school had so many good players, it was difficult for any one player to stand out. Watters had a hard time adjusting to not being the star of the team, and even phoned Holtz during games to ask for the ball more. "If his career didn't turn out as well as he expected, I'm sorry," Holtz told *Sports Illustrated.* "But I would do nothing different."

FIRST-YEAR FRUSTRATION. The San Francisco 49ers picked Watters in the second-round of the 1991 NFL Draft, making him the forty-fifth overall pick. The 49ers had been looking for a versatile running back to replace Roger Craig, the mainstay of their great Super Bowl championship teams. San Francisco already had quarterback Steve Young and all-time great wide receiver Jerry Rice, but they sorely needed a rushing attack to keep other teams off balance.

Unfortunately, Watters broke his right foot three days after reporting to training camp. He returned to the team in the fifth week of the season, but as a member of the practice squad. Just two weeks later he broke his hand. Watters tried to continue to practice with a splint on his hand, but the pain was too much. The team put him on the injured reserve list, meaning he would miss his entire rookie season.

The 49ers were worried about their high draft pick. "It was a question of, 'Do we have somebody here who is going to be hurt all the time?'" coach George Siefert declared in the *Sporting News.* "Everybody saw Ricky's ability, but there was still the question of how he would perform on game day."

Watters was cocky despite not playing his rookie season. He was loud and flashy and made sure his teammates all knew how talented he was. The 49ers squad was made up of numerous players with Super-Bowl experience, and they soon grew tired of Watters' bragging. "If you had asked me, I would have told you that the team had made a mistake in drafting him," San Francisco offensive tackle Harris Barton told *Sports Illustrated*.

Soon Watters became an outcast on the team. He gained 20 pounds and told his parents he wanted to give up football. Marie Watters advised her son to stick it out. "Anything you want in life doesn't come easy," she explained to her son, according to *Sports Illustrated*. "If it's handed to you, you won't appreciate it as much as if you earned it. God has his own time and way of doing things. You're being tested for a reason. Maybe you're not ready to be a 49er."

PUT UP OR SHUT UP. Watters decided to work hard to prepare for the 1992 season and prove to his teammates that he belonged in the NFL. He trained during the off-season and took up martial arts to improve his concentration. In training camp Watters toned down his bragging and worked hard during drills. Soon his teammates began to accept him.

Watters tried to explain his cockiness to *Sports Illustrated:* "I'll fire myself up to feel confident, and I'll try to instill that feeling of invincibility in my teammates," he said. "I try not to step on anybody's toes; I just want to have something to do with our success. We can all do things that we've never imagined. Whoever thought the great players would do what they have? They pursued a dream, and then they went beyond it. Someday I'd love to be one of the best who has ever played. I don't know if that will happen, but I can't be faulted for trying."

The new-and-improved Watters exploded on the rest of the NFL in 1992. He rushed for a team-leading 1013 yards and caught 43 passes for 405 more. Watters finished eighth in the NFL with 1418 total yards from scrimmage (rushing and receiving) and scored 11 touchdowns. His fellow NFL players voted him to the Pro Bowl all-star game.

Watters added an ingredient to the 49ers offense that had been missing since Craig had left the team. "In my ten years here, Ricky's the most-talented running back we've had," veteran center Jesse Sapolu admitted in *Sports Illustrated*. "Roger Craig ran on heart; his high knee action made him special. But if you talk about cutting and reading holes, Ricky is special. With Craig's work habits, he'll be great."

Unfortunately, Watters could not help telling everyone that he was the key to San Francisco's success. "The year I was hurt, they didn't even make the playoffs," he bragged in *Sports Illustrated*. "Same quarterback. Same wide receivers. Same tight end. Same offense. But no brand-name running back to take the pressure off Steve [Young]. I came in and made the offense work again."

The 49ers won the National Football Conference (NFC) West Division title with an NFL-best record of 14-2. Watters gained 83 yards rushing in his first playoff game as San Francisco defeated the defending Super Bowl champions, the Washington Redskins, 20-13. The 49ers came up one game short of reaching the Super Bowl themselves, however, losing in the NFC championship game 30-20 to the Dallas Cowboys.

RUNNING WATTERS. Over the next two seasons Watters established himself as one of the best all-purpose running backs in the NFL. Each season he led the 49ers in rushing (950 yards in 1993 and 877 yard in 1994) and also developed into a dangerous pass receiver, establishing career bests in both receptions (66) and receiving yardage (719) in 1994. Watters finished fifth in the NFL in 1994 with 1596 total yards and earned Pro-Bowl berths in each of his three seasons in San Francisco.

Proving he was a prime-time-performer, Watters saved his best games for the playoffs. In 1993, he set an NFL record with 5 touchdowns in a 44-3 blowout of the New York Giants. Watters was unstoppable in the biggest game he has ever played, Super Bowl XXIX against the San Diego Chargers. He scored 3 touchdowns, 2 through the air and 1 on the ground, as the 49ers crushed the Chargers 49-26.

Superstar

FLYS TO EAGLES. In his three seasons with San Francisco, Watters accounted for nearly 4300 yards of offense and scored 33 touchdowns. Still, he was never the 49ers' main man on offense, not with Young and Rice attracting most of the headlines. Watters became a restricted free agent following the 1994 season—meaning he could sign with any other NFL team, but San Francisco could match any offer—and he desperately wanted to have a chance to be a workhorse running back.

In February 1995, the Philadelphia Eagles signed 49ers' defensive coordinator Ray Rhodes to become their head coach. Rhodes realized that the Eagles needed a strong running game to be successful, and he had always liked Watters and respected his talent. Rhodes made it a priority to sign the San Francisco star, and in March 1995, Watters agreed to a three-year, $6.9 million contract, making him the highest-paid running back in the NFL.

San Francisco decided not to match the offer, so Watters became an Eagle. "We'd just won the Super Bowl and I scored 3 touchdowns," he stated in *Sport*. "Why would you want to break that up? It doesn't make sense to me. Fact of the matter is, I felt they didn't want me back."

THE MAN. Rhodes promised Watters that he would carry the ball a lot. "I could have played my whole life as a 49er," Watters explained in *Sports Illustrated*. "Done great things. But people always would have said, 'Well, he wasn't Emmitt Smith, he wasn't Barry Sanders.' Who wants to live with that for the rest of his life? I'd like the chance to prove that I'm as good as they are. I've never been the Man before. I never was at Notre Dame. In San Francisco I was one of the men. Now I'm the Man."

Rhodes discounted the criticism of those who called Watters selfish. "A lot of people think he's arrogant and selfish, but it's all about winning with Ricky," the coach told *Sports Illustrated*. "In San Francisco, with the system they had and all the players around him, a whole lot of his talents weren't exploited. He just wants the opportunity to show what he can do."

EAGLES FLY. Philadelphia started slowly in the 1995 season, going 1-3 in their first four games. "Early on, it was like playing for an expansion team—33 new guys, new coaching staff," Watters explained in *Sport*. "Even the go-to guys, like myself and [quarterback] Rodney Peete, were new guys. It was hard to get a rhythm. Some of our leaders gave up. At times, it was more than I could handle."

Watters again tried to inspire his teammates using his mouth. "Whether they thought I was crazy or a loose cannon or whatever, they see now," he declared in *Sport*. "I've been successful everywhere I've been. I always felt that some way, somehow we'd get into the playoffs." The Eagles turned their season around, finishing 1995 at 10-6 and earning a wild-card playoff spot. They defeated the Detroit Lions, 58-37, in the first round, but lost their next game, 30-11, to the eventual Super Bowl champions, the Dallas Cowboys.

Watters really was the main man of the Eagles offense. He accounted for 36 percent of the team's offense with 1707 total yards from the scrimmage line (fourth in the NFL). Watters finished sixth in the league in rushing with 1273 yards and led the team with 12 touchdowns. His teammates named him the Eagles' most valuable player, and he earned his third Pro Bowl selection, the first Philadelphia running back to do so since 1980, when Wilbert Montgomery was so honored. "I wanted to prove I wasn't just doing well on a great team in a great system and I think I did that," Watters told *Sport* after his first season in Philadelphia. "Next year, I'll be better than last."

LEADS LEAGUE. Watters had the best individual season of his career in 1996. He led the NFL in total yards with 1855, finished fourth in the league with 1411 rushing yards, and scored a career-best 13 touchdowns. Watters accomplished all this despite the fact that starting quarterback Rodney Peete was injured early in the season and backup Ty Detmer led the offense.

"Ricky lathered it up and carried the load for us," Rhodes declared in the Trenton, New Jersey *Times*. "He's been doing that all season. We have to do what we do best, and that's been running the ball. Is he the best? If he's not he's right up there with the best."

HOMECOMING. Philadelphia finished with a 10-6 record and earned a wild-card playoff berth for the second straight season. In the first round the Eagles faced the 49ers, marking the first time that Watters faced his old club. "I have a lot of friends still on that team, and my relationships with the guys on that team are still very positive," he stated to the Associated Press. "I have a lot of respect for that team and they have a lot of respect for me."

The homecoming was not a happy one for Watters, however, as San Francisco shut down the Philadelphia offense in a 14-0 victory. He gained only 57 yards rushing on 20 carries on a field made sloppy by heavy rains. "It was strange being on that sideline," Watters admitted to the Associated Press. "It was strange looking over there and watching those guys and playing against them. They played with total dignity and pride and they deserved to win."

OFF THE FIELD. Watters is single and lives in California. He earned a degree in design from Notre Dame. Watters is a good friend of heavyweight boxer George Foreman and has been in his corner for many of the champion's fights.

Watters is also active in charitable causes. In 1994, the American Cancer Soci-

CHOPPY WATTERS

Watters has always wanted to carry the ball as much as he can. Unfortunately, this desire has led to conflicts with his coaches and teammates at Notre Dame, San Francisco, and now in Philadelphia. In 1996 he argued with Rhodes, despite the fact that he carried the ball a career-high 353 times. "When I'm on the sideline, I can't be in the flow of the game," Watters complained to the Associated Press.

Many of Watters's teammates in San Francisco felt he was selfish, that he was concerned more with his individual statistics than with the success of his team. William Fuller, a defensive end with the Philadelphia Eagles, disagrees. "He thirsts for the football and there's nothing wrong with that," Fuller told the Associated Press. "I think if you take that away from Ricky you take his effectiveness."

Watters feels that his critics just do not understand him. "There's misconception all around the board," he explained in *Sport*. "People are usually nothing like you thought."

The Eagles star says that football fans should not expect him to change the way he plays. "I'm me, and they have to accept that," Watters told the *Sporting News*. "I am an emotional player, that's how I always have been."

ety named him Humanitarian of the Year. During the 1995 season, Watters donated $1000 for every touchdown he scored to Camp Okizu, a summer camp located in the San Francisco area for children suffering from cancer.

Despite his success in the NFL, Watters is still not satisfied. "I want a chance to prove I am the best, no, one of the best running backs in the league," he confessed in the *Sporting News*. "But to do that, you have to run the ball. I am not going to sit here and just talk. I intend to back it up by playing, too."

Sources

Sport, December 1994; October 1996.
Sporting News, November 9, 1992; December 7, 1992; September 11, 1995.
Sports Illustrated, December 7, 1992; September 11, 1995.
*The Times, (*Trenton) October 18, 1996; December 30, 1996.
Additional information provided by the Associated Press and the Philadelphia Eagles.

 WHERE TO WRITE:
C/O PHILADELPHIA EAGLES,
VETERANS STADIUM,
BROAD STREET AND PATTISON AVENUE,
PHILADELPHIA, PA 19148-5201.

Index

Series (ser.) is in *italic;* entries in Series 3
and their page numbers are in **bold.**

Series (ser.) is in *italic;* entries in Series 3 and their page numbers are
in **bold.**

Series (ser.) is in *italic;* entries in Series 3 and their page numbers are in **bold.**

Canadian Track and Field
Championships
Bailey, Donovan *ser. 3*, 16,
18
Candeloro, Phillipe *ser. 2*, 455-457
Canseco, Jose *ser. 1*, 173, 532; *ser.
2*, 509
Capriati, Jennifer *ser. 1*, 180, 510;
ser. 2, 382, 525-526
The Captain (See Penske, Roger)
Captain Comeback (See Harbaugh,
Jim)
Carew, Rod *ser. 1*, 116, 444; *ser. 2*,
139
Carlton, Steve *ser. 1*, 101, 473
Carner, Jo Anne *ser. 2*, 240
Carroll, Frank *ser. 2*, 29, 244
Carter, Joe *ser. 1*, 27, 29
CART Indy Car World Series
championship
Fittipaldi, Emerson *ser. 1*,
159
Unser, Al, Jr. *ser. 2*, 493-
494, 499-500
Cartwright, Bill *ser. 1*, 423
Casey, Jon *ser. 2*, 335
Cauthen, Steve *ser. 1*, 276
Cayard, Paul *ser. 2*, 305
Central Arkansas University *ser. 1*,
434
Pippen, Scottie *ser. 1*, 434
Cepeda, Orlando *ser. 1*, 532; *ser. 3*,
49
Challenger Division *ser. 1*, 6
Chamberlain, Wilt *ser. 1*, 55, 259,
424, 426; *ser. 2*, 327; *ser. 3*, 235
Championship Auto Racing Teams
ser. 1, 156
Chaney, Don *ser. 2*, 161
Chang, Michael *ser. 1*, 89-95, 475,
482
Charlotte Hornets
Bogues, Tyrone "Muggsy"
ser. 1, 69
Johnson, Larry *ser. 1*, 251
Mourning, Alonzo *ser. 2*,
322, 326
Chase, Sue *ser. 3*, 169
Chavez, Julio Cesar *ser. 3*, 51-52,
58

Chicago Bears *ser. 1*, 399
Harbaugh, Jim *ser. 3*, 97, 99
Chicago Blackhawks *ser. 2*, 177
Chicago Bulls *ser. 1*, 48, 113, 139,
244, 329, 540; *ser. 3*, 204
Jordan, Michael *ser. 1*, 255
Pippen, Scottie *ser. 1*, 436
Chicago Cubs *ser. 2*, 135
Maddux, Greg *ser. 1*, 347
Sandberg, Ryne *ser. 1*, 488
Chicago White Sox *ser. 1*, 28, 456
Jackson, Bo *ser. 1*, 229
Jordan, Michael *ser. 1*, 260
Thomas, Frank *ser. 1*, 530
Childress, Richard *ser. 2*, 75
Chmura, Mark *ser. 2*, 104
Christie, Linford *ser. 3*, 18-20
Cincinnati Bengals *ser. 1*, 272,
398, 400, 449; *ser. 2*, 436
Cincinnati Reds *ser. 1*, 80; *ser. 2*,
121
Cincinnati Stingers
Messier, Mark *ser. 1*, 376
Cinderella of the Ghetto (See
Williams, Venus)
Clark, Will *ser. 1*, 348
Clay, Cassius *ser. 1*, 165
Clemens, Roger *ser. 1*, 96-102,
172, 351, 443; *ser. 2*, 509
Clemente, Roberto *ser. 1*, 170
Clemson Tigers *ser. 2*, 428
Cleveland Browns *ser. 1*, 124-125;
ser. 2, 478
Cleveland Indians *ser. 2*, 114, 121,
198; *ser. 3*, 245, 264
Belle, Albert *ser. 2*, 9
Clinton, Bill *ser. 1*, 202, 393; *ser.
2*, 54, 464, 482, 518
Clinton, Hillary Rodham *ser. 1*,
393; *ser. 2*, 155, 464
Coal Miner's Daughter (See
Martin, Christy)
Cobb, Ty *ser. 1*, 171, 195, 492; *ser.
2*, 139
Coffey, Paul *ser. 1*, 321, 378; *ser.
2*, 111-113
Coleman, Derrick *ser. 3*, 201
College of William & Mary
Pride, Curtis *ser. 3*, 211
College Player of the Year

Series (ser.) is in *italic;* entries in Series 3 and their page numbers are in **bold.**

Series (ser.) is in *italic;* entries in Series 3 and their page numbers are
in **bold.**

Series (ser.) is in *italic;* entries in Series 3 and their page numbers are in **bold.**

Series (ser.) is in *italic;* entries in Series 3 and their page numbers are in **bold**.

M

Series (ser.) is in *italic;* entries in Series 3 and their page numbers are
in **bold.**

Mullin, Chris *ser. 3*, 233

Murakami, Masonori *ser. 2*, 340, 344

Murphy, Dale *ser. 1*, 82; *ser. 3*, 241

Murray, Brian *ser. 2*, 110

Murray, Eddie *ser. 2*, 13, 16, 122

Musial, Stan *ser. 1*, 567; *ser. 2*, 139

Mutombo, Dikembe *ser. 2*, 323, 326; *ser. 3*, **186-196**

Myricks, Larry *ser. 2*, 392

N

Nabisco Dinah Shore Women's Open
    King, Betsy *ser. 2*, 234, 237-238

Naismith Award
    Hardaway, Anfernee *ser. 2*, 150
    Kidd, Jason *ser. 2*, 230
    Leslie, Lisa *ser. 3*, 152-153
    Mourning, Alonzo *ser. 2*, 326
    Robinson, Glenn *ser. 2*, 409
    Swoopes, Sheryl *ser. 2*, 471
    Webber, Chris *ser. 2*, 517

Namath, Joe *ser. 1*, 268, 270, 367, 395

NASCAR championship
    Earnhardt, Dale *ser. 2*, 71-72, 75-77, 129
    Gordon, Jeff *ser. 2*, 77, 124-125, 130
    Labonte, Terry *ser. 2*, 131
    Petty, Richard *ser. 2*, 131
    Thomas, Herb *ser. 2*, 131

National AIDS Commission *ser. 1*, 244

National Association of Baseball Leagues *ser. 2*, 39-40

National Baseball Hall of Fame and Museum *ser. 2*, 45

National Basketball Association (See NBA)

National Collegiate Athletic Association (See NCAA)

National Footbal Conference (See NFL)

National Hockey League (See NHL)

National Invitational Tournament
    Bird, Larry *ser. 1*, 52

National Junior Olympics
    Jones, Roy, Jr. *ser. 2*, 204

National Junior Pentathlon Championship
    Joyner-Kersee, Jackie *ser. 1*, 264

National Junior Tennis League *ser. 1*, 35

National League Championship Series
    Bonds, Barry *ser. 1*, 80
    Dykstra, Lenny *ser. 1*, 117-118, 120
    Glavine, Tom *ser. 2*, 118-121
    Gwynn, Tony *ser. 2*, 135
    Maddux, Greg *ser. 1*, 348, 350
    Ryan, Nolan *ser. 1*, 468, 471
    Sandberg, Ryne *ser. 1*, 490-491
    Sanders, Deion *ser. 1*, 504-505
    Smoltz, John *ser. 3*, 262-263, 266

National Sports Festival
    Edwards, Teresa *ser. 2*, 83

Navratilova, Martina *ser. 1*, 176-179, 411-418, 508, 510-511; *ser. 2*, 175, 384

NBA All-Star game (See All-Star game, NBA)

NBA Defensive Player of the Year
    Mutombo, Dikembe *ser. 3*, 186-187, 193
    Payton, Gary *ser. 3*, 197-198, 203

NBA finals
    Barkley, Charles *ser. 1*, 48
    Bird, Larry *ser. 1*, 53-55
    Drexler, Clyde *ser. 1*, 113
    Hardaway, Anfernee *ser. 2*, 153
    Johnson, Earvin "Magic" *ser. 1*, 54-55, 241-244

Series (ser.) is in *italic;* entries in Series 3 and their page numbers are in **bold.**

Pippen, Scottie *ser. 1*, 257, 260, 433-439; *ser. 2*, 215; *ser. 3*, 204

Pitino, Rick *ser. 1*, 138

Pittsburgh Penguins
    Jagr, Jaromir *ser. 2*, 174, 176
    Lemieux, Mario *ser. 1*, 318

Pittsburgh Pirates *ser. 1*, 504; *ser. 2*, 118-119; *ser. 3*, 262-263
    Bonds, Barry *ser. 1*, 79

Pittsburgh Steelers *ser. 1*, 371; *ser. 2*, 95, 172, 429; *ser. 3*, 106
    Stewart, Kordell *ser. 3*, 269-270, 273
    Woodson, Rod *ser. 2*, 536, 539

Player of the Year, college
    Robinson, Glenn *ser. 2*, 406-407
    Swoopes, Sheryl *ser. 2*, 468-469, 471

Player of the Year, golf
    Nicklaus, Jack *ser. 2*, 357
    Norman, Greg *ser. 2*, 348

Player of the Year, high school
    Hardaway, Anfernee *ser. 2*, 147
    Robinson, Glenn *ser. 2*, 406-407

Player of the Year, LPGA
    Lopez, Nancy *ser. 1*, 340-343

Player of the Year, women's basketball
    Lobo, Rebecca *ser. 2*, 287-288, 293

Playmaker (See Irvin, Michael)

Portland Trail Blazers *ser. 1*, 244, 259, 358, 438, 540
    Drexler, Clyde *ser. 1*, 111

Powell, Mike *ser. 1*, 329; *ser. 2*, 389-397

Preakness Stakes
    Shoemaker, Willie *ser. 1*, 279

President's Council on Physical Fitness and Sports
    Griffith Joyner, Florence *ser. 1*, 202

Presley, Elvis *ser. 2*, 78, 450-451, 454

Priakin, Sergei *ser. 3*, 40

Price, Nick *ser. 1*, 146

Pride, Curtis *ser. 3*, **208-217**

Prime Time (See Deion Sanders)

Pro Bowl
    Aikman, Troy *ser. 1*, 20
    Bledsoe, Drew *ser. 2*, 22
    Elway, John *ser. 1*, 126
    Faulk, Marshall *ser. 2*, 89, 93-94
    Favre, Brett *ser. 2*, 98, 102
    Harbaugh, Jim *ser. 3*, 98, 105
    Irvin, Michael *ser. 2*, 164, 169
    Jackson, Bo *ser. 1*, 228
    Marino, Dan *ser. 1*, 370
    Rice, Jerry *ser. 1*, 448
    Sanders, Barry *ser. 1*, 498
    Sanders, Deion *ser. 1*, 503, 505-506
    Seau, Junior *ser. 2*, 423, 428
    Smith, Bruce *ser. 2*, 434, 436
    Smith, Emmitt *ser. 1*, 517
    Thomas, Derrick *ser. 2*, 475-476, 478
    Thomas, Thurman *ser. 1*, 546
    Watters, Ricky *ser. 3*, 297, 301-302, 304
    White, Reggie *ser. 1*, 559
    Woodson, Rod *ser. 2*, 536-537, 540, 543
    Young, Steve *ser. 1*, 585

Professional Football Hall of Fame
    Starr, Bart *ser. 2*, 105

Professional Golfers' Association (See PGA)

Puckett, Kirby *ser. 1*, 440-445; *ser. 2*, 119

Purdue University *ser. 2*, 160
    Robinson, Glenn *ser. 2*, 408
    Woodson, Rod *ser. 2*, 537, 539

Q

Quebec Nordiques *ser. 1*, 335
    Forsberg, Peter *ser. 3*, 85, 90

Queen Victoria *ser. 2*, 299

R

Series (ser.) is in *italic;* entries in Series 3 and their page numbers are
in **bold.**

Series (ser.) is in *italic;* entries in Series 3 and their page numbers are in **bold.**

Series (ser.) is in *italic;* entries in Series 3 and their page numbers are in **bold.**

King, Billie Jean *ser. 1,* 417
Navratilova, Martina *ser. 1,*
416-418
Tennis surfaces *ser. 1,* 107
Texas Rangers
Gonzalez, Juan *ser. 1,* 170
Ryan, Nolan *ser. 1,* 472
Texas Tech University
Swoopes, Sheryl *ser. 2,* 468-
469
Third and Long Foundation
Thomas, Derrick *ser. 2,* 481
Thomas, Debbie *ser. 1,* 571-572;
ser. 2, 28; *ser. 3,* 69
Thomas, Derrick *ser. 2,* 475-483
Thomas, Frank *ser. 1,* 527-533
Thomas, Herb *ser. 2,* 131
Thomas, Isiah *ser. 1,* 243-244,
534-541; *ser. 2,* 446
Thomas, Mary *ser. 1,* 536
Thomas, Thurman *ser. 1,* 496, 542-
548; *ser. 2,* 94, 437, 480
Thompson, Daley *ser. 2,* 363, 366
Thompson, John *ser. 1,* 135-136,
464; *ser. 2,* 324, 326; *ser. 3,* 189
Thorpe, Jim *ser. 2,* 363
Threet, Fannie *ser. 2,* 323
Thurman Thomas Foundation *ser.*
1, 548
Tiger (See Richardson, Dot)
Tomba, Alberto *ser. 1,* 549-555
Tomczak, Mike *ser. 3,* 274, 276-
277
Toney, James *ser. 2,* 202, 207
The Tornado (See Nomo, Hideo)
Toronto Blue Jays *ser. 1,* 120, 230,
444, 505, 532; *ser. 3,* 263
Alomar, Roberto *ser. 1,* 27
Fielder, Cecil *ser. 1,* 149
Glavine, Tom *ser. 2,* 119
Winfield, Dave *ser. 1,* 566
Torrence, Gwen *ser. 2,* 484-492
Tour de France *ser. 1,* 221
Armstrong, Lance *ser. 3,* 2,
6, 8-9
Induráin, Miguel *ser. 1,* 219-
221
Tour Du Pont
Armstrong, Lance *ser. 3,* 1-
3, 5, 7-9

Tracy, Paul *ser. 2,* 500
Tremblay, Mario *ser. 2,* 420
Trevino, Lee *ser. 1,* 144
Trinity Valley Community College
Kemp, Shawn *ser. 2,* 213
Trois-Rivieres Draveurs
Rheaume, Manon *ser. 2,* 400
Trottier, Bryan *ser. 1,* 188, 377
Tway, Bob *ser. 2,* 353-354
Tyler, Dani *ser. 3,* 79
Tyson, Mike *ser. 1,* 167, 208-209;
ser. 2, 207; *ser. 3,* 169
Tyus, Wyomia *ser. 2,* 489

U

UCLA (See University of
California, Los Angeles)
Unitas, Johnny *ser. 1,* 268, 367
United States Football League *ser.*
1, 271, 557, 582, 585; *ser. 2,*
436
University of Alabama
Thomas, Derrick *ser. 2,* 477
University of Arizona
Van Dyken, Amy *ser. 3,* 290
University of Arkansas *ser. 2,* 160;
ser. 3, 126
University of California *ser. 2,* 158
Kidd, Jason *ser. 2,* 229
University of California at Irvine
Powell, Mike *ser. 2,* 391
University of California, Los
Angeles *ser. 1,* 33, 198, 264;
ser. 2, 158, 168, 295
Aikman, Troy *ser. 1,* 18
Devers, Gail *ser. 2,* 57
Fernandez, Lisa *ser. 3,* 72-
73, 75
Miller, Reggie *ser. 2,* 309
Powell, Mike *ser. 2,* 391
Richardson, Dot *ser. 3,* 220
Strug, Kerri *ser. 3,* 286
University of Central Florida
Akers, Michelle *ser. 2,* 2
University of Cincinnati *ser. 2,*
516; *ser. 3,* 125
University of Colorado
Stewart, Kordell *ser. 3,* 270-
271

Series (ser.) is in *italic;* entries in Series 3 and their page numbers are
in **bold.**

Dolan, Tom *ser. 2,* 66
Van Dyken, Amy *ser. 3,* 291
World Track and Field
Championships
Bailey, Donovan *ser. 3,* 15,
17-18
Bubka, Sergei *ser. 2,* 33, 37
Devers, Gail *ser. 2,* 61-62
Griffith Joyner, Florence *ser.
1,* 200
Johnson, Michael *ser. 2,*
182-184, 186
Joyner-Kersee, Jackie *ser. 1,*
265
O'Brien, Dan *ser. 2,* 359-
360, 364, 366
Powell, Mike *ser. 2,* 390,
392, 396
Torrence, Gwen *ser. 2,* 484-
485, 488-490
World University Games
Bird, Larry *ser. 1,* 52
Powell, Mike *ser. 2,* 391
Torrence, Gwen *ser. 2,* 488
World Women's Basketball
Championships
Edwards, Teresa *ser. 2,* 84-
85
Leslie, Lisa *ser. 3,* 154
Swoopes, Sheryl *ser. 2,* 473
World Women's Soccer
Championship
Akers, Michelle *ser. 2,* 1-3,
6
Hamm, Mia *ser. 2,* 144

Worthington, Kimo *ser. 2,* 298,
301
Worthy, James *ser. 1,* 135
Wright, Mickey *ser. 2,* 240
Wylie, Paul *ser. 2,* 219
Wynalda, Eric *ser. 3,* 118

Y

Yachtswoman of the Year
Isler, J. J. *ser. 2,* 300
Yamaguchi, Kristi *ser. 1,* 575-580;
ser. 2, 28, 219, 221; *ser. 3,* 159
Yarborough, Cale *ser. 2,* 75
Yastremski, Carl *ser. 1,* 567; *ser. 2,*
507
Young America ser. 2, 302-305
Young, Brigham *ser. 1,* 581
Young, Steve *ser. 1,* 399, 401-402,
450-451, 581- 586; *ser. 2,* 103;
ser. 3, 296, 300
Yount, Robin *ser. 1,* 195
Yzerman, Steve *ser. 2,* 111-112;
ser. 3, 37

Z

Zaharias, Babe Didrikson *ser. 2,*
240
Zmelik, Robert *ser. 2,* 365
Zmeskal, Kim *ser. 1,* 383-384; *ser.
2,* 320-321; *ser. 3,* 280
Zmievskaya, Galina *ser. 1,* 38
Zo (See Mourning, Alonzo)
Zoeller, Fuzzy *ser. 2,* 352